The Human Aspects of Project Management

Managing the Project Team

Volume Three

The Human Aspects of Project Management

Volume One:
Organizing Projects for Success

Volume Two:
Human Resource Skills for the
Project Manager

Volume Three:
Managing the Project Team

The Human Aspects of Project Management

Managing the Project Team

Volume Three

Vijay K. Verma, P. Eng., M.B.A.

Project Management Institute
130 South State Road
Upper Darby, Pennsylvania 19082
610/734-3330

Library of Congress Cataloging-in-Publication Data

Verma, Vijay K., (1949–   )
    Managing the project team / Vijay K. Verma.
        p.   cm.
    Includes bibliographical references and index
    Contents: v. 3. Managing the Project Team
    ISBN: 1-880410-40-0 (pbk. : alk. paper)
    1. Industrial project management. 2. Matrix organization.
3. Work groups. I. Title.
HD69.P75V47   1995
658.4'04--dc20   95-40579
                                            CIP

ISBN: 1-880410-42-7   v.3

Book Team

Editor-in-Chief
James S. Pennypacker

Book Designer	*Editor, Book Division*
Michelle Owen	**Jeannette M. Cabanis**
Cover design by	*Editor, Book Division*
Michelle Owen	**Toni D. Knott**
Production Coordinator	*Acquisitions Editor*
Mark S. Parker	**Bobby R. Hensley**

PMI books are available at special quantity discounts to use as premiums and sales promotions, or for use in corporate training programs. For more information, please write to the Business Manager, PMI Publication Division, 40 Colonial Square, Sylva, NC 28779. Or contact your local bookstore.

The paper used in this book complies with the Permanent Paper Standard issued by the National Information Standards Organization (Z39.48—1984).

10   9   8   7   6   5   4   3   2   1

Table of Contents

Dedication   6
Foreword   7, 8
Preface   9
Acknowledgments   15
Change Management, Project Management, and Teamwork   17
    Understanding the dynamics of change   18
    Managing organizational change   25
    Teamwork—A key to managing change   32
    Managing changes in a project environment   42
    Summary   54
Team Dynamics and Cultural Diversity   59
    Groups and project teams   60
    Team dynamics and effectiveness   68
    Cultural diversity and project management   89
    Managing international projects   101
    Summary   107
Effective Team Building   113
    About team building   114
    Organizing the project team   122
    Practical guidelines for team building   133
    Summary   148
Developing Effective Project Teams   153
    Developing a project team for success   154
    Developing a team communication plan   159
    Effective team decision-making   171
    Managing project teams during the project   182
    Summary   189
Inspiring High Team Performance   193
    Managing communication challenges   194
    Developing trust and motivation   201
    Managing team morale   208
    Team leadership   216
    Summary   223
From Self-Managed Work Teams to Self-Motivated Project Teams   225
    About self-managed work teams   226
    Empowerment: A key element of SMWTs and SMPTs: (The self-motivated
        project team)   232
    Fostering an SMPT culture through empowerment   235
    Creating and maintaining SMPTs   242
    Leadership in SMPTs   256
    Summary   265
References   268
Appendix: Self-Assessment Exercises   280–292
Index   293

Dedication

For my late parents and Taya Ji for their inspiration; for Shiksha, my wife and my best friend; and for our children, Serena, Naveen, and Angelee, who taught me the practical side of dealing with people and teamwork.

Through teamwork, ordinary people can produce extraordinary results.

Foreword to *Managing the Project Team*

Like it or not, teams and teamwork are here to stay! Personally, as someone who was raised to cherish rugged individualism, I feel an ambiguity about this reality. When I think of working with others in a group, I get nervous about "groupthink." Could Einstein's theory of relativity have been created in a team environment? Could *Othello* have been authored by a team of writers?

Despite my concerns about groupthink, I recognize that in today's complex world, no one individual has the insights and skills needed to deal with many of the problems we commonly encounter. The need for team-based solutions is a reality we must reckon with. People who want to survive and thrive in today's messy business environment must reconcile themselves to this truth.

In attempting to conduct our affairs by using teams, we should be alert to the fact that it is mighty hard to put together effective teams. In their best-selling book, *The Wisdom of Teams*, Katzenbach and Smith point out that there is more to creating a team than simply putting a bunch of people together to work on a problem. Five people stuck in an elevator that is trapped between floors do not constitute a team. However, these same five people working together to deal with their problem do.

Most of the teams I run across in my work fall under Katzenbach and Smith's categories of preliminary teams, potential teams and pseudo teams. In each of these cases, team members are not working together to define common goals and to set out to achieve them through their mutual efforts. What Katzenbach and Smith define as real teams and high-performing reams are the ideals that we should strive for.

Vijay Verma has done an admirable job of providing us guidance on steps we can take to create real and high-performing teams. He begins with the premise that today's complex, competitive, fast-paced world demands that nontrivial problems be tackled by means of teams and teamwork. He also acknowledges that it is not easy to create effective teams. In addition to dealing with personality issues, team building requires leadership, coping with cultural differences, and gaining support from the organizational environment. Verma deals with these and other issues and offers us a road map to find our way to creating capable teams.

J. Davidson Frame, Ph.D., PMP
Director, International Center for Project Management Excellence,
George Washington University
Director of Educational Services, Project Management Institute
November 19, 1997

Foreword to *The Human Aspects of Project Management* Series

Today's ever-changing business environment requires new approaches to project management, which has become an important tool for dealing with time-to-market, resource limitations, downsizing, and global competition. As markets and project organizations become more dynamic, administrative and technical skills alone are no longer sufficient to deal with the complexities of modern project undertakings. Project managers who want to compete on a world-class level must understand the human side of their organizations and business processes. They must be social architects who can work across levels and functions of the organization, continuously improving the business process and fostering an ambiance conducive to innovation, risk-taking, self-directed teamwork, commitment, quality, and self-improvement.

The Human Aspects of Project Management series offers project managers and their teams the conceptual and practical guidelines for leading people effectively and confidently towards challenging project objectives. The series goes beyond the traditional, linear approach to project management, which assumes that project budgets and schedules can always be clearly defined and can form the cornerstone for tracking and controlling a project. By focusing on the human side, Verma offers a fresh approach to modern project management. He shows how to unleash higher levels of creativity, productivity, quality, and commitment from the project team by considering the human aspects.

With these books, the seasoned management practitioner or scholar who understands the conventional tools and techniques of project management but wants to go beyond the basic framework can gain a better understanding of the factors that drive project performance. *The Human Aspects of Project Management* provides a conceptual construct for managing modern projects. It offers concrete suggestions for dealing with diverse project teams, issues of delegation, empowerment, accountability, control, commitment, organizational linkages, alliances, and the intricacies of matrix management. Perhaps most important, the concepts set forth in this series will allow project leaders to build a true project team, which includes alliances with the business organization, support groups, and project sponsors. Such a project team establishes the foundation for an effective and productive project management system that can solve complex problems and produce quality results.

— *Hans J. Thamhain, Ph.D.*
Bentley College

Preface

Why This Series of Books?

Managing projects requires unique skills and techniques, different from those needed to manage ongoing operations. As project management moves into the 21st century, project managers face the challenges of operating in a project environment characterized by high levels of uncertainty, cross-cultural teams, and global competition for competent human resources. These challenges can be met by developing a clear understanding of human factors in project management and by effective use of the human resource management skills that are required to inspire project stakeholders to work together in order to meet project objectives.

Extensive literature and many software packages are available for the traditional aspects of project management: planning, scheduling, and reporting; cost control and risk analysis; and management of scope and quality. Yet most project managers agree that the real management challenges lie not in technical problems but in the behavioral and organizational aspects of projects.

We sometimes forget that, despite the recent information and technology revolution in project management, people are at the center of projects. People determine the success or failure of a project. They define project goals. They plan, organize, direct, coordinate, and monitor project activities. They meet project goals and objectives by using interpersonal and organizational skills such as communication, delegation, decision-making and negotiation. In project environments, people can be viewed as problems and constraints—or as solutions and opportunities.

Human resource management is therefore a vital component of project management. Many books on general management, personnel management, and organizational behavior contain concepts and techniques that support project management. But understanding the myriad complex human factors that determine project success requires research and experience specific to the project environment. The Project Management Institute has played a leadership role in this area by developing practical and thought-provoking literature and the *A Guide to Project Management Body of Knowledge,* which includes human resource management as one of the eight knowledge areas. This series gathers together these and many other resources on the human aspects of management. It focuses on making the most of human resources on projects. The emphasis is on people and how they can be organized to increase their overall effectiveness as individuals, as project teams, and as members of organizations.

Throughout my working life, I have always been fascinated by the degree to which human factors influence the success of project management. The ideas presented in this series developed from years of study and research; from my practical experience at TRIUMF; and from discussions with friends, colleagues, other project management professionals, family, clients, and those who have attended my classes and seminars. These ideas are not likely to become the last word in human factors in project management, but I hope they will incite an increased awareness, just as the efforts of researchers and project management practitioners who have successfully implemented creative leadership motivated me to think further about effective project human resources management. Project management will be more successful, and my efforts in writing this series well rewarded, if project management educators and practitioners are inspired to devote more energy to this important area.

One final note: As you read, you may occasionally come across a concept or an idea that you feel you already know. That may be true indeed. As Somerset Maugham said, "Basic truths are too important to be new."

About This Book

Volume 3: Managing the Project Team

Teams outperform individuals or a group of individuals in an organization, especially when high performance requires multiple skills, judgments, and experiences. As a result, the terms *"team"* and *"teamwork"* are frequently heard and are acknowledged as important by everyone. Most people believe that they understand the advantages of teams and how teams work. Organizations emphasize the importance of teamwork and team building. Yet people can work in the same department for many years, serve on task forces and committees, meet in management groups regularly, and still not be a part of a *team*.

For a team to function effectively, team members must be flexible, supportive, and committed to meeting team goals. There are countless books on this topic but very few that focus on managing teams in a project environment.

I initially believed that my experience, plus the existing body of research knowledge, would provide me with most of the information for this book. I was wrong. I expected to find the answers in *A Guide to the Project Management Body of Knowledge* but could not find sufficient depth on the dynamics of project teams or managing the project team. In order to develop practical ideas and concepts about building and developing effective project teams, I spoke to hundreds of people in several organizations. As expected, I found a lot of common sense in what makes project teams perform. However, I also kept running into "uncommon sense" that made a difference in project team performance.

Tough global competition has created an acute need for culturally diverse, fast, flexible, and competitive operations. Cultural diversity is a fact of life in managing joint ventures and international projects. It influences team dynamics and techniques for building, developing and inspiring project teams for high performance. Through this book, I have tried to highlight for the readers the important findings on this topic. I present some practical guidelines to manage project teams effectively by outlining the team dynamics and cultural diversity and then cover the steps of building, developing, empowering and inspiring teams to turn ordinary people and performance into *extraordinary* people and performance.

Projects, by their nature, are composed of unique, uncertain and non-repetitive sets of activities; hence they initiate and involve change. Changes in a project environment are inevitable and may happen at any time during the project life cycle. However, these being hard to anticipate, they often cause considerable stress to the project manager and project team members. Change can be managed more effectively and efficiently through teamwork because it encourages people to collaborate and work interdependently. This discourages the tendency to resist changes and challenges team members to find innovative solutions and creative approaches. Teams are critical to managing the major changes in skills, values, and behaviors essential to a high performing organization.

Today, most projects require a diverse mix of individuals who must be integrated into an effective unit—a project team. It's important to understand the difference between a *group* and a *team* and how their dynamics impact the overall performance. It's easy to gather a number of individuals together in a group. However, it requires special skills, attitude and commitment to shape those individuals into an effective team.

Project teams are very similar to sport teams in terms of human dynamics. Like team coaches, project managers should understand team dynamics and foster human synergy by effective team building. They must recognize the critical significance of the effective project team and the role of team building activities in facilitating project management performance.

The working relationship among members of the project team can affect not only their productivity but also team performance in relation to other stakeholders. Therefore, team building is essential for managing a project and developing effective project teams is one of the prime responsibilities of the project manager. Team building involves a whole spectrum of management skills required to identify, commit and integrate a group into a multidisciplinary, highly cohesive project team. While belonging to a really successful project team is very satisfactory, it is also rewarding for the project manager to use his or her qualities and skills to create such a team.

The success of project teams depends upon the ability of their team leaders in effectively managing and influencing the diverse mix of personnel. Because of the multidisciplinary, interdependent nature of project teams, project managers must learn team building skills in order to integrate the efforts of all project participants. They must understand the dynamics and the process of team development. They must create an environment where all team members are personally and professionally satisfied, are involved and have mutual trust. They must be able to create a clear compelling vision toward which team members work together with unity of purpose. They must build commitment for the vision through motivating, communicating effectively, and encouraging genuine participation in decision-making.

Management of both domestic and international projects requires effective planning, organizing, and controlling. However, management of international projects poses additional team building challenges especially in terms of communication, negotiation and human relations as a result of diverse cultural backgrounds of the project participants. Consequently, project managers must develop skills for operating in a multicultural environment and foster synergy within their project teams.

This book focuses on practical ideas that can help project managers to identify, build, maintain, motivate, inspire, and lead project teams to produce

12

high team performance and meet project objectives. It deals with the challenges of managing change and various issues associated with team building in the project environment. The drivers and barriers to high team performance are identified along with some suggestions and remedial actions to minimize the negative impact of barriers. This book also covers the development of effective project teams through motivation, effective decision-making and problem solving. The concept of empowerment and Self-Managed Project Teams (SMPTs) are described along with practical guidelines for creating, maintaining and leading SMPTs to enhance project success. Some practical concepts and ideas to inspire teams for continuous high performance by using open communication, managing conflicts in a constructive manner, building trust, managing the team morale, and providing effective team leadership, are presented in this book. It is organized around important issues and guidelines for managing project teams that project managers must learn and practice to manage projects effectively in the 21st century.

Topics have been organized in such a way that readers can easily find their particular areas of interest. No previous knowledge of team management and organizational behavior is required, but a keen interest in project management will be useful to thoroughly understand and apply the concepts presented. Each chapter deals with important aspects of managing teams in a project environment and outlines practical guidelines to help apply those techniques successfully. The concepts and ideas are illustrated by figures and the main points are highlighted by bullets.

Who Should Read This Book? Projects are accomplished by people with a diverse mix of skills, expertise, and cultural backgrounds, who must be integrated into an effective project team. The survival and growth of business organizations in the 21st century will depend upon their abilities to manage projects successfully. Effective teamwork is the key to successful project management.

Because it emphasizes the importance of team building in meeting project objectives and deals with skills and techniques for managing the project team and inspiring high team performance, this book should help anyone, from project management academics and practitioners to a novice in the field. It will help project management professionals learn the human skills needed to create a team environment that effectively integrates the efforts of all stakeholders and achieves human synergy. It will help top management, project managers, project team members, major project stakeholders, and all other project participants (functional managers, support personnel, etc.) increase their effectiveness in meeting project objectives by working together. Project management educators and academics can use this book to develop a short course, seminar, or training workshop on team building and managing the project team to achieve high performance.

The ideas presented here apply to projects in any industry, such as conventional construction, utilities, transportation, defense, manufacturing, petrochemical, service industries, systems development, computer and communications, pharmaceutical, education, research and development, high-tech, financial, hospitality, and the arts.

Learning Objectives. After reading this book and relevant reference materials, the readers should have an understanding of:

- Managing organizational changes and changes to the project process through teamwork
- The difference between a group and a team and characteristics of an integrated project team
- Stages of team development
- Team dynamics involving team context, team structure, team processes and team effectiveness
- Challenges of managing culturally diverse project teams; critical dimensions of culture
- Process, benefits and outcomes of team building
- Drivers and barriers to effective team building and how to eliminate or minimize barriers
- Organizing the project team by setting project goals and creating a conducive organizational climate
- Assembling the project team by selecting the right team members, clarifying roles and responsibilities and obtaining their commitment by using skill and responsibility matrix
- Managing communication challenges in a team environment by creating openness, managing conflicts through effective communication, and building effective team communications
- Developing a strong team for success by coordinating team efforts and using power and authority wisely
- Pros and cons of team decision-making, four decision styles in a team environment, and guidelines for effective team decision-making
- Importance of trust, motivation and team leadership in inspiring high team performance
- How to manage team morale throughout the project life cycle
- Empowerment, building empowered teams with their benefits and problems during transition
- Creating and maintaining Self-Motivated Project Teams (SMPTs).

Through this book, I would like to share with the readers my ideas and experiences about managing projects characterized by dignity, purpose, vision and competitive advantage. I hope you will enjoy reading this book and use it for years to come as a reference for managing projects *successfully* through managing project teams *effectively*.

14

Acknowledgments

Writing this book has been a labor of love. Like many challenges in life, writing requires diligence, perseverance, patience, and discipline—characteristics that don't come easily to many of us, and I am no exception. However, I am very fortunate to have people who encouraged me to stay on track and finish this book, despite many rewrites.

This book would not have been possible without the help of my friend, colleague, and mentor, R. Max Wideman, who stood by me throughout this project. If I acknowledge all Max's ideas and discussions, his name will be all over this book. Max helped me a great deal in developing my views, reviewing my manuscript, and discussing the topics covered. I cannot repay Max for the extraordinary amount of time he devoted to this project.

Another whose help was invaluable is Raso Samarasekera, who entered my handwritten manuscript into the computer. She went through several revisions cheerfully, with special attention to detail and quality. I am really grateful to Raso for her hard work. In addition, my colleague Mark Keyzer helped me in preparing figures and tables.

I am very grateful to Jim Pennypacker, Editor-in-Chief, PMI Publications Division, who encouraged me to stay with this project and played a significant role in expediting it. Another person who deserves special thanks is Jeannette Cabanis, my editor, whose patience, editorial guidance, and hard work were invaluable. I wish also to acknowledge the support of Michelle Owen, the book designer, and other staff members of PMI Publications Division who helped me to complete this project in a very professional manner.

I also wish to thank members of the PMI West Coast B.C. Chapter and my colleagues at TRIUMF with whom I shared my ideas and who gave me help and moral support in this endeavor. I especially wish to acknowledge the senior management members of TRIUMF—Dr. Erich Vogt, Dr. Alan Astbury, and Dr. Ewart Blackmore for their continuous support. Thanks are also owed to the participants in my classes and seminars for their excellent ideas and discussions.

On a personal level, I would like to thank my late parents and Taya Ji; my brothers, Rajinder and Sudesh Verma, and their spouses, Seema and Rita Verma; my sisters, Prem and Sangeeta and their spouses, Sat Parkaash and Surrinder Tony; my in-laws; and my special friends, Raksha and K.L. Toky. Although they are thousands of miles away, they have always inspired me in this endeavor.

Finally, special thanks to my daughters Serena and Angelee and my son Naveen, who supported me, suggested ideas about the basics of understanding people, and gave me an opportunity to complete this book while wondering what Daddy was doing at night in his study. Most of all, I am indebted to my wife, Shiksha Verma, for her love, understanding, and support. All that I am today, I owe to her love, friendship, and devotion. She does not truly know the extent to which she has helped me in completing this project. Shiksha, my appreciation for your support and love cannot be expressed in words, but thanks many times.

Vijay K. Verma
August 1997

Outline

Understanding the Dynamics of Change   18
Sources of pressure for change   18
Principles of change   19
Major types of change   21

Managing Organizational Change   25
Sources of resistance to change   26
Overcoming resistance to change   28
The behavioral side of change   30
Evaluating change   31

Teamwork—A Key to Managing Change   32
Teamwork and human resource management   34
Project team building   37

Managing Changes in a Project Environment   42
Types of changes in a project environment   43
Deciding what changes to make (tradeoff analysis)   50
Dealing with resistance to project changes   51
Evaluating changes and learning lessons for the future   52
The rules in making project changes   53

Summary   54

There is nothing more permanent than change.

— *Heraclitus*

Change Management, Project Management, and Teamwork

PROJECTS, BY THEIR VERY NATURE, are uncertain. Changes, conflicts and problems may occur at any time in the project life cycle. They are often hard to anticipate and therefore cause considerable stress to the project manager and team members. However, with proper planning, an understanding of the dynamics of change, open communications, and good teamwork, changes can be managed in a systematic and rational manner.

Sometimes a project itself may represent a change while, in other cases, projects implement a change. Projects may introduce a new aspect, dimension or perspective, or they may change the existing process, product or service in an organization. The first step in managing any type of project is to prepare the project plan. However, implementation of the plan rarely goes completely smoothly.

Thus, all projects, especially large and complex ones, involve unanticipated changes. Project managers define and evaluate the impact of these changes and formulate a strategy to deal with them. The impact of changes in terms of their impact on budgets and schedules varies according to the nature and size of the change, the number of parties involved, and the timing of the changes in a project life cycle.

Project managers face the challenge of managing projects characterized by high levels of uncertainty, rapid changes, cross-cultural teams, and global competition. They must convert change into opportunity by optimizing team members' performance through building cohesive teams and creating a true team "spirit." Communication, teamwork, leadership, and cultural ambiance are tools for managing project human resources and inspiring high performance. Good planning and effective teamwork help in dealing with the uncertainty of project changes and resistance to change.

Only through effective teamwork can resistance to changes be overcome and project objectives met successfully to the satisfaction of the client, the project team and other stakeholders. ■

Understanding the Dynamics of Change

Most people hate any change that doesn't jingle in their pockets.

— Anonymous

Change seems to be inevitable. It affects our lives dramatically, forcing us to change our plans over and over again. Organizations and projects are influenced by a variety of changes.[1,2] Therefore, the effective management of change can make the difference between success and failure—in projects as well as in life. In order to manage change effectively, it is necessary to develop an understanding of the dynamics of change.

Sources of pressure for change

If you want truly to understand something, try to change it.

— Kurt Lewin

For the last few decades, industrial activity in North America has been shifting from manufacturing to service industries. According to some experts, by the year 2000 the service sector will employ 80 percent of the work force. Globalization of markets, political realignments, technological advances in management information systems and production processes, corporate alliances, downsizing and flattening of organizations and many more factors are changing the structures of the corporations and their project management strategies.[3] Pressure for change is a worldwide phenomenon accelerated by global competition.

These pressures fall into four major categories.[4]

Globalization. Organizations face tremendous global competition. This is becoming more and more obvious in automobile manufacturing, consumer electronics, computers and communications and household manufacturing. Increasingly, the heavyweight players in the world's economy are large corporations involved in international or multinational projects. There is a global market and competition for most products and services and, in order to effectively compete in it, organizations must use creativity and transform their cultures, structures and operations. The emergence of these global organizations creates pressures on domestic organizations and projects to restructure and internationalize their outlook and operations. Because of these powerful forces for globalization, organizations must explore project opportunities all over the world.

Changing technology. Technology is changing at a rate greater than at any time in history. Among the most dramatic technological changes affecting the work environment is the rapid expansion of information system technology. This technological revolution is having a profound impact on project structures, power relationships and the management of complex project interfaces. Artificial intelligence, Computer Integrated Manufacturing and virtual reality are creating new project opportunities in terms of their development and applications.

18

Rapid product obsolescence. Fast-changing consumer preferences, combined with rapid and frequent technological changes and innovations, have shortened the life cycle of many goods and services. The effects of rapid product obsolescence can be dramatic for organizations that cannot adapt quickly enough. In the volatile pharmaceutical and electronics fields, some products become obsolete in as little as six months. Projects aimed at developing products and services in such industries must adapt to this rate of change in a cost effective manner.

The changing work force. Organizations must attract good employees from a workforce that is also changing very fast. A projection for the global workforce in the year 2000 concluded that:

- People worldwide will be better educated and developing countries will produce a growing share of the world's high school and college graduates.
- There will be increased diversity in the workforce, including minority groups, people with disabilities, and immigrants.
- The labor force will grow at less than half the rate that it did in the past.
- Women, especially in developing countries, will enter the workforce in greater numbers; three in five new workers will be women.
- The average age of the world's workforce, especially in developed countries, will rise to around thirty-five years.
- The ultimate effect of globalization will be to bring everyone to approximately the same level in terms of organizational positional power and information processing capabilities.[5]

Not only will the composition and values of the workforce continue to change, but, because of international and cross-cultural projects, interorganizational and international mobility also will increase.[5] If parent organizations cannot meet their needs for vocational or professional development, employees will simply leave. Employees are likely to become less loyal to a particular organization, but more strongly tied to their profession or skill. They may change occupations several times during their working lives to gain a variety of work experience, to gain more security, or to adjust to changing economic conditions. Consequently, it will be more common for individuals to have a variety of diverse occupations during their lifetimes.

Principles of change

Be patient; behavioral change comes in small steps.

— Anonymous

Success or failure in implementing change depends upon how well the situation has been analyzed, the quality of information collected, and an understanding of the strengths and weaknesses of the people involved in the change process. Organizational diagnosis should be carried out on a continuous basis to determine what changes should be made and how to implement them. Information needed to diagnose organizational problems can be gathered by questionnaires, interviews, observations or company records.[6] Managers and employees should recognize two factors when diagnosing organizational problems.[4]

First, organizational behavior is affected by many interacting forces. Problems may have multiple causes, as employee behaviors and personal problems interact with the current state of the organization. Attempts to isolate single causes for complex problems will lead to simplistic change strategies, which are usually ineffective.

Secondly, in the process of diagnosis, it is possible to gather information related to *symptoms* rather than *causes* of problems. Change strategies that merely respond to symptoms will not solve underlying problems. For example, rewarding employees for perfect attendance will not solve absenteeism because these problems may be caused by lack of interesting assignments, poor work policies and procedures and pressures created by excessive workloads.

The principles of organizational change must be considered when conducting an organizational diagnosis. First, you must understand the dynamics of change before implementing a change. And since organizational systems are complex, you must realize that it is hard to change just one element of a system; instead, the whole system needs to be analyzed.

In addition, people's resistance to change is normal. They are reluctant to tolerate discomfort, even for future potential gains. Thus change leads to conflict and stress. But these obstacles can be dealt with by explaining why the change is necessary and involving people in setting goals and developing change strategies. Such participation should be genuine—not lip service.[4,6]

The major forces that collectively influence the success of a change in an organization include the change agent; determining what should be changed and types of changes; gaining support from individuals affected by the change; and the evaluation of change.[7] The success of organizational change depends upon the techniques used by management to deal with these major factors when designing and implementing changes.

Project manager as change agent. One of the most important factors to be considered by organizations involved in large and complex projects and activities, is determining who will be the change agent. The term "change agent" refers to anyone inside or outside the organization who is *committed* to *direct* the change.[8] This change agent may be a member of the senior management team within the organization or an outside consultant, hired because of a special expertise in a particular area. The change agent must be able to determine the types of changes to be made and develop and implement these changes to accomplish the long-term goals of the organization.

Change agents must seek active participation from the various people likely to be affected by a change. They must anticipate some resistance to these changes and must be able to overcome this resistance at an individual and organizational level and gain the support of these individuals. This helps them gain their acceptance and their commitment, not only to the successful implementation of change, but to the positive outcomes from the change.

In reality, anyone in the organization can initiate and direct a change. For example, in a project environment, the project manager generally plays the role of major change agent. In this chapter, the terms *manager, project manager,* and *change agent,* will be used synonymously. The change agent must possess special skills to be effective in implementing changes. They must have an ability to determine why, what and how changes should be made, to solve change related problems, and to use behavioral science techniques and effective interpersonal skills to influence people appropriately during the change. Perhaps one of the most overlooked skills necessary to be a successful change agent is to determine how much change the stakeholder can withstand. It is imperative that top management chooses change agents with appropriate skills and expertise to implement the changes successfully. An organization may lose all potential benefits if changes are made inappropriately and by the wrong people.

Implementation of change in an organization can be considered a project that should be managed very carefully with special emphasis on human aspects because all changes involve people. A thorough front-end planning should be done that includes answering three key questions:

Why should the changes be made? Emphasize the importance of the changes and their impacts in terms of long-term goals of the organization.

What should be changed and when? Explore various alternatives and determine the priorities according to organizational constraints.

How the changes should be made? A plan should be developed showing the major steps to be followed along with human and other resources necessary to meet the plan.

Major types of change

Everything is changing. People are taking the comedians seriously and the politicians as a joke.

— *Will Rogers*

Organizations face several types of changes. In general, organizational effectiveness depends upon activities centering around four main classes of factors:[9]

- *People factors,* including attitudes, interpersonal skills, leadership skills, communication skills and other aspects of human resources
- *Structural factors,* including policies, procedures, organizational controls and organization structures, etc.

- *Technological factors,* which refer to the type of equipment or processes that help organizational members perform their jobs
- *Teamwork,* which has a significant impact on project effectiveness because it affects each of above factors. Effective teamwork helps in managing people, structural, and technological factors and creates human synergy.

Projects are similar to functional organizations but more specific in scope or smaller in size. Therefore, managing change in a project environment is similar to that process in a functional organization. Large, complex projects resemble an organization involved in multiple projects with similar relationships between people, structural, and technological factors. To optimize the effectiveness of the project management process, project managers must try to match appropriate people with appropriate technology and appropriate structure. These four factors are interdependent and project effectiveness is determined by the relationship among these three factors as shown in Figure 1.1.

Three types of changes, corresponding to three main determinants of organizational and project effectiveness as shown in Figure 1.1, are "people" change, structural change, and technological change.[7]

Change agents should conduct ongoing internal and external diagnoses of the situation to determine what changes would optimize the appropriateness of the people-structure-technology relationship and hence the overall effectiveness of management. For example, technological change emphasizes the need to modify the level of technology within a management system. It is highly technical and often involves outside experts. People and structural changes are complicated and interesting due to the dimensions of behavior, team and group dynamics and interpersonal relationships.[7]

"People changes." Although successful "people change" also involves some consideration of structure and technology, it primarily emphasizes increasing project or organizational effectiveness by changing its members. People change focuses on such factors as modifying attitudes, modifying interpersonal skills, modifying communication skills, and modifying leadership skills.

Change agents should try to make this type of change when the results of external and internal diagnosis indicate that problems and conflicts in managing human resources are the main cause of ineffectiveness in an organization.

Organization development (OD) is the process of people change. It focuses mainly on changing people based on an overview of structure, technology and all other organizational ingredients.[10] To demonstrate this organizational overview approach, it is important during organization development to identify and analyze both overt and covert components of the organization.[11]

22

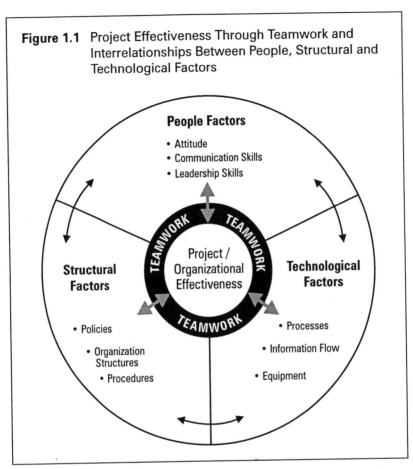

Figure 1.1 Project Effectiveness Through Teamwork and Interrelationships Between People, Structural and Technological Factors

People Factors
- Attitude
- Communication Skills
- Leadership Skills

Structural Factors
- Policies
- Organization Structures
- Procedures

Project / Organizational Effectiveness

TEAMWORK

Technological Factors
- Processes
- Information Flow
- Equipment

Source: Samuel C. Certo, Steven H. Appelbaum and Irene Divine, 1989, *Principles of Modern Management—A Canadian Perspective,* Third Edition, Allyn and Bacon, Inc., pp. 289. By permission of the publisher.

Overt factors include organizational structures, personnel and operating policies and procedures and planning/information systems, etc. These are generally cognitively derived and oriented to operational and task considerations. On the other hand, covert factors include sentiments, emotions, needs, desires, influence patterns and interpersonal relationships, and are difficult to identify. These are usually hidden, difficult to evaluate and are generally affective and emotionally derived and oriented to the general organizational climate plus psychological, behavioral, and process considerations.[7,11]

OD techniques suggest changes that emphasize both people and the organization as a whole. Management and change agents must be aware of the weaknesses of OD and use alternative techniques to work around them.

Change Management, Project Management, and Teamwork

Some guidelines that managers can use to improve the quality of OD efforts are:[12]

- Tailor OD programs to meet the specific needs of the project organizations
- Continually demonstrate (as part of the program) how people should change their behavior; model desired behavior
- Adjust organizational reward systems to reward those who change their behaviors according to an OD program.

Structural change. Structural change is aimed at increasing project/organizational effectiveness by changing controls, policies and procedures that influence organization members in their job performance. It focuses on modifying existing organizational structure. These modifications can take several forms. Organizations may clarify and define responsibility and authority; modify organizational structure to suit communication needs; or decentralize the organization, especially if it is very large and multinational or international in character. Decentralization has been shown to be helpful in achieving cost effective coordination, capitalizing on specialization, controlling subunits, increasing motivation through direct and closer contact among project team members; gaining greater flexibility, and delegating some decision-making at the local level (empowerment).[13]

Matrix structure is practical, particularly for managing projects that require team members with diverse backgrounds and skills who have been allocated to a project from various functional areas. Matrix structure leads to an effective use of available competing resources, but for a matrix structure to be effective and efficient, participants must be willing to learn and execute somewhat different organizational roles. This willingness is a personal characteristic that must be gauged by the change agent, along with the structural support available in the organization for such flexibility. These factors are interrelated and will vary from situation to situation.

There are some general advantages and disadvantages of making structural changes by adopting a matrix structure. These pros and cons are displayed in Table 1.1.[14] However, for a matrix structure to be effective and efficient, participants must be willing to learn and execute somewhat different organizational roles.[15]

To be successful, structural change should not overlook people and technology factors. Managers should only make structural changes if their internal and external diagnosis indicate that the present organizational structure is responsible for ineffectiveness.

Technological change. Rapid advancements in information systems technology and telecommunications are influencing the project management process and outcomes. These technological changes are eliminating the problems of physical distances. Audio and video conferences can create the personal interactions needed to work as a team. Robotics and com-

24

Table 1.1 Weighing the Value of Matrix Structure

Advantages	Disadvantages
Better project control	Creates more complex internal operations
Effective use of resources	Inconsistent application of company policy.
Better customer relations	A more difficult situation to manage (two bosses).
Shorter project development time	
Lower project costs	
Better professional development of team members.	

puter-aided design and manufacturing (CAD/CAM) techniques are proving to be very useful tools in managing projects in engineering and manufacturing industries. Other technological changes in the area of graphics, desktop publishing, multimedia presentation techniques, and easy production of three-dimensional pictures and photographs have improved the quality of presentation and reporting systems.

Technological changes have changed the way project participants work by themselves and interact with each other. Project managers must try to stay on top of technological changes in order to exploit new business opportunities.

Technological change emphasizes modifying the level and type of technology used within an organization or project management system. It may involve learning technical language (a "people" change), structural changes and outside experts.

Managing Organizational Change

When making a change, the change agent must consider the people who will be affected by it. A good assessment of what to change and how to change probably will fail without sufficient support of the participants. To gain their support, change agents must be aware of the usual resistance to change, understand the sources of this resistance and how to reduce it, and have some knowledge of the behavioral side of change.

Pressure to change is neverending. It is also inevitable that changes will be resisted, at least to some extent, by both individuals and organizations. Resistance to change is a complex problem and can take many forms. Overt resistance may lead to strikes, reduction in productivity, sloppy work, and even sabotage. Covert resistance may lead to increased absenteeism and tardiness, request for transfers, loss of motivation, lower morale and higher accident or error rates. One of the more harmful forms of resistance is lack of a genuine participation in and commitment to proposed changes by people even when they have opportunity to participate.[16]

Sources of resistance to change

Resistance to change may come at the individual level or from the nature or structure of the organization. Managers and team members must understand the reasons for and sources of resistance to change.[17]

Individual resistance to change. There are five sources of individual resistance to change (see Figure 1.2).[4]

Selective perception creates resistance because people tend to perceive only what they like or already believe in, for example, reading or listening only to what they agree with; conveniently "forgetting" any knowledge leading to other viewpoints; or misunderstanding communication that, if correctly perceived, would not fit with their values and attitudes.

An established *habit* represents a source of satisfaction and provides a certain comfort and security. People will change their habits only if they perceive advantages from changing some habitual behavior.

People who have a high degree of *dependence* on others will resist changes until the changes are endorsed and incorporated into the behavior of those they depend on. For example, some team members who are highly dependent on their team leader or project manager for feedback on performance will perhaps not agree to any new techniques or methods unless their leader personally endorses them and demonstrates to the team members how these changes will improve their performance.

Fear of the unknown is the most common source of resistance to change because every change carries with it an element of uncertainty. People affected by change may fear some personal loss, such as a reduction in prestige, a disturbance in established social and working relationships or personal failure in carrying out new job responsibilities. Uncertainty in such situations arises not only from the prospective change itself but also from the potential consequences of the change. As a result of fear, people sometimes refuse promotions that require relocating or that require major changes in job duties or responsibilities.

Economic reasons are a significant source of resistance. People resist changes that could lower their income either directly or indirectly; they have an investment in the status quo in their jobs. They have learned how to perform work successfully, how to interact with other team members and stakeholders and how to get good performance appraisals. Changes in established work routine may threaten their economic security, for example by lowering their value in the eyes of project manager and other team members.

These five sources of resistance, though common, are not the only reasons why individuals may resist any change. Whatever the reason, however, project

26

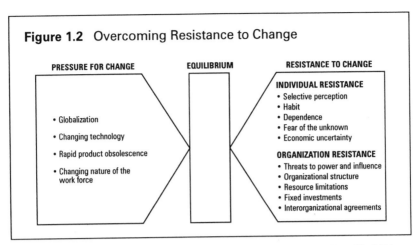

Figure 1.2 Overcoming Resistance to Change

PRESSURE FOR CHANGE   EQUILIBRIUM   RESISTANCE TO CHANGE

- Globalization
- Changing technology
- Rapid product obsolescence
- Changing nature of the work force

INDIVIDUAL RESISTANCE
- Selective perception
- Habit
- Dependence
- Fear of the unknown
- Economic uncertainty

ORGANIZATION RESISTANCE
- Threats to power and influence
- Organizational structure
- Resource limitations
- Fixed investments
- Interorganizational agreements

Source: Don Hellreigel, John W. Slocum, Jr., and Richard W. Woodman, *Organizational Behavior,* Sixth Edition, West Publishing Company, St. Paul, MN, p. 733.

managers can reduce resistance by pointing out the benefits of changes and involving people in developing plans to implement changes. For this reason, project managers must try to know their team members and other project stakeholders well, both formally as well as informally. This will help them identify sources of resistance, anticipate individual resistance to changes and develop strategies to manage changes successfully.

Organizational resistance to change. Organizations are often most efficient in doing routine things and may experience drop in performance, at least initially, when doing anything different for the first time. This pattern creates a strong defense against change to ensure operational efficiency and effectiveness. Moreover, change often opposes vested interests and violates certain territorial rights or decision-making powers that have been established and accepted over time. There are several significant sources of organizational resistance to change.[4]

People resist changes out of *fear of a threat to their existing power and influence.* "Power" can be defined as the control over something needed by other people, such as information or resources. Once such a power position has been established, not just by individuals but by an entire level of the organization, the preservation of that power and influence becomes an organizational imperative.

Organizations need stability and continuity to function effectively. Therefore, they tend to resist any major changes in *organization structure* that change the responsibility and authority relationships, span of control and flow of information.

Changes require resources: the investment of capital, time, and people with the necessary skills. Some changes are abandoned or deferred because of *resource limitations.*

Change Management, Project Management, and Teamwork

Fixed investments (of capital and people) limit the amount of changes that can be made. For example, in a large organization, senior people may not be making a significant contribution but may have enough seniority to maintain their jobs. Unless they can be motivated to increase their task performance and retrained for other assignments, their salaries and fringe benefits represent fixed investment that is hard to change.

Sometimes organizational change can be restrained by obligations imposed by *inter-organizational agreements*. Labor negotiations and contracts are pertinent examples. For example, the traditional rights of management to hire and fire, change task assignments, promotions and so on are subject to negotiations and fixed in the negotiated contract. Other kinds of contracts also restrain organizations.

Despite these barriers to change, organizations today are frequently forced to make changes in order to meet global competition. The survival and growth of organizations will depend upon their adaptability and the ability to change their strategies, structure, operations and resources.

Overcoming resistance to change

Praise can be your most valuable asset as long as you don't aim it at yourself.
— O.A. Battista

Project participants often face difficulties in clearly understanding situations that involve change because of the large number of variables associated with change. However, project managers and team members can learn to identify, analyze and overcome resistance to change and become more effective change agents.

Force field analysis. One tool that can assist them in this process is Kurt Lewin's *force field analysis*,[18] which is based upon the idea that change is not just an event, but a dynamic balance of opposing forces. Force field analysis suggests that any situation can reach a state of equilibrium resulting from a balance of forces pushing against each other. Forces such as technological change and a changing workforce tend to push for change. At the same time, other forces (such as individual and organizational resistance) act in the opposite direction. The combined effect of these forces is shown in Figure 1.2.[4]

Therefore, in order to initiate change, the project manager must act to modify the current equilibrium of forces by either increasing the strength of pressure for change, reducing the strength of resistance to change, or changing resistance into pressure for change by convincing people that the change is necessary and will benefit them.

The force field analysis model helps us understand the process of change and has two primary advantages.[4] It stresses the role of upfront analysis. Before making any change, both the project managers and team members must analyze the current situation by evaluating the forces pressing for

28

and resisting changes. This helps them better understand the relevant aspects of any changed situation.

In addition, this model highlights the factors that *can* be changed and those that *cannot*. Thus project managers can avoid wasting time and effort battling forces over which they have little, if any, control. Instead, the energy can be focused towards the forces that will be effective in implementing change successfully.

Guidelines to overcome resistance to change. Realistically, we cannot expect resistance to changes to cease completely. But we can reduce resistance by using the following guidelines.[4,19]

Avoid surprises. No one likes surprises, especially if they are unpleasant. Project managers should give people who are likely to be affected by the change sufficient time to evaluate the proposed changes. They should inform them of the reasons for change, the type of change being considered and the probability that the change will be implemented.

Promote real understanding through empathy and support. Opposition to a proposed change is reduced by reducing the fear of personal loss.[20] It is useful to understand how people are experiencing changes, to identify those who are troubled by the change, and to understand the nature of their concerns. When project participants feel that the project managers or other change agents are open and sympathetic to their concerns, they provide necessary support and information. This, in turn, creates a collaborative team and problem-solving atmosphere and helps overcome barriers to change.

Effective communication. People resist changes when they are uncertain about its consequences. Change agents should provide adequate information and help prepare people for change. Effective communication can reduce gossip and unfounded fears and develop better and sincere understanding among all parties affected by the change.

Positive attitude towards change. Positive attitude and enthusiasm is contagious. It is hard for project managers to push for a change without their hearts in it. Changes should be made not just for the sake of changing but should be aimed to increase overall effectiveness. To emphasize this attitude towards change, management should earmark some portion of rewards for those change agents (champions) who prove to be most instrumental in implementing constructive changes.

Participation and involvement. Perhaps the most effective strategy for overcoming resistance to change is to involve those who are likely to be affected by the change directly in planning and implementing change. Involvement and participation in planning changes increases the probability that the concerns and interests of the parties involved are accounted for and this reduces their resistance to change.

Through involvement, people buy into proposed changes and the change process. Participation leads to better acceptance and hence stronger commitment to implement the changes successfully and make them work.

Start with tentative change. Resistance to change can be reduced by implementing changes on a tentative basis. This is the best way of reducing feared personal loss. Project participants may evaluate the effects of change during this trial period. Using this tentative approach means that those involved can test reactions to new situations before committing themselves irrevocably and that they can acquire more facts on which to base their attitudes and behavior toward the change. Having time to get used to the idea, they may be less likely to consider the change as a threat.[21]

Those with strong preconceptions can evaluate the change more objectively and may consequently review their preconceptions and modify them. Management can also evaluate the method of change and make any modifications before carrying it out full scale.[21]

Careful analysis of a situation does not, however, always guarantee a successful change. If, after analysis, a project manager elects to increase the pressure for change as the strategy for producing the desired change, such an increase in pressure may lead to unpleasant short term changes that are disruptive to the team climate and unbalance the project organization.

The behavioral side of change

Not everything that is faced can be changed but nothing can be changed until it is faced.

— *James Baldwin*

Positive results from any change depend upon corresponding changes in the behaviors of the people involved. Almost all changes require some modification in human behavior. Therefore, project managers or change agents should not only select the best people-structure-technology relationship but should also try to make changes in such a way that related human behavior is effectively changed.

According to Kurt Lewin, behavior changes through a three-step process of unfreezing, changing and refreezing.[22]

Unfreezing. This step involves reducing those forces that represent status quo. Unfreezing can be accomplished by showing people discrepancies between current behaviors and desired behaviors. Old behaviors may be difficult for individuals to "throw out" because of strong beliefs and positive attitudes they traditionally associated with that behavior.

Changing. Changing involves developing new behaviors, values and attitudes through changes in organizational structures and processes. This step shifts the behavior of individuals to a new level. People begin experimenting with new behavior with the hope of increasing their effectiveness.

According to Edgar Schein, this change is most effective if it involves both identification and internalization,[23] *identification* being the process

30

by which individuals perform new behavior by copying an expert in their organization, and *internalization* being the process by which they try to make these part of their normal behavior, making the new behaviors useful over a longer time.

Refreezing. This step stabilizes the individual or organization at a new state of equilibrium. In this state, people see their new behavior as part of themselves. Refreezing can be accomplished through the use of supporting mechanisms and positive reinforcements that will reinforce the new organizational state, such as organizational culture, policies, norms and structures.[24]

Evaluating change

As an important part of the management function, change agents should evaluate the changes they've made in order to assess their impacts on the overall effectiveness of the organization. The main purpose of this evaluation is to determine how the change itself can be modified to increase overall productivity and also how the various steps used in developing and implementing the change process can be modified for future use.

It may be difficult to correctly evaluate the impact of changes because of unreliability in the data related to outcome of the change. However, change agents must include the evaluation as an important element of the change process because of an opportunity to learn lessons for implementing changes in the future. Evaluation of change involves watching for symptoms that indicate that further change is necessary. However, senior managers should be careful not to make changes simply based on observation symptoms. They must analyze their internal and external environment and collect more objective information before deciding about the need for changes. In general, additional change in an organization is justifiable if it:

- Improves its overall financial and organizational effectiveness
- Improves trust between all stakeholders
- Improves its competitive situation
- Improves the quality of work life for its employees
- Contributes to professional growth, self-esteem and job satisfaction of its employees
- Contributes to society as a whole.

Teamwork—A Key to Managing Change

Snowflakes are one of nature's most fragile things, but just look at what they can do when they stick together.

— Anonymous

Change, conflict, and stress are interrelated, as shown in Figure 1.3. Symptoms of resistance to change include loss in productivity, "sick-outs," and work slowdowns as well as some more subtle symptoms such as apathy, hostility and justifications of why the changes won't work. All these symptoms, taken together, may be called the *change resistance syndrome.*[25] According to

Change Management, Project Management, and Teamwork

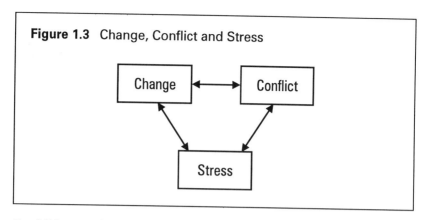

Figure 1.3 Change, Conflict and Stress

Roethlisberger, the resistance to change syndrome follows a reciprocal pattern that begins when management introduces a change and immediately the workers counter with resistance.[26] To overcome this resistance, management may take various approaches, such as explaining the need for the change and its benefits; hiring consultants to justify the change or to help facilitate its acceptance; using feedback sessions to emphasize the realities behind the change; or sending stressed managers for training to learn how to cope with change and handle resistance to change.[25]

When these approaches fail, management may resort to positional authority by punishing the holdouts and rewarding the collaborators. Such approaches only lead to more serious people problems because they poison the working relationships and mutual trust between both parties. The battle continues until either the ringleaders quit, the workers reluctantly accept the change, or management gives up and forgets the whole thing. In a project environment, at this point, project and team organization may look stable on the surface, but the resentment and bitter feelings linger, making the next innovation and its acceptance very difficult. Consequently, many desirable changes are avoided, brushed aside and minimized by both the management and the workers until organizations are forced to face the change process again because of internal or external pressures.[27]

In spite of our managerial knowledge about handling change, the change resistance syndrome is still very common and a serious problem. Change can only be managed successfully through effective communication, mutual trust, cooperation and collaboration—the main characteristics of an effective team. In a sense, resistance to change is a failure in teamwork. In a true team environment, the resistance to change either does not emerge, or if it does, the team members proactively collaborate in managing the change process. Teamwork minimizes the resistance to change by encouraging genuine participation and facilitating cooperative interactions between all team members, regardless of their positional status, to accomplish the common team objectives.

32

Building, developing and maintaining an effective project team is not easy. Whenever teamwork is left to chance, project managers experience passive behavior characterized by resistance to change. While management interprets this resistance externally as poor behavior, resulting in a negative evaluation of resistant workers, the workers' opposition to change is merely their internal response to the perceived need to protect their work environment and social character. Teamwork and effective team building bridges the gap between these external and internal processes during change. To manage the change effectively through teamwork, both the project managers and the team members must understand this process and behaviorally respond to each other in a way that leads to cooperation, collaboration, and shared commitment.

Team building is one of the primary responsibilities of the project manager. As discussed earlier, project managers can be viewed as change agents. To manage change effectively, they must appreciate the importance of team building and the role of communication, leadership and cultural diversity to manage project human resources effectively. Dramatic increases in project complexity require individuals with a diverse mix of backgrounds, skills and expertise to be integrated into an effective unit—a project team. In a team environment, people work *interdependently* rather than *independently*. Increasingly, stringent project performance requirements mandate a high level of sustained cooperative effort within the project team. Project managers must recognize the critical significance of the effective project team and the role of team building in facilitating this high performance standard.

Project managers must understand interpersonal and group dynamics to optimize productivity at the individual as well as at the team level. While belonging to a successful project team is very satisfying, creating such a team is equally rewarding for the project manager. Beyond that, project managers must continue to provide routine care and feeding of team members.

The working relationships among the project team members affect not only their individual or team productivity, but also affect their performance in relation to the client and the support groups. Therefore, teamwork is a critical factor for project success and developing effective project teams is one of the prime responsibilities of the project manager. Team development involves a whole spectrum of project management skills to identify, commit, and integrate the project participants from traditional functional organizations into multidisciplinary and highly cohesive project teams.

Project managers must create an environment that facilitates real teamwork and fosters human synergy. They must acquire skills to identify, build, maintain, motivate, lead, and inspire project teams to achieve high team performance and to meet or exceed the project's objectives. They must understand the issues associated with teams in the project environment, such

Change Management, Project Management, and Teamwork

as the importance of team building; the team building process; and the major tasks in building project teams to suit the various phases of the project life cycle. The drivers and barriers to high team performance must be identified and solutions developed to minimize the negative impact of these barriers. Project managers should continually motivate their team by providing challenges and opportunities, by providing support as needed, and by recognizing the team members for good performance. High team performance can be inspired and real teamwork achieved by using open and effective communication, developing trust among team members, managing conflicts in a constructive manner, and encouraging collaborative problem-solving and participative decision-making.

Teamwork and human resource management

Teamwork leads to human synergy.

— Anonymous

In order to develop the appropriate skills for operating in a global and multicultural environment, project managers must develop a clear understanding of the human aspects of project management and of effective management of project human resources. A balanced combination of basic management, project management, interpersonal, and leadership skills are required to meet project objectives. Figure 1.4 shows a model for effectively managing project human resources and inspiring high team performance, that consists of four key factors:[28] *communication, teamwork, leadership, cultural ambiance.*

Communication, teamwork, and leadership are vital components of effective management of project human resources. These incorporate all major skills required to accomplish project objectives successfully. They are all interrelated and critical to project success. Although voice mail, e-mail and other information technology communication tools may help in communicating messages efficiently, it is not certain that these are highly effective because of missing nonverbal (body language) components of communication. Project management today faces greater challenges because of the increased need for joint ventures and international projects characterized by cultural diversity in project teams and stakeholders. Cultural ambiance plays a significant role by itself in dealing with people and also influences communications, teamwork, and leadership in a project environment. Project managers must develop appropriate organizational designs and project management strategies to facilitate open communication, effective teamwork, and a leadership style that inspires high performance of all project participants throughout the project life cycle.

Teamwork is what creates human synergy and helps increase the performance of all project participants. Project managers must be aware of all the important elements of the effective project human resource management model and how these can be combined to optimize project success.

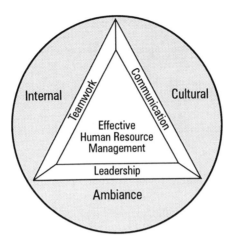

Figure 1.4 Model for Effective Project Human Resource Management

Internal · Cultural

Teamwork · Communication

Effective Human Resource Management

Leadership

Ambiance

Cultural ambiance impacts overall human resource management, as well as influencing Teamwork, Leadership, and Communication.

Hence, effective Project Human Resource Management is a function of Teamwork, Leadership, Communication and Cultural Ambiance.

This is the essence of project management integration.

Teamwork and communication. Communication is a vital element of project human resource management. A project manager uses communication, more than any other skill set in the project management process, to ensure that team members work cohesively on the project and resolve their mutual problems effectively. Successful project leaders rely heavily upon their ability to communicate vision and inspire project participants towards high performance.

Communication can be defined as a process by which information is exchanged between individuals through a common system of symbols, signs, or behavior.[29] In project management, the importance of communication is emphasized by Sievert, who says "A high percentage of the frictions, frustrations, and inefficiencies in working relationships are traceable to poor communication. In almost every case, the misinterpretation of a design drawing, a misunderstood change order, a missed delivery date, or a failure to execute instructions result from a breakdown in communication."[30]

Communications can make or break a project. Project managers must establish appropriate communication channels and design project organizational structures that facilitate open and effective communication and foster creativity, real team spirit, and human synergy.

Listening skills. Effective listening is perhaps the most important component of communication, but it is a skill that some project managers, selected primarily on the basis of their technical and quantitative skills, may lack. Alliances with major stakeholders can only be built and maintained through active listening and opening up communication channels to keep messages flowing in both directions. In addition to improving project communications, this usually facilitates the development of mutual trust, respect, and good working relationships, enhancing overall team performance.

Effective listening in a team environment implies that we attend to:[28]
- What people want to tell you
- What they don't want to tell you
- What they cannot tell you without help.

Effective listening reduces social distances and softens social status differences in teams. It facilitates better understanding and cooperation. Also, through effective listening, project managers gain more knowledge and information from others that should help them take appropriate actions. It also reinforces team members because they feel they are listened to and their ideas are valued and put into practice when appropriate.

Listening is an excellent tool for creating teamwork. Most projects fail because of lack of teamwork, which is mainly caused by communication breakdown and poor interpersonal skills.

Listening is highly related to perceptions. A good listener must be conscious of his or her own behavior, attitude and feeling, and feel completely responsible for how they affect others. Teams have a diverse mix of people. Listening requires a willingness to see, appreciate, and even accept different viewpoints. Often feelings and sentiments prevail over facts and logic. Project managers must recognize that generally team members act in accordance with the sentiments of their teams. It is through effective listening that project managers can understand the emotions, feelings and sentiments of individual team members and then develop appropriate strategies to build teams and achieve effective teamwork.

Communication is complex. Yet since competent communication leads to effective leadership, interface management, integration, and high team performance, project managers must work at removing communication barriers (caused by themselves or by other project personnel) to achieve effective project communications throughout the project life cycle.

Teamwork and leadership. Effective teamwork is the by-product of good leadership. There is an ample body of literature on communication, teamwork, and leadership. However, it is still not very clear what project leadership is and how it relates to project management. Verma and Wideman dealt with this issue in addressing the questions: Is it leadership or management that is most needed to managing projects successfully in the next century? Do we need different leadership styles/blends during different phases of the project life cycle?[28]

For a more in-depth discussion of this topic, see Volume 2 of this series, *Human Resource Skills for the Project Manager*, Chapter 7.

Teamwork and cultural ambiance. The increased need for joint ventures and international projects leads to increased cultural diversity among project team members and other major stakeholders. Management of both domestic and international projects requires effective planning, organizing, and controlling. However, management of international projects and joint ventures poses additional human resource management challenges related to communication, teamwork, and leadership, as a result of the diverse cultural backgrounds of the project participants. This presents interesting challenges in negotiating, motivating, and human relations. This topic is discussed in detail in Chapter 2.

Project team building

Teamwork can make ordinary people produce extraordinary results.
— *Anonymous*

Projects today have dramatically increased in complexity, requiring individuals with a diverse mix of background, skills, and functional specialties who must be integrated into an effective unit—*a project team*. To manage projects with multifunctional activities, project managers must cross organizational lines and deal with people over whom they have little or no authority. Increasingly stringent project performance requirements are mandating a high level of sustained cooperative effort within culturally diverse project teams. Project managers must recognize the critical significance and role of an effective project team and must acquire appropriate team building skills to foster cultural synergy within their multicultural team and inspire high team performance.

What is a team? A team approach is a distinctive way of working that harnesses the collective skills, strengths, and energy of team members. Teamwork leads to synergy and improves performance of everyone (see Figure 1.5). A team is a group of people, but all groups do not qualify as teams. At times, a group may be formed just for administrative purposes or for achieving personal goals or for social affiliation. At other times, committees can stifle creativity and hinder decision-making. However, occasionally, a group of people combines high morale, effective task performance, and a clear relevance to the organization.[31,32] A team is a group of people who work interdependently, who are committed to common goals, and who produce high quality results. Figure 1.6 shows the differences between a collection of people, a work group and a team with respect to their stage on the maturity continuum and management role.[33]

Characteristics of effective teams. Effective teams produce high quality results and succeed in spite of many difficulties and cultural or philosophical

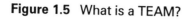

Figure 1.5 What is a TEAM?

T — Together

E — Everyone

A — Achieves

M — More

differences. Team members help each other resolve problems, and feel responsible for the output of the team as a whole. Effective teams have several task-oriented and people-oriented characteristics.[32]

Task-oriented characteristics relate to direct measure of project performance by focusing on tasks and results. Such characteristics include:
- Commitment to technical success
- On schedule, on budget performance
- Committed to producing high-quality results
- Innovative and creative
- Flexibility and willingness to change
- Ability to predict trends.[32]

People-oriented characteristics influence indirect measure of project performance. These characteristics are more associated with people skills and working relationships among team members. People-oriented characteristics of effective teams include:
- High involvement, work interest and high energy
- Capacity to solve conflicts
- Good communications
- Good team spirit
- Mutual trust
- Self-development of team members
- Effective organizational interface
- High need for achievement and growth.[32]

Teams can be judged by their output, objectives, energy, structure and atmosphere. In a nutshell, effective team is composed of a group of people who work interdependently, who are flexible, committed to achieving common objectives, work well together and enjoy it, and produce high quality results. Effective teams can easily recognize barriers to their own effectiveness and then develop and implement actions to remove those barriers.

38

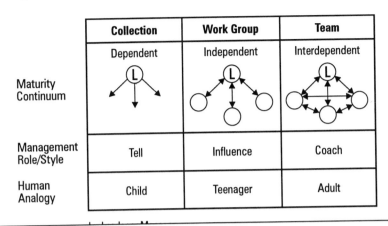

Figure 1.6 A Group Does Not Make a Team

	Collection	**Work Group**	**Team**
Maturity Continuum	Dependent	Independent	Interdependent
Management Role/Style	Tell	Influence	Coach
Human Analogy	Child	Teenager	Adult

Adapted from materials presented in a seminar on Coaching & Team Building Skills for Managers & Supervisors, by Skill Path Inc., 1994, Mission, Kansas. p. 8. By permission of publisher.

What is team building? Building effective project teams is one of the prime responsibilities of project managers. Team building is the process of transforming a group of individuals with different interests, backgrounds, and expertise into an integrated and effective work unit. It can also be seen as a process of change. In this transformational process, the goals and energies of all team members merge and support the objectives of the team. The team building process is important for all types of projects but will vary in complexity depending upon the nature and size of the project.

In the process of team building, project teams have to answer ten questions:

1. What are we here to do?
2. How shall we organize ourselves?
3. Who is in charge?
4. What are our roles, responsibilities and relationships?
5. Who cares about our success?
6. How do we resolve problems and conflicts?
7. How will the performance be measured?
8. How are the awards decided?
9. How do we fit in with other groups?
10. What benefits do team members need from the team?[31]

These questions do not arise at specific and predictable times and need not be answered in a step-by-step process. However, in practice, these issues must be addressed and resolved as they arise and or they may become significant obstacles to team progress. The project team becomes stronger, and a high-performance team, if it successfully works through its obstacles in a

Change Management, Project Management, and Teamwork

Figure 1.7 Role of Management and Leadership in The Five Stages of Team Building

Stage	Management Skills	Leadership Qualities	Task & Relationship Behaviors	Task & Relationship Outcomes	Theme
1. Form	Organizing Teaching Setting accountabilities Setting standards Goal setting	Being open & honest Vision and values-driven Solutions-oriented Trustworthy Listening	Orientation *Dependency*	Commitment *Acceptance*	Awareness/ Orientation
2. Storm	Counseling Active listening Assertiveness Job analysis Performance assessment Conflict management	Being patient Being flexible Being creative Kaleidoscopic thinker	Resistance *Hostility*	Purpose *Belonging*	Conflict/ Control
3. Norm	Communicating Giving constructive feedback Affirming Coaching	Playfulness Humor Entrepreneurship Networking	Communication *Cohesion*	Involvement *Support*	Cooperation
4. Perform	Consensus-building Problem solving Decision making Rewarding	Managing by walking around Stewardship delegation Mentor Futurist Cheerleader/champion	Problem Solving *Interdependence*	Achievement *Synergy*	Productivity
5. Adjourn/ Reform	Evaluating Reviewing Improving	Celebrating Bringing closure	Closure *Celebration*	Recognition *Satisfaction*	Separation/ Moving on

Adapted from materials presented in a seminar on Coaching & Team Building Skills for Managers & Supervisors, by Skill Path Inc., 1994, Mission, Kansas. p. 14-15. By permission of publisher.

timely manner; likewise, if it fails to clear the obstacles, success in achieving objectives is unlikely. Team building involves going through all difficulties and obstacles until a working group becomes high performing and effective. One of the most important characteristics of an effective team building process is that all problems are resolved by the team members themselves rather than having problem-solving done for or to them.

All teams go through five stages of development, which include:

1. Forming (testing)
2. Storming (infighting) also known as conflict/floundering
3. Norming (getting organized)
4. Performing (mature closeness)
5. Adjourning (re-forming).[31, 33]

Teams follow a specific developmental sequence that has three characteristics:

Table 1.2 Management vs. Leadership

Management	Leadership
• Uses positional power	• Uses personal power
• Administers	• Innovates
• Feels challenged by complexities	• Feels challenged by change
• Focus on tasks and processes (what? and how?)	• Focuses on people (why? what for?)
• Transactional (exchange)	• Transformational (empowerment)
• Control	• Direct
• Driven by objectives	• Driven by vision
Does things right.	**Does the right thing.**

Cyclical. All stages occur naturally and in order. How long a team stays at a particular stage depends upon team dynamics, team size, and team leadership.

Developmental. There are several issues and challenges at each stage that must be resolved before the team can go to next stage. Again the speed at which a team progresses to next stage depends upon maturity level of the team members, facilitation skills of team leader, and commitment to meet common goals.

Thematic. There are themes and corresponding behaviors for each stage. Themes fall into two main categories: they are either task-oriented (relates to getting the work done) or relationship-oriented (relates to keeping the group together and helping it work effectively).[33]

Figure 1.7 shows five stages of team development, along with themes, main issues and corresponding task- and relationship-oriented behavior of the team members during each stage.[33] Project managers must learn team building skills to take the members smoothly through all stages to the fourth stage when teams become high performing. Project managers need to use a combination of management and leadership skills as the teams go through all stages of development. Table 1.2 shows major differences between management and leadership.[33]

Team building is not a one-shot deal. It should be an ongoing process. To build effective project teams, project managers must obtain top management support, commitment of team members, introduce appropriate rewards and recognition, create a conducive environment, manage conflicts effectively and above all expedite communications among all channels and links and provide good team leadership.

Teamwork is essential to manage change. The project manager can play an active role as change agent and use human skills to overcome resistance to change. Effective management of human resources—the most valuable assets and resources in a project—can be achieved if project managers evaluate and use all four factors (communication, teamwork, leadership, and cultural ambiance) to build an effective intercultural team and integrate the efforts of a diverse mix of team members. They must recognize that change is inevitable and therefore focus on developing appropriate project management strategies to convert change into opportunity by optimizing the performance of all human resources in a project. Teamwork can provide a useful way to involve team members in any change program and to increase collaborative and supportive behavior.

Managing Changes in a Project Environment

Managing a project is creating a change.

— *Anonymous*

All projects, especially large ones, involve changes and problems that were not anticipated in the original plan. Yet despite the numerous legitimate reasons for making changes in a project, change creates a lot of uncertainty and is a common source of tension and resistance in projects. It can have a detrimental effect on team productivity and interpersonal relationships among project participants.

The project plan is the most fundamental element of strategic change management. It is the first line of defense when dealing with project uncertainty. Well-developed project plans can help deal with change systematically and rationally, while the efficient management of change can make the difference between project success and failure.

There are really only four primary factors that can affect a project plan. They are changes in goals or objectives, staffing levels, budgets, and/or schedules.[34]

There are also some secondary factors—quality, risk and contract management—that can affect a project plan. All of these factors are interdependent; each of them may affect other aspects of the plan. In essence, making project changes is a matter of replanning the project to accommodate the change. Because a project is a multidimensional interrelated system of objectives having dimensions of scope, quality, time and cost, it is difficult to change one dimension of this system without affecting the other. For example, any changes in the staffing level may affect the project schedule, budget and performance (quality). A change in schedule may force changes in the budget and staffing requirements. A change in budget may affect the scope of work or objectives that can be accomplished, which in turn affects everything else. To change a project plan, the project manager must work through the original relationships in the plan and evaluate all project dimensions in order to adjust everything that will be affected by the change. As these adjustments are made, each change and its impact should be documented and communicated to top management, the client and project team members.

Some common reasons for changes in a project environment are:

- A change in organizational policy that affects project priority
- A reorganization in the company that creates staffing adjustments on the project
- Changes in the composition of the project team based on phase of the project life cycle
- A cutback in expenditures that reduces the project budget
- A major new source of competition that requires quicker completion of the project
- Political situations (environmental studies, government regulations and major funding decisions) that seriously affect the start and overall life cycle of the project.
- A new breakthrough (especially in R&D projects) that changes the emphasis of the project.[34]

At some stages of the project life cycle, changes are more beneficial and should be encouraged. For example, during the conceptual and planning phase, the iterative process of scope development and front-end planning is an evolutionary process involving enormous changes. Since the plans are only being developed during these early phases and very little real capital is invested, changes to the overall project plan and project management approach developed during these phases are more cost effective. Changes are better made during these phases rather than during the implementation phase when the cost of changes can be very high and the net benefits are sometimes questionable. Also, in order to optimize overall project success, changes during an implementation phase or at the later stages of the project life cycle should be discouraged if possible since they are not only too expensive but are also very disruptive. Such changes are naturally resisted by project personnel and hence pose additional human relations challenges in the management of the project. This leads to considerable conflict and stress.

Project managers must study the types of changes to be made and select the ones that are likely to be most effective in increasing overall productivity. They must carry out a tradeoff analysis and deal with common resistance to changes.

Types of changes in a project environment

Changes to the project will inevitably occur in the baseline of scope, quality, schedule, budget and resource allocation. These changes must be analyzed and evaluated to determine correction actions to be taken when necessary. Two types of major changes that can significantly affect a project are scope changes and baseline changes.[35]

Scope changes. Scope management is the most fundamental element of project management. Changing the scope of a project refers to making additions, modifications and deletions to the end product or service. Although scope changes (after the scope is finalized) can be managed with proper project controls and administration procedures, it has a significant impact on overall project performance, team morale and other human factors in a project. Common sources of scope changes are:

Project specification changes. This, the most common type of scope change, is normally initiated by the client. Its purpose is to get additional capability or feature that was not included in the original specifications but is considered important enough to be included later. It may have significant impact on the overall budget and schedule.

Design change. These are initiated when someone comes up with a better way to produce or provide the end product.

Technological changes. As a project evolves, new types of technology in equipment, material, communication, and/or expertise may become available.

Business cycle. Circumstances within the business environment change over time. Announcements by competitors, international agreements, exchange rates and labor disputes can force changes in project scope. Organizations need to be more proactive rather than reactive to adjust the project scope.

Personnel changes. As a project progresses, the people involved may change. The key client representative may leave, new clients may be brought into the picture (by mergers and acquisitions), the project manager or administrator may be transferred to another project considered more important by top management, or a key expert from the project team may be pulled off the project. Such changes require timely adjustments to project requirements, design, technology and business perceptions.

A sound change control procedure must be designed and implemented to track and evaluate the changes initiated by any of these sources. Without effective change control in place, project managers may become overinvolved in trivial things and miss the original project outcomes within time, budget and resource baselines. Unfortunately once the baselines start slipping, costs escalate, questions arise, people start finger-pointing and the project team's time is wasted in non-constructive activities. To cope with these issues, it is important to implement an effective mechanism for change control.

Procedures for managing scope change. Scope changes have a significant impact on the project and its people because they deal with the end product or service. Change control procedures should be based on following the objectives to facilitate effective and efficient scope changes.

- Define options for project managers when project scope changes.
- Establish a process for submitting the change and evaluating its impact on the current project baseline that is agreeable to all parties concerned.

- Help approve or disapprove the time, effort and money required for the change, based on constraints and sound business principles.[37]

Here are five major steps that may be used to accomplish these three objectives:

Design a change control form. It should describe "what" and "why" aspects of scope changes. This form may have to be completed by the person requesting the change or by the project manager (especially for politically sensitive projects). Figure 1.8 shows a typical change control form.[37]

Record the change control details on a change control log. The change controller can then place such changes on the agenda for the change control committee.

Approve the change for further investigation. This is done by a change control committee composed of members from the technical and business area, as well as a decision maker from the organization responsible for paying for the investigation and implementation of the proposed change.

Evaluate the change. This may be done by the investigation team, which may be composed of change control committee members with some additional members having specially needed skills. It involves carrying out a cost/benefit analysis and making recommendations. The team may find the proposed scope change may seriously affect the budget, schedule, manpower requirements, may have political ramifications or may place the organization in jeopardy. The investigation team completes its evaluations and returns the change control to the change controller to proceed to the next step.

Approve the change. The approval committee is made of same members as the change control committee with the possible addition of appropriate decision makers. The decision makers should consider the impact of such changes on the project and organization as a whole.[35]

These procedures, although too formal for small projects, are particularly useful for large projects. Project managers may require a project review chart which is a document that describes the change of scope, compares the current completion date, effort needed, project personnel and cost associated with the proposed change. Figure 1.9 shows a typical project review chart that also should show recommendations and approvals by appropriate personnel.

Baseline changes. Project baseline refers to the project specifications, required standards and targets with respect to budget, schedule, resource use, and capital asset utilization. Baseline changes, which are associated with the project plan, are easier to anticipate than scope changes because they can be tracked against actual performance by the project manager, team members, and functional managers. Some common types of baseline changes are client-driven, regulatory-driven, externally driven and internally driven (with a number of sub-types). Some of these changes are common in projects and can be identified and taken care of quickly, while others are more

Change Management, Project Management, and Teamwork

Figure 1.8 Change Control Form

Change Control Form

| Change Order # _____ |

REQUESTER
Project Description _____   Date _____
Project Number _____
Change Initiated By: _____
Description of Proposed Change:
_____
_____
_____

Reason for Change: _____
_____

CHANGE CONTROL COMMITTEE
Impact on the Project:
  Effect on Schedule _____
  (short term/long term)

  Effect on Budget _____
  (short term/long term)

  Effect on Manpower _____
  (short term/long term)

Actions
  ☐ Cancel, Do Not Proceed
  ☐ Proceed with Engineering only
  ☐ Proceed all the way. Extra costs as accepted
  ☐ Hold... pending detail estimate of time and cost
  ☐ Other (explain) _____

FOR CLIENT _____   **DATE** _____

subtle and can sneak up on the project team causing serious cost and schedule overruns. Figure 1.10 shows major sources of changes to the baseline.[35]

Client-driven change. Client-driven change occurs for a variety of reasons, but there are three interrelated elements of changes driven by the client. Baseline changes in scope, as noted earlier, are initiated by the client's desire to change the characteristics of end product or service. Changes in cost come about because the client is concerned with total cost as well as cost distribution (quarterly, fiscal year, etc.). Sometimes clients may want to change the periodic cost to meet their budgetary surplus or deficit. The client may be fo-

46

Figure 1.9 Project Review Chart

Project Review Chart

Project Name _____   Project # _____

Project Manager _____

BASELINE

Baseline Completion Date _____

Baseline Project Budget (total) _____

Baseline Personel Requirements
(total in person years)   _____

Special Constraints/Assumptions _____

_____

AS OF LAST REVIEW

Review Date _____

Completion Date _____

Project Budget
(Forecast to complete) _____

Personnel Requirements _____

Actions Approved _____

REVISED

Date _____

Status of Action Items _____

_____

Completion Date _____

Project Budget _____

Personnel Used to Date   Forecast to
(person years) _____   Complete _____

DEVIATION
  ☐ Withing Contingency   ☐ More than Contingency

PROPOSED ACTIONS _____

_____

_____

  ☐ Approved   ☐ Disapproved

Signatures
         _____   Date _____
         Project Manager

         _____   Date _____
         Owner/Client

---

cusing on total cost or on cost schedule relationships. Schedule changes refer to the alteration of completion dates and/or interim milestones.

    Regulatory-driven change. These changes are caused by regulations and mandatory directives imposed on the project team. In the matrix

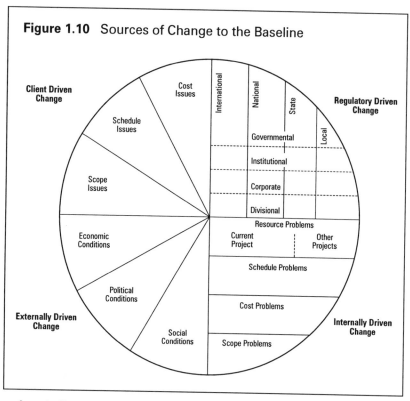

Figure 1.10 Sources of Change to the Baseline

Source: Joan Knutson and Ira Bitz, 1991, *Project Management—How to Plan and Manage Successful Projects,* AMACOM, A Division of American Management Association, New York, NY, p. 103. By permission of the publisher.

shown in Figure 1.10, one side of the matrix represents the sources of regulations: governmental or quasi-governmental, institutional, corporate or divisional (departmental). The other side represents the level from which these regulations are initiated and imposed: local, state, national and international. Thus, there is a 16-cell matrix of potential sources of regulatory changes to the project baseline.

Externally driven change. Externally driven change originates from the environment in which the project operates. There are three main types of environmental changes that may affect the project. Economics can affect project progress, rather than the end product itself. For example, the baseline of a computer systems project may change because of the cost and delivery of key hardware components or introduction of relevant software to the marketplace. Political change can be caused by an event or circumstance that alters the customer environment for the organization (for example, the impact of the Valdez oil spill on Exxon). Socially driven change can be caused by factors that affect the organization's responsibilities within the community and society as a whole. For example, some busi-

48

nesses may decide not to deal with the countries that violate human rights or with companies that pollute the environment.

Internally driven change. These represent forces exerted on the project team by altered conditions or problems within the organization. Some major types of internally driven change, which may or may not be under the direct control of the project team, are changes caused by scope or technical problems, cost problems, schedule problems, and/or resource demands.

Procedures for managing baseline changes. In reality, baselines are not static. They change as the project progresses. Here are some general steps for managing baseline changes that will help project managers manage their time efficiently.

- All baseline changes must be processed through one person—the project manager.
- All changes must be communicated to the project manager.
- Clear rules must be established regarding the timing (e.g., weekly, biweekly, etc.) for submission of baseline changes, so that tracking can be done systematically. Baseline changes are tracked to warn project participants (wave red flags), to document and analyze problems, and to negotiate for assistance in managing baseline changes in the most effective way.

Project managers should not hesitate to address the reasons for changes in the baseline whenever the project gets into a crisis. It takes time to revise plans, reissue them and deal with the reasons for deviations from baselines. However, as soon as the project manager suspects the possibility of a baseline change, he or she must take a bold, calculated view of reality and evaluate its impact on the balance of the project. Each project manager may establish his or her own baseline change procedure by following the guidelines described below.[35]

- The person in charge of processing baseline changes should also coordinate the change among project team members.
- Baseline changes should be made on a scheduled basis rather than at random.
- Do not panic, follow the formal baseline change process when the project gets into a crisis.
- Communicate the changes that have been approved and made to various levels, the rest of the team members, and the client.
- Clarify authority and approval points. For example, you can authorize slippage in a task as long as it has float, but go to the client before slipping the entire project completion date.
- Define reserves in time, resources, or dollars.
- Allow changes to be made by authorized personnel only. The functional manager can authorize a change in personnel, in consultation with the

project manager, but a team member can't arbitrarily trade off with someone else.

- Consider possible impact on the overall project before approving any change.
- Study alternatives. Work within the constraints given. Ask for tradeoffs only when absolutely necessary.
- Don't be afraid to change the baseline when necessary, but work with the client.
- Don't overreact. Allow time for the baseline change to take effect and its impact to be evaluated before implementing another change.
- Document the change thoroughly; when it was made, why, by whom it was approved, and how much did it cost. This will help explain the rationale of decisions later and will help build a better database for future references.
- Track the change to ensure that there are no unanticipated ramifications.[35]

Deciding what changes to make (tradeoff analysis)

Changes are expensive. Select them and implement them carefully.

— *Anonymous*

Project changes involve four fundamental parameters—cost, time, quality and scope. A systematic approach should be used to understand the tradeoffs in making project changes. It should be based upon a clear understanding of the impact of changing one parameter on the others. The following steps summarize a step-by-step method for analyzing project changes.[34]

Step 1: Gather information on the problems or the change. Focus on the rationale behind making changes that may be related to human errors or failures, unexpected problems or external environment. Basically project managers should seek an answer for the question: *What changes are required now that were not when the project was originally planned?*

Step 2: Review the project goals and objectives. Project goals and objectives should be reviewed and validated in light of the new problems or circumstances. Any modifications to goals and objectives, if necessary, should be made at this time to adjust the project plan accordingly.

Step 3: Establish the relative priorities for project schedule, budget and performance criteria. This should help determine the impact of project changes on the firm's profit picture and strategic plan. The following questions should be addressed during this step, before deciding on a course of action.

- Is a cost overrun acceptable?
- Is it better to change project specifications?
- Cost overruns versus schedule delays: which would be worse?
- Will "crashing" costs shorten the completion time?

50

Step 4: Review the status of each aspect of the project. Gather up-to-date information and review schedule, budget, quality, priorities, task sequences and communication system.

Step 5: Generate alternatives to accomplish objectives of the changes. This step can be very useful if done right. The project manager can hold a brainstorming session with the project team and appropriate project stakeholders to generate alternatives to manage the proposed changes. Creativity and freedom to express ideas should be encouraged.

Project modifications may involve one or more of the following inter-related options, which can be mixed and matched in various degrees to accomplish the desired result:[34]

- Hold the project performance specifications constant: review the impact on cost and schedule without additional resources.
- Freeze the budget for the project: this may affect the schedule and performance specifications.
- Adjust a combination of goals, budgets and/or schedule; this may lead to significant modifications to the project plan.
- Change the project team: this may affect schedule and budget.
- Add equipment: this may solve schedule or technical performance problems but can have significant impact on the budget.
- Change operating and administrative procedures: Avoiding bureaucracy and using the KISS principle ("Keep It Short and Simple!") can increase overall efficiency.
- Scrap part or all of the project: this will seriously affect performance, budget and schedule, therefore it needs a careful review of organizational priorities.

Step 6: Analyze the alternatives. Analyze the risk of each alternative and carry out a cost/benefit analysis before selecting the best alternative.

Step 7: Make the decision and revise the project plan. The changes should be documented and approved by the appropriate members, just like the original plan.

During each step of this tradeoff analysis, it is important that the project manager, the project team, functional managers and client (when appropriate) work as a cohesive team and contribute their ideas and priorities regarding the impact of the problems and changes.

Dealing with resistance to project changes

Most people may agree with the change but disagree with the change process.
— Anonymous

Unfortunately, implementing changes in a project is not always as simple as changing the plan. Because of human and behavioral factors, change causes tension. Uncertain outcomes lead to resistance to changes in projects. Project participants start feeling comfortable with the original project plan and strongly resist any changes to this plan. Some resistance to change in a project also comes from misunderstandings about the rationale behind the change, fear of unknown, fear of personal loss, and political self-interest.

When dealing with resistance to change, project managers generally hear things like:

- We already planned it this way and this is the way we want to do it.
- We have been doing it like this for years.
- Let's talk about something else.
- I liked the plan better before.
- Forget about new ideas and let's keep going.
- Let's not get carried away.
- Changes will slow us down a lot.
- Changes will cost us too much.

The manifestations of resistance to changes include attitudes of skepticism, lethargy, procrastination, lower morale, anxiety, tension and lower productivity in general. Implementing change will go more smoothly is there is adequate communication to create understanding and comprehension. The project manager must encourage inquiries and explain with patience. This will help gain acceptance for the change and commitment to the change process.

The change agent must ensure that the proposed changes are communicated effectively (expressing the reasons for and importance of the changes), understood by the people affected (questions and feedback are encouraged without imposing your views too strongly) and accepted as necessary and appropriate. These steps will help get a stronger commitment from people involved in making the changes work successfully.

Some practical tactics that should be followed in dealing with resistance to changes in a project environment include:

- Openly discuss tensions or frustrations
- Use leadership abilities to motivate enthusiasm and shared vision
- Focus people on the positive aspects of the change, while being honest about the situation.
- Clearly define any new expectations, measurement criteria, or rewards, and be tough when you need to be.
- Don't let personal agendas get in the way; accept the change and show your support.[34]

Evaluating changes and learning lessons for the future

People resist change only when they are not an active part of it.

— Anonymous

In addition to spending time and effort in defining, analyzing and implementing change, change agents or project managers must evaluate the changes they make. The purpose of this evaluation is not only to gather feedback on how the change itself can be modified to increase project effectiveness but also to determine if and how the overall change process and the steps used in this process can be improved for the future.

According to Margulies and Wallace,[36] this evaluation may be difficult because outcome data from individual changes may be hard and/or unreliable to measure. However, project managers should still try their best to evaluate a change in order to increase its effectiveness on the project. The evaluation process involves watching for symptoms that may indicate the need for further change. A word of caution: changes should not always be made on the basis of observing symptoms. The decision to make any changes in a project should be based upon objective information resulting from thorough and well-executed internal and external diagnoses of the project situation. In general, a change in a project can be justified only if it:

- Improves the means to accomplish project goals in a cost effective manner with respect to its budget, schedule and performance criteria
- Increases profitability of the organization as a whole
- Promotes professional development of project team members
- Increases the synergy effect of team building
- Contributes to individual satisfaction and social well being of project participants.

Figure 1.11 shows major factors discussed in this section which are highly interrelated and have a great deal of collective influence on the success of a change in a project environment.

The rules in making project changes

In order to define and manage a change in projects, based on major factors and ideas outlined in this section, following are some practical rules that should be followed in making project changes:

- Never get angry.
- Never commit to changes without understanding their impact on the project.
- Remember there is always more than one way to accomplish an objective.
- Always involve team members when exploring alternatives and adjustments.
- Always work from the original plan and document changes in relationship to the baseline.
- Always evaluate impact on the entire plan, not just the component that is being changed.
- If changes in scope, budget or schedule are involved, always ask for approval unless authorized to do so.
- Always evaluate, document and communicate risks to decision makers.
- Always make sure the changes are clearly communicated to the project team after they are approved.[34]

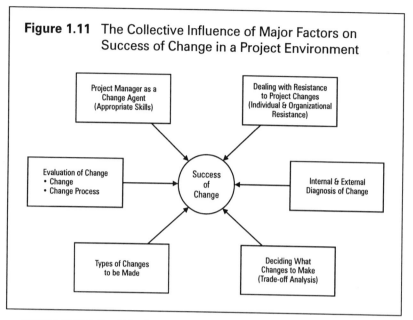

Figure 1.11 The Collective Influence of Major Factors on Success of Change in a Project Environment

Source: Samuel C. Certo, Steven H. Appelbaum and Irene Divine, 1989, *Principles of Modern Management—A Canadian Perspective*, Third Edition, Allyn and Bacon, Inc., pp.287. By permission of the publisher.

Summary

Resistance to change is inevitable. Any attempt to impose the change process and its outcomes leads to serious problems in terms of poor working relationships, lack of trust, breakdowns in communication and significant loss in productivity. Resistance to change can be overcome by teamwork. Project managers should be used as change agents and trained in human aspects of project management.

A high proportion of project problems are caused by some kind of communication breakdown including lack of active listening; uncohesive teams; uncoordinated teamwork; and poor project leadership. General project management faces additional challenges because of the increased need for joint ventures. Moreover, international projects are characterized by the cultural diversity of the project teams and the project stakeholders. These factors emphasize the need to manage project human resources effectively through the understanding and use of a model that includes three elements: teamwork(T), leadership(L), and communication(C), otherwise known as TLC (tender loving care).

A strong project team is the nucleus of a successful project. Effective team building and teamwork is crucial to optimize performance of project participants. When the concept of team building is well understood and applied at all levels, it becomes much easier to transform work groups into "real" teams throughout the organization. Team building is also one

54

of the most critical project leadership qualities that determines the performance and excellence in a project environment. Although the process of team building and taking team members through all stages of team development can entail frustrations, yet the rewards are great.

Teamwork is a useful tool to involve people in change program and increase cooperative and collaborative behavior to manage the change effectively. In a project environment, importance of teamwork, team building, and enhancing trust among team members must be emphasized. Teamwork will not only help meet project objectives within the given constraints, but will make work "fun" by increasing the morale of team members and hence their productivity and team synergy.

Tough global competition and a rapidly changing world places many demands on top management, project managers, project team members and other project stakeholders associated with the need to plan and manage project changes effectively. Changes in a project seem to be inevitable and can happen at any time in the project life cycle. Even though there may be valid reasons to make a change in a project, changes should be planned for and dealt with effectively. Project changes do not only affect the project plans but changes affect the people—stakeholders and constituents. The impact of implementing changes can be measured in terms of overall project performance by comparing to the baseline plan. With a sound and well documented original plan, the impact of any changes can be assessed and managed.

Pressures for change stem from many sources, including globalization, changing technology, rapid product obsolescence and changing nature of work force. The impact of changes in a project in terms of overall budget, schedule and performance may vary depending upon the timing, nature, size of the change and the number of parties involved. Project managers (as change agents) must have a clear understanding of the types of changes to be made and use a trade off analysis to determine what changes are most effective to meet project goals and objectives depending on project situations and circumstances.

Change is a common source of tension and resistance in projects. Resistance to change is a common and natural reaction of human beings. This resistance to change happens at an individual and organizational level. Individuals resist change through selective perception, habit, dependence, fear of the unknown (personal loss) and economic uncertainties. Organizational resistance to change can be caused by a threat to power and influence, the organizational structure, resource limitations and inter-organizational agreements. Special emphasis must be placed on effective communication, better understanding and comprehension (rational behind change) and gaining acceptance and hence commitment of people affected by the change through their sincere involvement and participation in planning and implementing the change.

Change Management, Project Management, and Teamwork

To be effective change agents, project managers must possess special skills to determine when, what and how changes should be made, solve change-related problems, and use a behavioral science approach in managing the three-stage change process. Interpersonal skills and effective communication are crucial in influencing people appropriately during the change. They must encourage pressures for change, discourage resistance to change and evaluate the change depending on the phase in the project life cycle.

chapter

2

Outline

Groups and Project Teams   60
  About groups   60
  About the project team   63

Team Dynamics and Effectiveness   68
  Developmental sequence of project team members   69
  Team context   74
  Team composition and roles of team members   75
  Major team issues   79

Cultural Diversity and Project Management   89
  What is culture?   89
  Cultural diversity and projects   92

Managing International Projects   101
  Attributes of international projects   101
  Primary factors in cross-cultural settings   104
  Challenges in managing international projects   105

Summary   107

Teamwork: the ability to work together toward a common vision and to direct individual accomplishment toward organizational objectives.

2

Team Dynamics and Cultural Diversity

ONE OF THE MOST IRRITATING things for sports fans is to watch a favorite team fail to play together. We can see immediately when team members are acting more as individuals than as a team, being either too dependent or overly independent and not coordinated at all. We can see examples of poor teamwork—missing a message, failing to pass at the right time, failing to assist team members who are in trouble, trying to shine at the expense of others or failing to pass on information to the leader. We "coach" from our armchairs on matters of behavior, attitude and performance.

Project teams are very similar to sports teams in terms of human dynamics. Like team coaches, project managers must understand team dynamics and foster human synergy by effective team building.

The performance of project managers is dependent upon the output of the project team: a group of individuals with different needs, backgrounds and expertise. The smooth running of a project team becomes more challenging with increased project complexity, a diverse mix of skills and cultural diversity. Special attention must be given to the quality of the interpersonal skills and team dynamics within the project team to understand and influence its productivity in a project environment.

Many people think of a "team" as simply "a group of people with a common goal." Such an erroneous assumption makes it difficult to develop a group into an effective cohesive and high-performing team. A team is a group of people who are committed to common goals, who depend on each other to do their job (working interdependently and relying on cooperative efforts), and who produce high quality results.

Cultural diversity poses special project management and team-building challenges. Some ideas to capitalize on cultural diversity and achieve synergy within a multicultural and cross-functional team are presented in this chapter, along with information on managing international projects. ∎

Groups and Project Teams

Take care of each other, share your energies with the group. No one must feel alone or cut off, for that is when you do not make it.

— *Willi Unsoeld, mountain climber*

The word *team* is often used loosely, sometimes merely as a synonym for a group. Instead of handling an assignment as a project, management may appoint someone as a task leader to get that task done. The task leader may assemble a group of people, divide the task into subtasks and assign a responsibilities to specific members of the group. The task leader may assume that he or she has assembled a *team* whereas in reality, it is simply a *work group*. There is a big difference between the group/work group and a team in terms of its dynamics, the roles of its members, their level of commitment, and authority and reporting relationships among its members.

Cleland has suggested a framework for analyzing team situations in a project management environment, which centers around the following questions:

- What are the challenges and problems presented by the situation?
- What is the difference between a group and a team?
- How do we move effectively from a group to a team?
- What are the characteristics of an effective project team?
- What are the major factors underlying team dynamics and team effectiveness?
- How can we capitalize on cultural diversity and achieve synergy?[1]

About groups

Two heads are better than one.

— *Anonymous*

A group is a collection of people who communicate with one another over a period of time. The members of the group are often few enough so that each member can communicate with all the others one to one, not secondhand through other people.[2] Three conditions must be met for a group to exist:[3]

- Members are able to see and/or hear each other.
- There is interpersonal communication among all members.
- All members see themselves as members of the group with shared goals.

Some examples of groups are clubs, classes, or civic groups.

Individual-group relations. Many people believe in the importance and centrality of the individual, while others are more oriented towards group goals and norms. Two important concepts regarding individual-group relations are:

Individualism/collectivism, one of the dimensions of culture, refers to the role of individual versus the role of group. *Individualism*, which is more dominant in Europe and North America, places emphasis on individual decisions while *collectivism*, which dominates in Japan and China, emphasizes group decisions. The cultural belief in individualism creates

60

uneasiness and uncertainty over the influence that groups should have in organizational decision-making and other actions. The cultural belief in collectivism has the opposite effect.[4]

Group versus individual interests. The interests of a group and those of the individuals that comprise it are often compatible.[5] However, sometimes their interests may conflict.

In a group, everyone may not contribute equally. A *free rider,* for example, refers to a group member who gets benefits from group members but does not make a proportional contribution towards generating the benefit.[6] Students sometimes experience this problem when an instructor assigns a group project for which everyone gets the same grade. In such a case, the non-contributing member obtains the benefit of the group grade but does not carry a proportional share of workload required to earn it.

Free riding is harmful to group performance in many ways. It violates equity standards; it violates a standard of social responsibility; and it violates a standard of reciprocity or exchange. When group members feel that one or more members are free riders, a *sucker effect* may occur. In other words, some group members may withhold their efforts because they feel that the free riders are planning to withhold their efforts, thus "sucking" the energy and commitment out of the group.[3,7]

Group types and development. Individuals usually belong to many types of groups that can be classified in numerous categories depending upon a person's perspective. People join formal and informal groups to satisfy their psychological needs, social needs and desires to accomplish personal and project objectives.[3]

Friendship and task groups. This classification is based upon the primary purpose the group serves. A friendship group is an informal group that develops naturally because of common interests, ties, hobbies, or social status. It serves the primary purpose of meeting its members' personal needs of security, esteem and belonging. A task group is formally created by management to accomplish organizational objectives. For example, small teams of eight to ten specialists formed in an industrial organization to develop and market a new product are examples of task groups. Task groups are sometimes referred to as *work groups* or *teams.* A single group in an organization may serve both friendship and task purposes.

Interdependence in task groups. Task groups or work groups can be further classified depending on how the group members depend on each other in accomplishing some tasks or project objectives. The three types of task groups based upon interdependencies are:[8]

- *A counteracting group* exists when group members interact to resolve some conflict through negotiation and compromise. For example, a labor-management negotiating group is a counteracting group because both parties believe that at least some of their goals conflict.

Table 2.1 Key Differences Between Groups and Teams

Area	Groups	Teams
Purpose	1. Think they are placed together for administration purposes only.	1. Have been coached to meet goals.
Mode of Working	2. Work independently and sometimes at cross-purposes. Members attempt personal gain at expense of group (turf wars not uncommon).	2. Work interdependently and help each other win. Members contribute to team goals (promote constructive attitudes and team welfare as a priority).
Level of Participation	3. Not actively involved in setting goals (only act as hired hands).	3. Actively involved in setting goals. (feel ownership for their tasks).
Trust and Communication	4. Distrust each other's motives. Roles have never been clarified. Disagreements seen as personal attacks.	4. Work in a climate of trust and open communication. Accept that different roles enable different perspectives and enhance problem-solving.
Working relationships	5. Play politics which may harm other's credibility. (no sincere working relationships).	5. Are open and honest because leader is open and honest. Information is readily given. (Long-term relationships are important).
Conflict Resolution	6. Indulge in difficult conflict situations. Supervisor puts off conflict resolution until serious damage is done.	6. Have been trained to turn conflict into opportunity to generate new ideas and deepen relationships.
Decision Making	7. Do not participate in decisions affecting the group. Conformity, not results, is the desired outcome.	7. Team leaders encourage teams to make their own decisions. Coach shows confidence in their competence and experience (eventually leading to self-motivated project teams).

- A *coaching group* exists when group members perform their jobs relatively independently in the short term. For example, once project planning is done, various work package managers can work independently for a relatively short time but they must act interdependently for systems integration.
- An *interacting group* exists when a group cannot accomplish its tasks until all members have completed their share of the task. For example, in an automobile manufacturing plant, an assembly team of eight to ten people may perform separate jobs required to assemble a component. If any of the jobs is not completed, the component cannot be assembled. Common forms of interacting groups include committees, task forces, advisory councils, work crews, review panels, project teams and so on. It is not only managers and professionals who work in groups but an increasing proportion of the workforce must work in a team environment.[8,9]

Difference between a group and a team. Many people confuse groups with teams. However, there are some key differences between groups and teams in terms of levels of commitment, interdependencies and shared responsibility.

A work group possesses most of the following characteristics.[10]

- The group works on assigned tasks.
- They have a common task (or a set of individual tasks) that tend to be explicit.
- Relationships are functional.
- The group is often temporary.
- Leadership tends to go with competence.
- Members think of themselves as a group; they have a collective perception of unity and conscious identification.
- Members communicate with one another, influence one another, and react to one another. [10]

What is a team? What makes a good team? These are simple questions and we tend to think we know the answers—until someone asks!

A team is more than just a work group. It is a group of people who are committed to common goals, who depend on each other to do their job (work interdependently), and who produce high quality results.

A team can also be defined as a group of people in which the individuals have a common aim and in which the jobs and skills of each member fit in with those of others.[11]

The two components of this definition—*a common task* and *complimentary contributions*—are essential to the concept of a real team. An effective team may be defined as one that achieves its goals efficiently and is then ready to take on more challenges if so required.[10,11]

Table 2.1 shows some key differences between groups and teams.

About the project team

Achievement is a WE thing, not a ME thing, always the product of many heads and hands.

— J.W. Atkinson

In general, a project team is a work group of two or more individuals who must interact and work interdependently with each other to accomplish project objectives. Effective team work produces a synergistic effect, i.e., the output of the team is more than the sum of the output from its parts.

Project teams are united by a common purpose and the concept of share responsibility. According to Francis and Young, a team is an energetic group of people who are committed to achieving common objectives, who work well together, are interdependent on each other, and who produce high quality results.[12]

Because of rapid changes in technology, unpredictable funding, complex task environments, and interpersonal dynamics, it is essential to develop a project team in which individuals share common objectives and skills of each member, brought together from several functional areas, complement and fit with those of others. In a project, the performance of a project manager is affected by the actions of the project team. The project team works directly with the project manager in planning, coordination, interfacing and control functions.

Just as a high-energy group of committed individuals can boost the project manager to new heights of effectiveness, an effective project team leader can optimize the strength of all team members and create an environment to blend their talents and thus multiply an overall performance of the project team. Before getting into the benefits and process of team building, it will be helpful to identify and understand what project teams need to know and the characteristics of an integrated project team.

What does the project team need to know? Few things are more satisfying in life than belonging to a successful project team. Project team leaders must understand organizational and behavioral variables and create a climate to maximize the satisfaction of all individuals on the project team while optimizing the performance of the project team as a whole. Project managers, at the start of the project, should talk with each team member on a one-to-one basis and must make sure that the project team members know: [13]

- Project objectives and importance to the overall organization
- Selection and assignment criteria for team members
- Roles and reporting relationships of team members
- Why the team concept is being used and how it should work
- The hindering/helping forces on the project
- Impact of the project on their careers and professional development
- What rewards (team or individual) might be forthcoming if the project is successful
- What basic rules, policies and procedures will be followed in managing the project
- How much autonomy the project team has
- What level of support is available from top management (tolerance for failures, extra training, etc.)
- The style of the team leader
- How decisions will be made
- How performance will be evaluated and documented.

A frank and open discussion of these items with each team member is likely to reduce anxiety and allow the team to focus on project objectives. In spite of the fact that sometimes such discussions may increase the anxiety level of some team members, generally these discussions help to identify and deal with the source of the anxiety. Dealing with their anxieties and making team members feel that they are an integral part of the team will lead to high performance of the team as a whole.

Types of interacting teams. The process and outcome of team building depends upon the type of interacting teams. Like groups, there are various types of interacting teams. A team environment in an organization often involves one or more of the following types of interacting teams.[3]

Problem-solving teams may consist of five to twenty employees drawn from different functional areas. These employees could be hourly or salaried; they might volunteer or be nominated to be on these teams. They may meet one to two hours a week, or as needed, to discuss ways of improving quality, productivity or efficiency, and the work environment. In some organizations, these teams are called *quality circles*. The formal authority of problem-solving teams to implement their ideas varies from none to limited but they can influence improvement in quality and reduction in costs. However, they do not basically reorganize the project tasks, structure, or the role of managers and employees.

Special purpose teams are common in a project environment. These teams may consist of five to thirty employees, drawn from various functional departments and sometimes two management levels. They are involved in a wide variety of tasks that can include:[3]

- Designing and introducing work reforms and new technology
- Liaison with customers and vendors to improve inputs and outputs
- Integrating the functions of marketing, finance, and human resources
- Increasing product or service innovations
- Encouraging concurrent engineering by integrating engineering and manufacturing, and fostering creativity in improving overall performance
- Establishing better links between strategic and tactical plans and decisions
- Introducing creative techniques for training, professional development and career development.

These teams emerged in early to mid-1980s and are spreading rapidly, including into unionized organizations. They operate with a greater degree of empowerment than problem-solving teams.

For example, Oryx Energy Company, a Texas-based oil and gas exploration and production firm, formed twenty-six teams to improve effectiveness and efficiency. One team worked on the destructive competition between Oryx's exploration and production division, which had often fought over new projects and capital. Today, a team with members from both units meets to share information on projects and work through mutual problems.[14]

Self-managed or self-directed teams normally consist of eight to fifteen functional groups of employees who share a responsibility for a particular unit of production (including a major identifiable product or a service). The members of self-managed teams perform multiple tasks, manage themselves with minimum supervision and are responsible for the whole work process, which includes planning, scheduling, organizing, implementing, evaluating, and making decisions as needed. Team members are cross-trained in all technical skills necessary to complete the tasks assigned and they share responsibility for the success of the team.

Team Dynamics and Cultural Diversity

Self-managed project teams are more beneficial than traditional work groups. A survey of the transition to self-managed teams in seven countries showed improved productivity, quality, and employee attitudes as well as lower operating costs.[15] Self-managed teams became popular in the late 1980s and appear to be the wave of the future. For example, at Volvo in Kalmar, Sweden, teams of fifteen to twenty employees elect their own leaders and divide their tasks, although production goals are set by higher management.[16]

Self-managed project teams fundamentally change how project tasks are organized by empowering the team members to control the techniques of performing their jobs. The self-managed and self-motivated project team is discussed in detail in Chapter 6.

The characteristics of an integrated project team. The interdependence of project team members and the satisfaction and pleasure that they derive from their association with the team are some of the unique characteristics of an integrated project team. Some of the important characteristics of a fully integrated project team are:[1]

- A common reason for working together (commitment to project objectives)
- Strong sense of belonging (cooperation and cohesiveness)
- Pride and enjoyment in group activity (strong belief in team work)
- Interdependency (members realize that they need each other to succeed)
- Shared interests (collaborate and help each other win)
- Commitment to the team concept (no *prima donnas* allowed)
- Strong performance norms and results orientation (high expectations of each other to produce quality work)
- Acceptance of group accountability for success or failure (members help each other when needed)
- High degree of intragroup interaction (develops mutual understanding)
- Respect for individual differences (different views are listened to and acknowledged)
- Climate of trust and healthy conflict (express ideas, opinions and disagreements freely).

With spiraling technological and cultural complexity in organizations, and megaprojects involving several disciplines, countries and currencies, it is difficult, if not impossible, for a single human being to manage a project. Even on smaller projects with modest task complexities and unpredictable tasks, the team approach produces better results.

Don't let the project team become a committee. Project teams often face tough questions related to project priorities, human aspects and scope management. In the absence of strong leadership, well-directed focus and self-management, a project team may wander away from their real project goals and become a committee, leading to loss of productivity. According to Tom Peters, "committees deliberate and project teams do and accomplish."[17] The following recommendations for avoiding the commit-

66

tee trap are based on the observations and experiences of successful teams at 3M and Apple.[17]

Set goals and hard target dates for key subsystem tests. Projects consist of several subsystems (or subprojects) and milestones. Successful project teams are characterized by clear goals. Six to ten strict due dates for testing key subsystems help achieve a smooth rate of progress.

Assign personnel on a full-time basis. Team members must be obsessed by the project. Team members responsible for key functions should be assigned on a full-time basis right from the beginning to avoid potential priority conflicts.

Have members commit their functions. Top management should urge all team members to commit their functions to goals and due dates. Conditional commitments from one's home function area lead to a committee environment and should be avoided.

Be sure project leaders appraise team members' performance. In order to increase team productivity, project managers, not home functional managers, should do performance appraisals of team members for the duration of the project.

Promote the idea of a career as a string of projects. In a multiproject environment, team members should be able to get better career opportunities by doing well on a string of projects having multifunction tasks.

Live together. Team spirit and commitment come through "hanging out" together. All key team members should have office areas in close proximity and away from their functional colleagues.

Pay attention to the social element. High spirits are not accidental. Team leaders must create a comfortable social environment to make team members feel that everyone is in it together. They should facilitate bonding by having "signing up" ceremonies, frequent milestone celebrations, humorous awards for successes and setbacks alike.

Encourage external stakeholder participation. External stakeholders such as principal vendors, distributors, lead customers (future test sites), main contractors, etc., not only contribute directly but also add authenticity and a sense of distinctiveness and task commitment. Therefore, project team leaders should encourage active participation of external shareholders according to the phase in the project life cycle.

Create self-contained systems. Project team members should have their own work stations, local area networks, database etc. However, the project team leaders should be careful not to go too far in order to avoid integration problems with the rest of the organization.

Members pick their own leader. Project team leaders appointed by top management may have the formal authority to manage the project, but successful project teams usually select and rotate their own leaders, or even choose to be without a leader. It should be recognized that leadership may change as the project progresses depending upon the project life cycle.

Management should honor project leadership skills. "Management by projects" is one of the most effective approaches to competing on a global level. However, it requires a wholesale reorientation of the organizational structure from "vertical" (functional specialist dominance) to "horizontal" (multifunction teams). Horizontal project leadership must become a desired skill in the organization, rewarded by promotions and dollars. Good team member skills for junior members must be cherished and desired as well.

A project-focused management approach requires more than appointing teams. If not managed well, project teams and task forces may add to bureaucracy rather than subtract from it.[17] However, by using these guidelines and recommendations, project leaders should be able to increase team performance and avoid the project-turned-committee trap.

Team Dynamics and Effectiveness

Coming together is a beginning; keeping together is progress; working together is success.

— *Henry Ford*

The behavior of a group is not the same as the sum total of each individual's behavior. This is primarily because individuals act differently in groups than they do when they are alone. Most people join groups to satisfy some of their needs: security, status, self-esteem, affiliation, power, or goal achievement. Teams are replacing individuals as the basic building blocks of organizations because teams are most effective in achieving human synergy and high performance, and thus meeting many of these needs for their members. How do teams develop? What are the characteristics of effective teams? Why do some groups have a stronger team spirit than others? How can we increase team effectiveness to satisfy team members' needs and at the same time achieve organizational goals? These questions have interested many organizational theorists and many models of team dynamics and team effectiveness have been proposed over the years.[18, 19, 20]

Team effectiveness refers to how the team affects the whole organization, project environment, its individual team members, and the team's existence.[21] It determines the extent to which the team is successful in terms of project objectives and organizational goals, the satisfaction and well-being of team members, and the team's ability to survive.[19]

The main factors influencing a team's effectiveness can be classified in four categories:[18,19]

- The developmental sequence of team members
- Team context and goals, which include external environment, team goals, and task characteristics
- Team composition and roles of team members
- Major team issues, which include norms, cohesiveness, and leadership.

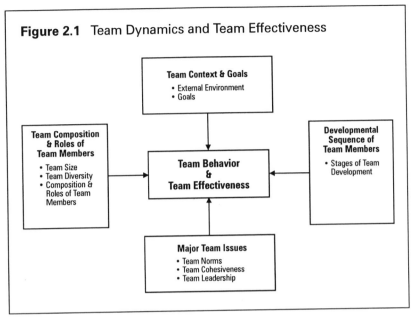

Figure 2.1 Team Dynamics and Team Effectiveness

Adapted from: Steven L. McShane. 1995. *Canadian Organizational Behavior*, Second Edition, Chicago, IL: Richard D. Irwin, p. 302 and Don Hellreigel, John W. Slocum, Jr., and Richard W. Woodman, *Organizational Behavior*, Sixth Edition, St. Paul, MN: West Publishing Company, p. 319. By permission of the publisher.

The effectiveness of a project team depends upon its ability to maintain the commitment of its team members, especially as the team progresses through stages of development. Without this commitment, team members leave and the project team will quickly fail. Figure 2.1 shows the main factors that influence team dynamics and team effectiveness. All these factors are interdependent and must be diagnosed and analyzed independently and in relation to each other to gain a better understanding of team dynamics, behavior and degree of effectiveness. For example, elements of the context or external environment of the team, such as encouragement or discouragement from top management, will influence the project team's goals, norms and roles.[18,19]

Developmental sequence of project team members

It is constant and determined effort that breaks down all resistance and sweeps away all obstacles.

— *Claude M. Bristol*

To increase the effectiveness of individual team members and help them grow, team members must move sequentially on a maturity continuum from dependence through independence to interdependence.[22] In a group, people may work independently, taking responsibility for assigned tasks, but real synergy and teamwork is accomplished when people work interdependently.

Whenever people work as a group or as a team, group dynamics comes into play and influences their overall productivity, which refers to how competent the group is in the knowledge and skills that determine its ability to complete tasks, and develop morale, which refers to group commitment as measured by motivation, confidence, and cohesion.

There are four main stages of group development—orientation, dissatisfaction, resolution and production, which correspond to the stages of team development discussed in Chapter 1 (forming, storming, norming, and performing).[23]

Stages of team development. When project teams are built, most of them go through four predicable stages of development as shown in Figure 2.2.[24] These stages can be represented by four sectors of a team development wheel and can be described as follows:[3,24,25,26]

Forming (floundering). All new teams start in this stage with milling around and confusion because of the high degree of ambiguity in terms of their roles and relationships. *Awareness* and *orientation* are dominant themes in this stage as members focus their efforts on defining goals and developing procedures to perform their tasks. Team members in this stage of development try to get acquainted with each other and understand their own roles and those of other team members and the project leader. The project manager should recognize that individual team members in this stage might:

- Keep feelings to themselves until they know the situation
- Act more securely than they actually feel
- Experience confusion and uncertainty about what is expected of them
- Be nice and polite, or at least not hostile
- Be more impersonal and businesslike
- Try to evaluate personal benefits relative to the personal cost of being involved in the project team.

Storming (conflict). After floundering, project teams progress to confronting the issues and other team members in order to acquire control and understand their roles, objectives and relationships. Normally this happens regardless of what is done or whether any leadership is applied or not. In the storming stage, things start becoming serious. Conflicts may emerge over relative priorities, responsibilities, task behaviors, and the role of the project team leader (with regard to task direction and guidance). *Competition* over leadership roles and *conflict* over goals are dominant themes that may generate emotional tension and consequently some team members may withdraw or isolate themselves. The project team leader must be able to resolve conflict during this stage rather than withdraw or suppress it. Suppressing conflict may create bitterness and resentment that will last long after team members attempt to initiate the conflict by expressing their emotions and differences. Withdrawal may convey the message that the team leader does not care, which will cause

70

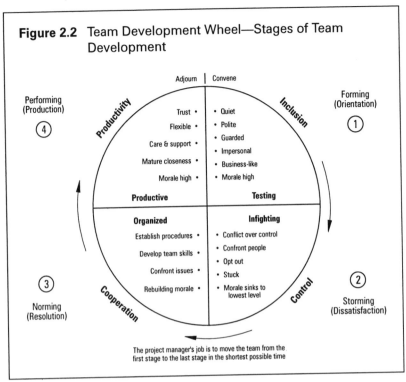

Figure 2.2 Team Development Wheel—Stages of Team Development

Adjourn | Convene

Performing (Production) ④

Forming (Orientation) ①

Productivity

Inclusion

Trust •
Flexible •
Care & support •
Mature closeness •
Morale high •

• Quiet
• Polite
• Guarded
• Impersonal
• Business-like
• Morale high

Productive

Testing

Organized

Infighting

Establish procedures •
Develop team skills •
Confront issues •
Rebuilding morale •

• Conflict over control
• Confront people
• Opt out
• Stuck
• Morale sinks to lowest level

Cooperation

Control

③ Norming (Resolution)

② Storming (Dissatisfaction)

The project manager's job is to move the team from the first stage to the last stage in the shortest possible time

Adapted from several sources, including, R.B. Lacoursiere, 1980, *The Life Cycle of Group Developmental Stage Theory*, New York: Human Service Press; and presentation by Gary Robinson, PMI West Coast British Columbia Chapter, Oct. 1992.

the team to fail more quickly. In this stage, conflict is inevitable and should be embraced as productive, if handled appropriately.

Norming (productive). By this stage, the team members are organized to work together and meet project objectives. *Cooperation* and *cohesiveness* within the project team is a dominant theme in the norming stage. Task-oriented behavior leads to sharing of information, mutual acceptance on opinions and goals and positive attempts to reach mutually agreed upon goals. Relationship-oriented behavior emphasizes empathy, concern and positive expression of feelings, leading to team cohesion. A sense of shared responsibility and cooperation develops in the project team. During this stage, project teams really get organized because procedures are established, issues are confronted and resolved, and team skills are developed.

Performing. This is the final stage of team development during which the team members are open, effective and willing to help each other win. A high level of mutual *trust* and high *performance* are dominant themes in this stage. During this stage, the roles of individual team members are accepted

Team Dynamics and Cultural Diversity

and understood. Team members demonstrate how effectively and efficiently they can perform their tasks. They understand when they should work independently and when they should help each other. In this stage, the team members are flexible and trust each other. They provide care and support for each other which increases the overall team performance.

Beyond this stage, the team may proceed in one of two ways: Some teams continue to develop themselves and learn from their experiences and new input, thereby improving their effectiveness in managing the project, while others—especially those that have not developed high achievement norms—may only perform at the survival level. [3] A marginally adequate level of performance may be the result of excessively self-centered behavior of some team members, poor team leadership, development of norms that inhibit high performance, or other factors.[27]

While most project teams go through all four stages of team development, the time taken to progress from one stage to the next may vary from team to team, influenced by the maturity level of the team members, the project manager and overall project environment. In addition, project teams sometimes get stuck in the conflict stage or swing back and forth between conflict and floundering.[25] Only the project team members can determine if and when to advance to the next stage.

There is always the possibility of failure of the whole development process. Team members may lose confidence in the process, lose team leaders, or abandon the project team. Some teams may reach their optimum level of productivity at the end of norming (productive stage) and not advance to performing because they may not have the capacity or the need to be high performing.[25]

Project team members normally ask questions reflecting the task-oriented and relationship-oriented (social) behaviors that may differ from stage to stage. Table 2.2 shows possible task- and people-oriented questions for each stage.[25]

The major characteristics of high performing teams are that the project team members are flexible, open and supportive. They trust each other and help each other win. They are self-led and the leadership is informal, ad hoc and shared.[24,25]

The successful project manager strives to move the team from first stage to the final stage in the shortest possible time. The challenge is to maintain a high level of morale, motivation and productivity on a long-term basis while making sure everyone is having fun while working on the project. To achieve this, project managers should either hire expert facilitators or learn effective facilitation skills themselves. These skills will be essential for guiding project team members through the four stages of team development to ensure high performance and optimum team synergy.

Adjourning the project team. After completing the four stages of team development, most organizations face the dilemma of what to do after the

72

Table 2.2 Questions that Reflect Major Task and Relationship Issues for Each Stage of Team Development

Task-Related Questions	Relationship-Related Questions
Forming	
What do "they" really want?	What will get me in trouble?
What is the goal?	What will get me rewarded?
What do we need to achieve goals?	Who can I trust?
Storming	
What are the issues/problems?	Who's in charge?
Are we doing the right thing?	What are the limits?
What will really solve the problems?	What are the roles/responsibilities?
How will we accomplish the work?	
Norming	
What are the tasks and deliverables?	What's acceptable? What's not?
What are the performance standards and measurement criteria?	How can we establish work patterns that work for us?
How will we control work and report status?	How will we resolve conflicts?
Performing	
How can we make it more creative or perfect?	How can we gain more autonomy?
How do we keep up the challenge, achievement and satisfaction?	How can we support each other?
Adjourning	
What am I going to do when this project is over?	How can we sustain our working relationships in the future?

Adapted from seminar material on "Facilitating Groups to Get Results," presented by Erica Jones at PMI Annual Seminars & Symposium, 1994.

project is finished. This is the natural and inevitable stage of adjourning the project team.

Adjourning involves the termination of task behavior and disengagement from relationship-oriented behavior. Adjourning must be done in a carefully planned manner and, whenever possible, efforts should be made to assign another challenging project to the team before it is too late and the members disappear.

Sometimes teams that are formed to meet long-term goals, such as quality improvement, go on indefinitely. Adjourning for this type of team is more subtle and happens when one or more of the key members leaves the organization. The new leader may then change the goals and membership of the team.

Team context

> *It's not so much where we are, but in what direction we are moving.*
> — *Anonymous*

A team's context is formed principally by the *external environment*, which can influence each of the factors shown in Figure 2.1, as well as directly influencing the team's behavior and its effectiveness. The team's context encompasses several features of organizational environment as well as other conditions and factors that are not directly controllable by the team, such as:[18, 19]

- Technology (information technology and communication tools)
- External competition (stimulates creativity and cohesiveness)
- Physical layout and location (tight matrix)
- Supportive management (emphasis on team approach)
- Formal rules and procedures (team's autonomy)
- Reward system (individual versus team reward)
- Organizational values (affect team norms).

A team's effectiveness increases when it communicates effectively, there are sufficient resources to perform the tasks, and management provides genuine support and training for team building and team development. Also, an appropriate reward system can motivate project team members to work together. For example, according to one recent survey, teams often fail because team members are rewarded for individual effort rather than team effort.[28]

Team goals combined with clear compelling directions increase the team's effectiveness. Goals influence the efficiency and effectiveness of individuals, teams, and organizations, each of which has multiple goals.[18] There may be both compatible and conflicting goals within and between individuals, teams, and organizations. Typically teams have two types of goals: Relationship-oriented goals and Task oriented goals.

Teams are generally more effective when project tasks are well defined and are easy to implement.[29] On the other hand, more complex tasks involving creativity and innovation require a diverse mix of skills and experience that challenges the team to work together and increases cohesiveness. Teams are particularly effective for interdependent tasks because people coordinate better when working together than individually. That is

74

why in projects involving new product development, concurrent engineering teams are more effective than individuals because the highly interrelated tasks of design, manufacturing and marketing are better coordinated by a cross-functional team than by individuals working in separate functional departments.[19]

Team composition and roles of team members

The effectiveness of a project team depends upon its size, diversity, and composition in terms of similarities and differences among team members and the roles they prefer to assume in a team. Effective teams must have members who are motivated to perform the team's tasks, who agree on team goals, who work together and abide by the team's rules of conduct, and who demonstrate a collectivistic attitude that values mutual dependence.

Team size. The size of a work team influences team behavior and effectiveness. What should be the optimum size of a team? It can range from two to twenty with twelve being the biggest size where each member can easily interact with each other.[30] Teamwork is more easily achieved in smaller teams because of the convenience of getting to know each other and exchanging information and ideas. Also, coordination and acceptance is easier in smaller teams. For example, executives at Bata Footwear shifted from large manufacturing operations to smaller plants in which fewer employees worked on a product line. Employees could more easily see the big picture, which led to better teamwork and hence to the plant's success.[31]

With a team of optimal size, there is enough diversity of skills and experiences, yet the team is small enough for team members to know each other well, develop good working relationships, exchange ideas, and agree on team goals. As team size increases, more time and effort is required in coordinating roles and activities and resolving differences. Getting commitment from team members becomes harder because of difficulties in getting wider acceptance of strategies, plans and decisions of the project team. Large teams may break into smaller informal subgroups around common interests and work activities, leading to reduced commitment to team goals. One way to handle this problem is illustrated by a solution in use at GE Canada's Bromont plant. There, teams of up to eighty people are divided into several informal groups based on common interests, work hours and home locations.[19]

Table 2.3 shows some of the possible effects of team size. It shows ten dimensions of teams in three categories (leadership, team members and team process).[18,32] It is obvious from this table that a team of seven or less interact differently than a team of thirteen to sixteen. The effects identified in this table need to be qualified.[32] Adequate time and the commitment level of team members towards team's tasks and goals, among other

Table 2.3 Some Possible Effects of Size on Teams

Category/Dimension	Group Size 2-7 Members	8-12 Members	13-16 Members
Leadership			
1. Demands on leader	Low	Moderate	High
2. Differences between leaders and members	Low	Low to moderate	Moderate to high
3. Direction by leader	Low	Low to moderate	Moderate to high
Members			
4. Tolerance of direction from leader	Low to high	Moderate to high	High
5. Domination of team interaction by a few members	Low	Moderate to high	High
6. Inhibition in participation by ordinary members	Low	Moderate	High
Team Process			
7. Formalization of rules and procedures	Low	Low to moderate	Moderate to high
8. Time required for reaching judgment decisions	Low to moderate	Moderate	Moderate to high
9. Tendency for subgroups to form within team	Low	Moderate to high	High
10. Tendency toward polarization	Low	Moderate	Moderate to high

Source: Don Hellreigel, John W. Slocum, Jr., and Richard W. Woodman, *Organizational Behavior,* Sixth Edition, St. Paul, MN; West Publishing Company, p. 323. By permission of the publisher.

factors, influence whether or not the size of a team impacts on optimum effectiveness.

Diversity. Diversity adds complexity to understanding team behavior and its effectiveness. There is growing diversity among team members in terms of age, gender and race. Also most project teams have team members with a diverse mix of backgrounds, skills, norms and experiences. Based on diversity, teams can be divided in two categories:[19]

Homogenous teams include members with common technical expertise, values, ethnicity and norms. Members in homogenous teams experience higher satisfaction, better interpersonal and working relationships

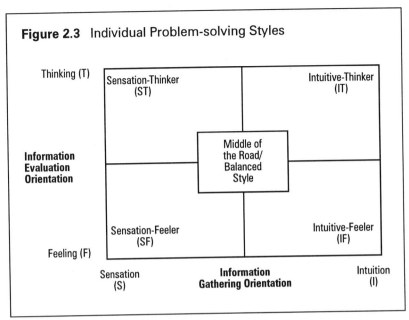

Figure 2.3 Individual Problem-solving Styles

Source: Don Hellriegel, John W. Slocum, Jr., and Richard W. Woodman, *Organizational Behavior,* Sixth Edition, St. Paul, MN; West Publishing Company, p. 151. By permission of the publisher.

and less conflict because of similar backgrounds. Homogenous teams are effective for tasks that require a significant amount of cooperation and coordination, such as emergency response teams or string quartets.[33]

Heterogeneous teams are characterized by diverse personal characteristics, cultural backgrounds, and values of their team members. Since heterogeneous team members tend to see problems or opportunities from different perspectives; heterogeneous teams are generally more effective than homogeneous teams for complex projects and problems requiring innovative solutions.[34] Heterogeneity leads to quality decisions and creative problem solving because of a broader knowledge base. Diversity among team members encourages them to obtain a wide network of cooperation and support.[19]

Roles of team members. The characteristics of team members and the roles they play influence the team's performance. A team must be composed of members with a variety of problem-solving styles and behavior roles (task-oriented, relations-oriented and self-oriented).[3,19]

Problem-solving styles. Problem-solving styles can vary widely among project team members. In general, the problem-solving style of individual team members depends upon two dimensions: their preferred style of obtaining information from external sources (by sensation or intuition), and their preferred way of reaching a decision (by thinking or feeling).

Hellreigel and Slocum, Jr., developed a model containing four basic types of problem-solving styles: sensation thinker (ST), sensation feeler (SF), intuitive thinker (IT), and intuitive feeler (IF) as shown in Figure 2.3.[35]

Sensing people seek specific factual data and information from their environment, whereas intuitive people gather global or more abstract data. After gathering data, people make decisions based on their thinking or feeling. Thinking people tend to solve a problem by breaking it into logical parts and then analyzing them, whereas feeling people make decisions based on instinct.[35]

One problem-solving style is not better than another. Many people exhibit characteristics of each style at various times and in different situations. In a project environment, it is important to achieve a balance by integrating all four psychological functions.

The particular combination of problem-solving styles of team members can affect the team process and its decisions.[36] For example, there is likely to be more conflict and divergence in a team with three strong sensation thinkers and three intuitive feelers than if all six members have the same problem-solving style. Although different view points should stimulate creativity and innovative solutions, if differences are not facilitated properly, those can also lead to conflict, which may hurt the team spirit.[36]

Behavior roles. Behavior roles of team members influence the team process, its behavior and effectiveness. These roles can be classified as task-oriented, relations-oriented and self-oriented.[18,37]

The **task-oriented role** of team members facilitates and coordinates decision-making tasks. It consists of the following subroles:[18,37]
- *Initiators* offer new ideas and suggest solutions.
- *Information handlers* may be either information seekers who clarify suggestions and obtain authoritative information or information givers who offer facts or generalizations that relate experiences pertinent to team problems.
- *Coordinators* coordinate team members' ideas, suggestions and activities.
- *Evaluators* assess the team's functioning and question the practicality, logic or suggestions of other team members.

The **relations-oriented role** of team members deals with team tasks, sentiments and viewpoints. It consists of the following subroles:[18,37]
- *Encouragers* praise and accept the ideas of others; they convey warmth and solidarity toward other members.
- *Harmonizers* relieve tension and resolve intragroup conflicts.
- *Gatekeepers* encourage participation of other team members by saying such things as: "Let us hear from you, Cathy, about developing contingencies," or "Bob, do you agree with this project plan?"
- *Followers* serve as friendly members and follow others.
- *Group observers* tend to give feedback from arm's length.

78

- *Standard setters* suggest team standards, evaluate quality process, raise questions about team goals, and assess team's actions towards meeting these goals.

The self-oriented role focuses only on the needs of individual team members, sometimes even at the cost of the team. It consists of the following subroles:[18,37]

- *Blockers* are negative and reject the views of others.
- *Recognition seekers* try to get attention, boast and report on personal achievements, and monopolize discussions.
- *Dominators* try to manipulate the team by asserting their superior status; they interrupt the contribution of others.
- *Avoiders* maintain a distance from others and resist new ideas and teamwork.
- *Devil's advocates* bring up alternative viewpoints; overdoing in this area can lead to negative results.
- *Topic jumpers* continually change the subject.

In effective problem-solving teams, members play both task-oriented and relations-oriented roles. Often each member plays two or more subroles. The project manager and the project team value and respect the team members who play the roles leading to high team performance. Project managers must discourage self-oriented roles because teams dominated by members playing these roles are often ineffective and fail in meeting project objectives.

Self-Assessment Exercise A (see Appendix) provides a questionnaire for evaluating your task oriented, relations-oriented, and self-oriented behaviors as a team member. The scale indicates how often you perform each role. Scores of 24 to 32 on task-oriented behaviors, and 6 to 12 on self-oriented behaviors would suggest an effectively functioning team.[38]

Major team issues

Accept the challenges so that you may feel the exhilaration of victory.
— General George S. Patton

The levels of commitment and performance of some teams are much higher than others. These high-performance teams develop norms to regulate and guide the behavior of their members. They are more cohesive and members are highly satisfied and motivated to remain on the team. Their task performance remains high because their team's norms do not conflict with project and organizational objectives. When team members are inspired by their team leaders they are often prepared to give more than 100 percent to the project. Team leaders are able to create a true team spirit, develop mutual trust, and better working relationships among team members, and provide them with compelling directions and necessary support.

In addition to the team's context and goals, developmental sequence of team members, composition and roles of team members, there are some other issues that significantly influence effectiveness. Three of these team issues are: *norms, cohesiveness,* and *leadership*.

Team norms. Why are employees in some departments eager to leave immediately when their normal work day ends, whereas people performing similar functions in a team environment stay to finish their tasks? This is mainly due to *norms*—the informal rules, expectations and patterns of behavior that teams establish and that are also accepted by team members.[39] Team norms regulate the behavior of members and exist only for behaviors that are important to the team.[40] Norms guide many aspects of organizational life, including how the team deals with the client, how team members share and negotiate resources, and how willing team members are to put in extra time and effort. [19] For example, a team norm of minimizing and correcting defects increases the quality of team's output and also the quality standards of the organization.

Norms improve coordination and communication and hence team performance as long as they do not conflict with corporate culture and the leadership style of top management. Project managers must be aware of the key issues related to team norms.[18,19]

Team norms versus organizational rules. Norms are different than organizational rules in the sense that organizational rules are written and distributed to employees in the form of policy manuals, whereas team norms are generally unwritten. Also, organizational rules may not be accepted by employees whereas team norms are accepted by team members and they abide by them. Norms are generally backed up by some type of a power or influence system. If a team member violates team norms, other members indicate their disapproval and sanction that individual in some way. Sanctions can range from rewards for compliance, to a threat of exclusion or noncompliance or even, in extreme, dysfunctional cases, physical abuse.[18]

Project managers must ensure that all team members are aware of team norms and are willing to follow those readily. Any unconscious team norms should be brought to the level of conscious awareness. Conscious acceptance or rejection of team norms increases the potential for achieving individual and team freedom and maturity and maximizes the potential for influencing team effectiveness in a positive, rather than a negative, way.[41]

Team norms versus team goals. Team norms are often related to team goals and project teams often adopt norms to help them achieve their goals.[42] Project managers should continually evaluate to determine if team norms are consistent with, neutral to, or conflicting with team and project goals. For example, sometimes team norms may specify not to produce too much and not to make too many changes. Team members may justify

80

such norms by claiming that overworking to produce too much will burn out employees, lead to more stress, accidents and absenteeism, and reduce productivity in the long run. A team norm of restricting individual output (beyond a certain level) is acceptable to all team members, especially if their primary goal is to increase social interaction. This illustrates following points about team dynamics in organizations:[18]

- Team goals may be different from organizational goals.
- Peer pressure can significantly influence individuals to follow certain norms and goals.
- Employees are concerned about both task-oriented and relations-oriented behaviors. *Project managers may encounter significant team resistance if they try to change task-oriented behavior without evaluating its impact on relations-oriented behavior.*

Conditions for enforcing norms. Team norms do not apply in every situation. Most teams form and enforce norms related to behaviors and expectations that are important to meet team goals. Major reasons of enforcing norms developed by the project team include:[18]

- Team norms aid in team survival and possible benefits. For example, the project team member may not discuss salaries and fringe benefits with other individuals in the organization to avoid feelings of inequity.
- Team norms simplify or establish predictable desired behavior of team members. For example, when team members go out for lunch together, teams may develop a norm to avoid uncomfortable concerns about how to split the bill.
- Team norms help to avoid embarrassing interpersonal problems. For example, teams may develop a norm about not discussing personal affairs (to avoid surfacing moral values) and not getting together socially in member's homes (to avoid differences in taste or income).
- Team norms emphasize the central values or goals of the team. Team norms clarify what is distinctive about the team's identity. For example, project teams involved in fashion industries expect their members to be trend-setters.[43]

How team norms develop. Teams develop norms to help accomplish their goals. Norms represent certain behaviors that help team members function more effectively. Three main factors that contribute to the development of team norms include:[19]

- Positive statements that contribute to a team's success or survival. Such statements are made by team members or outsiders. For example, a CEO or a team leader might frequently emphasize the importance of good customer relations, which urges the team to do whatever is necessary to achieve customer satisfaction.
- A critical event in the team's history may trigger a norm. For example a serious injury caused by a cluttered work area may urge the team to develop a norm to keep its work area clean and organized. Also, a team

may develop a norm to lock up its tool crib and facility doors after an expensive tool or equipment is stolen.

- The primacy effect may influence the team norms. This is a tendency to quickly form opinions and it causes initial team experiences to set the tone for future behaviors.[44] For example, the participative leadership style of the team leader may create an open team environment and encourage team members to give their suggestions and ideas freely.
- Belief and values of team members contribute significantly to the development of team norms. For example, a project team may develop a norm to keep meetings short and start and end meetings on time if team members strongly believe in punctuality and time management.

Conformity to team norms. Everyone has felt peer pressure at one time or another.[45] Coworkers may make sarcastic remarks if a team member does not complete his or her part of the project on schedule, does not meet team expectations, or is frequently late for a meeting. In extreme situations, the team may use coercive power to enforce its norms, threatening to exclude those who don't conform to team norms. The pressures to adhere to norms may result in conformity. There are two basic types of conformity.[18, 45]

Compliance conformity occurs when an individual's behavior becomes or remains similar to the team's behavior because of real or imagined peer pressure. Sometimes, teams only get compliance conformity to team norms from their team members because they personally don't think that the norms are appropriate and desirable. In spite of this lack of personal acceptance, people often comply because they:[18]

- Feel that unity is necessary to accomplish team goals
- Want to become popular and be accepted by others
- Feel that cost of conformity is lower than that of non-conformity (fear of ostracism)
- Feel that personal relationships and harmony may be jeopardized.

People change their behavior and their effort to comply.

This is particularly strong in new members because they are not sure of their status and want to demonstrate their strong membership in the team.

Personal acceptance conformity is based upon positive personal support of team norms. It occurs when an individual's natural behavior, attitudes and beliefs are aligned with the norms and goals of the team. This type of conformity is stronger because the individual believes in team norms and therefore *wants* to rather than *has* to comply to team norms.

Norms are directly reinforced through praise from top management or team leader, more access to valued information and resources, or other rewards available to team.[46]

Norms and conformity to them influence team effectiveness. Without this the teams would be chaotic and consequently it would be difficult to meet project objectives. However, at the other extreme, excessive and

82

blind conformity threatens ethics as well as the team's potential to deal with project changes, uncertainties and complex problems.

The power of conformity to team norms is illustrated in the classic story of an employee assigned to work with a small team of pressers in a pajama factory.[47] In this case, the employee initially increased her output (units pressed per hour) and exceeded the team norm of fifty units, but had to reduce it to conform to a level acceptable to the team. Later when the team was disbanded, leaving the criticized employee to work alone, she increased her performance and maintained her output to ninety-two units per hour compared with forty-five units in the presence of coworkers.

Many organizations benefit from team conformity to control safety, performance, attendance, and other work behaviors. The following collection of examples illustrates how the power and politics of peer pressure may significantly influence team performance, while, at the same time raising ethical questions about controlling employee behavior through coworkers.[48]

Dunkley Lumber, the independently owned sawmill near Prince George, British Columbia, Canada, reduced lost time because of accidents by introducing a safety program that involved putting employees into small safety teams to watch each other's safety behavior. Peer pressure to "do it all or not at all" had a powerful influence on employee behavior in reducing accidents.[49]

In many Japanese companies, peer pressure forces people to work beyond the formal workday. Japanese auto manufacturers applied the power of group conformity to reduce absenteeism at their North American plants. They accomplished this by urging team members to carry the extra workload when a co-worker was absent. Employees did this rather than face humiliation or possible exclusion from the team. Although the company was able to maintain low absenteeism rate by using this strategy, it raises some ethical concerns in the workplace. Mumir Khalid, a union leader at McDonnell Douglas Canada does not approve of using teams for this type of conformity. "Team work leads to competition between teams, speed-up, and peer pressure within teams," he warns. "It also leads to team members reprimanding fellow workers if they are absent or can't keep up for any reason."[50]

Many employees at CAMI Automotive Inc., in Ingersoll, Ontario, Canada, agree with Khalid's statement. In 1989, the joint venture of General Motors and Suzuki, opened with a strong emphasis on teamwork to solve problems and achieve high performance. During the first year, only 19 percent of employees agreed with Khalid's statement but in a more recent survey 44 percent felt that teams are used as a control system to reduce absenteeism and boost job performance.[50]

Changing team norms. Although norms are deeply ingrained, project managers must try to change those norms that may undermine team performance. Two approaches to accomplish this are using the primacy effect by introducing performance-oriented norms upfront, and selecting team members with desirable norms. For example, if the project team wants to emphasize safety, project manager should select team members who value high safety standards.

Selecting team members with positive norms may be effective in new project teams but it is hard to change counterproductive norms in existing teams. To achieve this, project managers must be tactful and use persuasive communication and a team-based reward system. If everything fails, as a last resort the group can be dissolved and replaced with team members having desirable norms.[51, 52]

Unfortunately, the pressure to conform to counterproductive norms is sometimes stronger than the financial incentive.[52] This is illustrated by the story of employees in a pajama factory. Team norms are very powerful in terms of influencing output. The project manager should avail every opportunity to introduce performance-oriented norms throughout the team development process and select team members who will bring favorable norms to the team.

Team cohesiveness. The performance of a team depends upon the level of its cohesiveness. Cohesiveness refers to how much people like the team and how motivated they are to remain as team members.[53] It determines how strongly the team members feel bonded to each other. It is the glue or esprit de corps that holds the team together and ensures that all team members fulfill their individual as well as collective obligations.[19] Cohesiveness is related to the following three main functions of teams which also represent the three main reasons of why people join teams:[19]
- Accomplish goals (individual's and team's)
- Gain status and fulfill social affiliation needs
- Get emotional support (during crisis or trouble).

Most people like to become and remain team members because they believe that the team will help them meet their personal needs and objectives.[54]

Because it influences the team's effectiveness and performance, it is important to understand the following issues related to cohesiveness:[19]

Causes of team cohesiveness. Team cohesiveness depends upon various factors (see Figure 2.4) that influence the identity of a team member, working relationships among team members and usefulness (perceived or actual) of the team in fulfilling individuals' needs.[55] Teams become more cohesive as they progress through the four stages of team development outlined earlier. The following factors affect team cohesiveness:[19]

Similarity among team members influences cohesiveness because members with similar ideas, opinions, outlooks, and attitudes feel comfortable with each other and therefore interact better.[56] Due to this similarity, members easily agree on team objectives, plans of actions, and ground rules to achieve teamwork. This enhances trust and reduces destructive

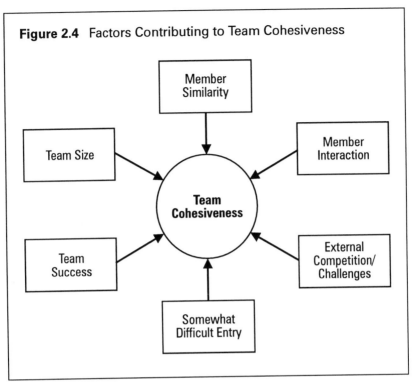

Figure 2.4 Factors Contributing to Team Cohesiveness

Member Similarity

Member Interaction

Team Size

Team Cohesiveness

Team Success

External Competition/ Challenges

Somewhat Difficult Entry

Source: Steven L. McShane. 1995. *Canadian Organizational Behavior,* Second Edition. Chicago, IL.: Richard D. Irwin, p. 310. By permission of the publisher.

conflict. That is why homogenous teams are more cohesive than heterogenous teams.

Interaction among team members increases team cohesiveness.[57] Interaction increases when members work on interdependent tasks and in close proximity. Project managers should recognize that the physical arrangement (e.g., a tight matrix) normally encourages interaction among team members but may reduce interaction with other people in the organization or in other teams.[58] Maintaining interaction becomes a challenge when several team members telecommute, work in the field, are on the road, or are physically located far from others and the project office. It is important to bring them together periodically to renew team support. For instance, a software technology company having up to eighty engineers working at customer sites held frequent lunches, parties and social gatherings at company headquarters to maintain cohesiveness by keeping everyone in touch with each other.[59]

External competition and challenges energize the team and increase its cohesiveness. This is particularly true when most members feel that they can meet the challenges and competition only through teamwork rather than by working alone.

Somewhat difficult entry may increase the perceived prestige of the team. Existing team members accept and support new members after they have gone through the same entry experience.[60] It should be recognized that entry should be made somewhat difficult in the sense that it should challenge the members in terms of required skills to contribute to project success rather than making the entry simply very expensive or too awkward.

Team success increases the team's cohesiveness.[61] People like to be associated with successful teams because they believe that such teams will help them grow. Successful teams provide a sense of achievement and opportunities for promotions.

Team size may influence the team's cohesiveness significantly. Smaller teams are more cohesive simply due to logistics in achieving effective communication and coordination. However, teams should be large enough to provide a broader base of knowledge experience and problem-solving skills to evaluate alternatives and make proper decisions

Maintaining a high level of cohesiveness is a challenge. However, a better understanding of these factors should help project managers increase cohesiveness of their team.

Consequences of team cohesiveness. Cohesiveness is essential for achieving teamwork.[62] It is an important characteristic of effective teams. Following are the main consequences of cohesiveness:[19]

- High motivation to remain in the team and make a contribution
- More sensitivity to each other's needs which leads to better working relationships
- More mutual trust and open communication
- Less dysfunctional conflict and effective conflict management strategies
- Information is shared readily and more frequently
- Increased social and emotional support to each other in stressful situations.[63]

Cohesiveness and team performance. The purpose of team building is to achieve human synergy. The team performance is influenced by its cohesiveness depending upon the compatibility between team norms and company goals.[64] Figure 2.5 shows that team performance is the highest when team cohesiveness is high and team norms are aligned with organizational goals. However, if team norms do not support the organizational goals, high team cohesiveness leads to lower task performance than low cohesiveness. This happens because high cohesiveness motivates team members to primarily conform to team norms even if it results to lower performance, whereas in low cohesive teams, norms are less important and therefore the team performance may not be driven too low even if it is so desired according to team norms.[19]

Strategies to develop team cohesiveness. Firstly, project managers must focus to ensure that team norms are consistent with overall objectives and

86

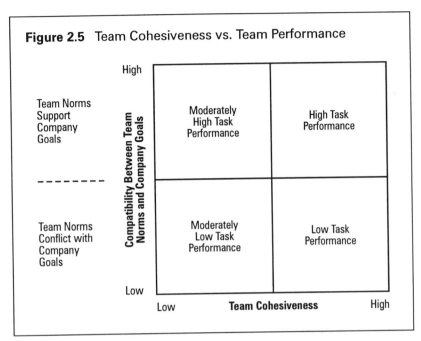

Figure 2.5 Team Cohesiveness vs. Team Performance

Team Norms
Support
Company
Goals

Team Norms
Conflict with
Company
Goals

Compatibility Between Team
Norms and Company Goals

High

Low

Moderately
High Task
Performance

High Task
Performance

Moderately
Low Task
Performance

Low Task
Performance

Low   **Team Cohesiveness**   High

Source: Steven L. McShane. 1995. *Canadian Organizational Behavior,* Second Edition. Chicago, IL.: Richard D. Irwin, p. 312. By permission of the publisher.

then they should develop cohesiveness in order to increase team performance. Following are some practical ideas to develop team cohesiveness:[19]

- Select team members with similar goals, attitudes, values, work ethics, professional interests, and experiences.
- Encourage interaction among team members by using a tight matrix and creating an open environment. Close proximity increases cohesiveness.
- Keep the team size small without losing the depth and breadth of combined knowledge and experiences needed to meet objectives.
- Ensure that the team is aware of external competition and threats and help them develop strategies to be well prepared.
- Provide challenges which can only be met through teamwork.
- Maintain high entrance standards. Team members will value their potential to become and remain team members.
- Expedite communication.
- Celebrate team success. Recognize team performance with appropriate rewards.
- Provide sufficient resources to accomplish the task.
- Provide proper training to resolve conflicts promptly. Unresolved dysfunctional conflicts reduce cohesiveness.

Team cohesiveness is not easy to achieve. Project managers must evaluate the consequences of cohesiveness and factors that contribute to team cohesiveness. By using these ideas, conducting team building exercises regularly, and nurturing the project team, project managers should be able to increase team cohesiveness and hence high team performance provided team norms are consistent with organizational goals.

Team leadership. Another team issue which affects effectiveness is leadership. Informal or emergent leadership is more effective in achieving goals in smaller teams. An informal leader emerges with time and is able to significantly influence the team because of his/her ability to help the team meet its objectives. Successful team leaders must demonstrate multiple leadership as well as effective situational leadership.

Multiple leadership. In teams, members must work interdependently on tasks with a common commitment to meet team goals. Therefore, teams have both task-oriented and relations-oriented goals which must be met to optimize team effort. Instead of having two different leaders (one for task-oriented goals and another for relations-oriented goals), one team leader is expected to provide multiple leadership to achieve both goals which may be difficult because of different personal characteristics required to meet each goal.[65]

It is likely that informal leaders who look after task-oriented goals in a team would emerge only when formal leaders neglect their task-related responsibilities or are not capable of doing them.[66] On the other hand, more people are likely to emerge as informal leaders to help meet relations-oriented goals.

Effective team leadership. An effective team leader influences all factors associated with the team dynamics and team effectiveness model shown in Figure 2.1. For example, an effective team leader must be aware of external environment (the team context) in terms of technology, external competition and relationships with external stakeholders. They influence the selection of team members by defining the selection criteria. They must be able to take team members through the four stages of team development quickly and smoothly without letting the team fall apart. They influence the team composition, roles of team members (task-oriented, relations-oriented and self-oriented behavior roles) and team size to ensure that team norms are consistent with project goals and overall organizational goals.

It is clear from Figure 2.1 that achieving a high degree of team effectiveness is quite difficult because of complex team dynamics and several factors affecting team behavior. It becomes even more challenging for project leaders due to increased cultural diversity among team members. However, a better understanding of the factors shown in Figure 2.1 and the practical suggestions outlined in this section should help project managers build more effective teams.

Cultural Diversity and Project Management

Culture is a kind of "mental software"—the collective programming of the mind which distinguishes the members of one group of people from another.
— *Geert Hofstede*

Before identifying the major elements of culture, it is important to understand its basic nature, general definition, and key characteristics. These are briefly described as follows:[67]

What is culture?

Culture represents the distinctive way in which a group of people related by geography, religion, ethnicity, or some other unifying principle, lead their lives.[68] It refers to a commonly shared set of values, beliefs, attitudes and knowledge. Culture can be created both by people and environment and can be transmitted from one generation to the next through family, school, social environment and other agencies.[69] Culture is difficult to define precisely and is a complex subject because of its several dimensions and elements. Hofstede describes culture simply as a kind of "mental software ... the collective programming of the mind which distinguishes the members of one group of people from another."[70] Culture can also be defined as acquired knowledge that is used to interpret the experiences of a group and which forms the basis of its behavior.[71] Here are some key characteristics of culture:

- Culture is acquired by learning and experience.
- Groups, organizations and societies share cultures.
- Culture is transferred from generation to generation.
- Culture is based on symbolic representations.
- Culture has a pattern characterized by its structure and integration.
- Culture is a variable. Groups, organizations and societies may change according to changes in their environments.[71]

Major elements of culture. Today more project managers operate in an environment characterized by cultural diversity. Cultural differences may significantly influence success in project management and especially in negotiations for international projects.[69] More business organizations are now investing in educating global managers to develop their cultural sensitivity and increase their intercultural communication skills. To achieve this, it is important to understand and analyze the major elements of culture. Martin identified seven major elements of culture (see Figure 2.6) which are briefly described below:[69]

Material culture. This refers to physical objects created by people or results of technology.[72] It includes the tools and skills of local workers, their work habits and attitudes towards work and time. Project managers need this information to plan for any negotiations with international partners of different cultures.

Figure 2.6 Major Cultural Elements Affecting Projects

Cultural Element	What It Means or Implies	Impact on Project	Recommendations/ Comments
Material Culture	• Refers to tools, skills, work habits and work attitudes	• Determines technical and manpower constraints	• This formation is needed for planning and negotiations
Language	• Medium of communication • Words and experiences may differ	• Affects communications • Influences understanding of beliefs and values	• Learning foreign language develops better understanding and rapport
Aesthetics	• Arts, music, dance, traditions and customs	• Encourages informal and open communication • Influences success directly	• Relationships are enriched by encouraging informal communication
Education	• Transmission of knowledge through learning process • Approach to problems and people	• Affects project planning and negotiations	• Knowledge of education system helps in determining level of skills and expertise (helpful in project planning and negotiations)
Religion, Beliefs and Attitudes	• Mainspring of culture • Affects dress, eating habits, attitudes of workers towards work, punctuality and work site	• Emphasizes on promptness and punctuality	• Appreciation of religion, beliefs and values develops mutual trust, respects and improves cooperation and team spirit
Social Organization	• Organizations/groups (labor unions, social clubs) • Relate to social classes	• Influences formal/informal communication • Affects business contacts for negotiating	• Social skills can lead to better results than formal meetings
Political Life	• Government involvement in joint ventures with foreign companies • Concerned about treatment of people, jobs, financial, economic and safety factors	• Affects delivery of materials, supplies and equipment • Influences permits and licenses	• Staying in tune with political life helps identify the strengths, constraints and business contacts

Adapted from: M. Dean Martin. 1981. The Negotiation Differential for International Project Management. *Proceedings of the Annual Seminar/Symposium of the Project Management Institute.* Drexel Hill, PA: Project Management Institute pp. 450–453.

Language. Language is a mirror of any culture.[73] It is the primary medium of communication, which is vital in managing projects. Language includes words and expressions that may mean different things in different cultures. To learn the language of a culture is to know its people and this helps in understanding beliefs, values, ways of life, and points of view.[74] Project participants of other countries appreciate the efforts other people make to learn their language and this helps in developing better rapport among all project participants.

Aesthetics. This refers to the art, music, dance, traditions and other customs. Aesthetics may not directly influence project activities but an appreciation of aesthetics of different countries enriches relationships and encourages the informal and open communication that may influence project success.

Education. The cultural component of education deals with the transmission of knowledge through the learning process.[69] It outlines how people from different cultures approach problems, and relate to other people and foreigners. Knowledge of the educational system can lead to better understanding of a culture and help in project planning and negotiations.

Religion, beliefs and attitudes. Religion is often called the mainspring of a culture; it significantly influences each of the other elements of the culture. It affects dress, eating habits, attitudes of workers towards work, punctuality and work site.

Hall indicated that different cultures have different attitudes towards time.[75] For example, in the United States and Germany, promptness and punctuality is valued whereas in some other cultures, appointments cover a general time interval rather than a precise time. It is important that the project manager recognizes that culture can and does affect these critical variables that may influence communication and project outcomes.

Social organizations. This cultural element deals with the organization of individuals into groups and the way they structure their project activities to accomplish proper goals and objectives. It includes family relationships, labor unions, social clubs and other societal references that influence attitudes and values.[69] Social organizations also relate to social classes in society. A better understanding of social organizations helps the project manager in terms of business contacts, time scheduling and formal/informal communication and networking. For example, sometimes project managers may attain more success at informal social meetings than at formal-daytime meetings in an office environment.

Political life. Often foreign governments get involved in joint ventures between their local companies and foreign companies entering their market. This is increasing with the growth of multinational corporations and the need to compete globally through partnering and collaborations with other countries.[76] The foreign government's concerns relate to the amount of profits, economic and financial transactions, number of jobs created, treatment of its people and safety and environmental factors. They can approve or disapprove issuance of licenses and permits, import and export of equipment, supplies and materials, or can in various other ways make the job of a project manager easy or difficult. Resolving some of these problems by bribing local officials raises a question of ethics. In some cases, foreign governments may demand that their representative be involved actively in front-end project planning and decision-making depending upon the nature of the projects, the amount of money, level of technology, and the amount of government support needed for the project.

All these elements of culture can significantly influence a project's outcome. In addition, project managers should be familiar with the following conditions in approaching another culture:[69]

Self-reference criterion. According to this criterion, the individual evaluates others in terms of his or her own value system. Project managers with such an attitude set up barriers that may cause conflicts and breakdowns in communication. For example, a project manager who criticizes the language, food and religion of a foreign country may offend the people of that country and thereby reduce mutual understanding and open communication.

Culture shock. This occurs when an individual is away from the known and familiar and is faced with differing customs and ways of doing things. However, there is always more than one way to do a job. Project managers should focus on getting things done, rather than on trying to teach people their own values and work styles.

Cultural diversity and projects

People have one thing in common; they are all different.

— *Robert Zend*

In a multinational project environment, culture is a dominating variable. Project managers can face serious problems related to project cost, schedule, quality and people if they are unable to recognize and deal with the major elements of culture and appreciate cultural differences among project participants. Owens has outlined some major dimensions of cultural differences and their implications for project managers and how cultural synergy may be achieved.[67, 77]

Critical dimensions of cultural differences. Hofstede[77] identified major critical dimensions of cultural differences. Each dimension can be described as an aspect of a culture that can be measured relative to other cultures. An appreciation of these critical dimensions of cultural difference should help project managers understand the dynamics of culture and its effect on a team's behavior. Critical dimensions of cultural differences are as follows:[67, 77]

Power distance. This dimension evaluates how a particular culture deals with inequality. Hofstede described the concept of a power distance index (PDI) that refers to the degree of "dependence relationships" in a particular country.

In order to obtain the PDI, Hofstede conducted a study in which questions were addressed to employees from over fifty countries who worked for one large multinational firm. These employees were asked to determine their perceptions and preferences about the decision-making styles of their managers and the extent to which they were afraid of expressing their disagreement with their managers.[78] PDI scores indicate the extent of dependency expectations of a particular project team member from that country. Hofstede summarized the significance of PDI scores as follows:[78]

Low PDI scores obtained in the U.S., U.K. and most Western European and Scandinavian countries indicate a relatively limited dependence on bosses and a preference for consultation and participation. Hence, there is interdependence between boss and subordinate.

High PDI scores obtained in Latin countries (including Spain and France) show a considerable dependence of subordinates on bosses. Sub-

92

ordinates either demonstrate their dependence by preferring an autocratic or paternalistic boss and following their orders without asking any questions, or show their counter-dependence by rejecting their bosses entirely. The emotional distance in a country with a high PDI score is large between bosses and subordinates, which implies that subordinates are unlikely to approach or contradict their boss directly.

Individualism-collectivism. This cultural dimension examines the role of the individual versus the role of the group, as briefly discussed in Chapter 1. Hofstede summarized several key differences in organizational practices between these two types of societies.[79]

In collectivist societies, personal relationships are given higher priority than the task, whereas in individualist societies, the task is supposed to prevail over any personal relationships. If a business person or a project manager from a Western country (individualistic) tries to force a quick decision in a collectivist culture (Eastern and Latin countries), he or she will be criticized for failing to conform to cultural norms.

Gender role identification (masculinity-femininity). Hofstede described countries as having either dominant masculine or dominant feminine cultures. A "masculine" society is one in which social gender roles are clearly distinct and where men are supposed to be dominating, assertive, tough and want material success. In a "feminine" society, roles overlap and men and women are likely to be more equal, tender and concerned with quality of life. In such a society, organizational rewards are based on equality.[80]

Uncertainty avoidance. This dimension focuses on tolerance for ambiguity or uncertainty in the workplace. Hofstede found that different cultures cope differently with uncertainties and ambiguities. For example, in a culture with strong uncertainty avoidance such as in Japan, Mexico, Germany and Italy, people tend to have a high need for security, formal and structured organizations, and a resistance to conflict-inducing situations. On the other hand, in countries with low uncertainty avoidance (the U.S., U.K., Canada and Sweden), there tends to be a greater tolerance for different ideas, and creativity and innovations are encouraged. [77]

Project outcomes are not always certain. Depending upon the home culture, project team members may feel uncomfortable or even threatened by uncertainties and ambiguities in a project and may take particular actions to cope with it. To successfully manage projects in such situations, project managers must be aware of the reactions of different team members to ambiguous situations.

Time. This relates to time horizon, value of time, and focus.

Time horizon (long-term/short-term orientation). According to Hofstede, long-term orientation shows an inclination towards strategic/long-term plans, future rewards, perseverance and thrift; whereas short-term orientation focuses on present and past, with a particular respect for tradition, preservation of "face" and fulfilling social obligations.[81]

Value of time (punctuality/flexibility). Value of time is determined by the way punctuality is defined and valued. In the United States and Northern Europe, punctuality is defined precisely (e.g., meetings start on time and deadlines are taken seriously), whereas punctuality is defined somewhat loosely in Italy, Spain and Latin American countries.[82]

Focus (single focus/multiple focus). The United States and Northern Europe cultures tend to emphasize on single focus which implies concentrating on one task at a time and having high commitment to schedules and plans.[82] On the other hand, people in Southern Europe, Middle East and Latin America are multiple-focus oriented, which implies that they put more emphasis on relationships than schedules and deadlines.

Fully industrialized Asian cultures (Taiwan, Japan, Singapore, Hong Kong and South Korea) have a single-focus orientation to time and also maintain a focus on building good relationships. On the other hand, people in lesser developed South East Asian countries tend to be more multi-focused.

Attitude towards life (quantity vs. quality of life). This relates to the value system of people in different cultures with respect to their desire for material things. *Quantity of life* people tend to be more competitive. They emphasize achievements and the acquisition of money and material goods. *Quality of life* people value quality of life more than quantity. They are more cooperative. They tend to emphasize relationships, concern for others, and interdependence.

Major cultural variables and related orientations. In addition to six critical dimensions of cultural differences, there are five major cultural variables with specific associated orientations that influence the behavior of people in different cultures.[82] These cultural variables have been derived from the work of several anthropologists and business consultants. The cultural variables of *Environment* and *Action* are derived from the studies by Kluckhohn and Strodtbeck[83] and Hall;[84] the *Communication* and *Space* variables are based on the work of Hall,[84] and the *Thinking* variable is based on the work of Rhinesmith[85] and Stewart and Bennett.[86] These variables are briefly described below.

Environment. Environment influences the behavior of people with respect to the orientations of control, harmony and constraint.[82,83]

Control. People feel that they have full control of their environment and they can change it to fit their needs and meet their goals. This is typical of people in the United States and Northern European countries.

Harmony. People with this orientation believe that it is better to live in harmony with the environment and others and unity permeates all forms of life. This orientation is very common and popular in Asia. For example Japanese value the concept of Wa (harmony), and in Chinese culture most

94

individuals and organizations consider "feng shui" regarding the construction of homes and industrial buildings; buildings are located and oriented according to ancient beliefs and rules in order not to disrupt the flow of *chi,* or life force energy. They believe that feng shui principles must followed in order to live and conduct business and to safeguard good luck and future fortune.

Constraint. Some people, especially in Middle East and Latin countries, stress influence of external forces. They believe that fate, luck and chance can significantly influence our outcomes. They believe that God has ultimate power and controls our lives; and unforeseen circumstance will impact the results of our efforts.

Action. Cultures can determine how aggressive or passive people are. People's orientation to action can be classified in following two categories:[82,83]

Task Orientation. People with task-oriented cultures emphasize on achievements and accomplishments of their objectives. For example, U.S. and Northern European culture is action-oriented and emphasize accomplishing measurable objectives. When people in such cultures ask *Who are you?* the answer is usually a job title or job description.

Relationship Orientation. People in Africa, the Middle East and Latin America emphasize relationships and experiences. They value character, affiliations and personal characteristics more than just work and achievements. When people in such cultures are asked *Who are you?* they normally tell their tribe's name, family, clan or other affiliation.

Communication. This is the most important dimension or variable of cultural differences. Different orientations to communication can cause communication breakdowns, which can lead to serious problems in sales, negotiations, conflict management, and achieving teamwork. Cultural orientation to communication can be classified in following categories:[82,84]

High Context. This refers to emphasis on implicit communication. Building and maintaining relationships is an important first step toward conducting business. Communication is more nonverbal than verbal. High context orientation is common among people in Middle East, Asia and Latin America, where they want to find out about family background, education, character and political connections, in addition to an individual's technical skills and experience.

Low Context. People with low context orientation stress exchange of facts and information rather than relationships. People in the United States normally have a low context orientation because in the United States information is given in words and the meaning is expressed explicitly. Communication is direct and minimal relationship is considered adequate to conduct business. In a project environment, engineers and technical specialists are more low context-oriented than sales and marketing people.

Direct. This refers to straightforwardness. Managers in the United States practice a direct style of communication: they mean what they say and say what they mean. They prefer to identify a conflict, analyze it, find its cause and then manage it. However, while project managers in the United States are businesslike, they also often soften the delivery of a direct message to an extent that German project managers, who value even more directness, may feel that U.S. managers are not direct and trustworthy.

Indirect. People with indirect orientation prefer to avoid conflict in order to allow other party to save face, and preserve honor and respect. This is common in many Asian and Latin American countries. For example, people in Japan and China often say "yes" when they may mean "I am not sure" or "I understand." On the other hand, in the U.S., conflict avoidance is interpreted as low assertive and low cooperative behavior.

Expressive. People in the Middle East and Latin America have an expressive communication style, in the sense that they display emotion, use more body language, and stress relationships.

Instrumental: People in the United States, Japan, Western and Northern Europe, use instrumental style of communication. They emphasize facts and objectivity more than emotions, and body language.

Formal. People in Asia, the Middle East, Latin America and Eastern Europe have a formal orientation to communication. They stress following protocols and social customs. They emphasize status or formal authority and tend to follow customs in greeting their business associates, dress codes, and exchanging business cards and gifts.

Informal. People in Canada, the United States and Australia tend to use an informal style of communication. There is less emphasis on rigid protocols, ceremonies and customs. People in business start using first names immediately, whereas in other countries this is done only after developing closer business relationships. In the United States, people often shake hands firmly with a smile and direct eye contact, whereas in Japan, they are more formal, exchanging business cards with a bow, only a minimal eye contact, and no handshake. In some Native American cultures, making eye contact is considered rude and displays lack of respect.

Space. Different cultures have different requirements about their personal space (distance between individuals); division of physical space into private or public spaces; and how these are used while communicating with others. A culture's orientation to space can be classified in following two categories:[82,84]

Private. People with this orientation tend to prefer distance (at least an arm's length) between individuals. For example in the United States, people like to have a private office or a private space in large offices. In private space environments, there are more closed door meetings, minimal disruptions and interruptions and people are expected to get permission to enter private space.

Public. This orientation is common in Asia and Latin America. People with this orientation prefer close proximity and offices are open. Managers often sit with or near other employees. There are frequent interruptions and people feel free to enter another's space.

Thinking. This refers to the process of interpretation and the way something is thought about and analyzed. A culture's orientation to thinking can be classified in following categories:[82,85,86]

Inductive. Reasoning is based on experience and experimentation with emphasis on *how* something can be done rather than *why.* This is typical in the United States and most of Northern Europe.

Deductive. Reasoning is based on theory and logic with emphasis on intellectual principles, ideas and theory; *why* rather than *how.* Most French project managers follow deductive thinking and may say "That sounds very well, but it is correct theoretically?"

Linear. This refers to analytical thinking, in which people tend to break problems into smaller, manageable packages. Many project managers in the United States (especially in technical fields) tend to analyze events, concepts and diagnose problems. This type of thinking may appear cold, impersonal and overly objective.

Systemic. This refers to focusing on the big picture and interrelationships between components. People in Japan, China and Brazil tend to use more of a systemic thinking style.

A U.S. thinking style focuses on action and getting things done, with emphasis on achieving measurable results. Most U.S. project managers tend to use realistic and operational thinking and like to classify information in a linear cause-and-effect manner. On the other hand, people with Japanese, Chinese and Brazilian cultures are more systemic than analytical. For example, the Japanese like to get specific details about people and organizations rather than insisting on logical or linear connections, while Europeans often stress abstract theory.[82]

A cultural orientation model with eleven elements as shown in Figure 2.7 can be developed by incorporating the six critical dimensions and five cultural variables explained earlier. Project managers must recognize all eleven elements of this model and be aware of their associated orientations in order to recognize and capitalize on cultural differences to achieve synergy and teamwork.

Cultural diversity and the project manager. We are a community of learners. Project managers must be on alert to learn from people of diverse cultures. Project managers in multicultural projects must try to learn relevant customs, courtesies and business protocols before taking on the responsibility of managing an international project. Hofstede emphasized the importance of all six dimensions of culture in learning to understand

Team Dynamics and Cultural Diversity

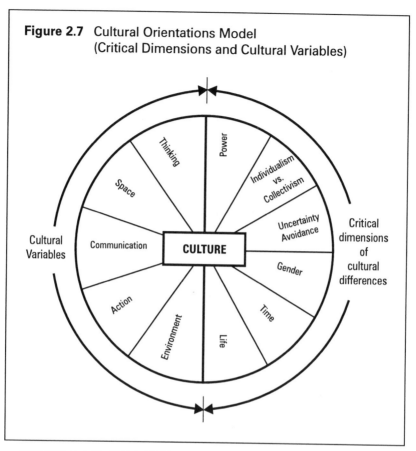

Figure 2.7 Cultural Orientations Model
(Critical Dimensions and Cultural Variables)

Adapted from the work of Geert Hofstede, 1993, *Cultures and Organizations: The Software of the Mind* (McGraw Hill, 1993) and *Cultural Dimensions in People Management: The Socialization Perspective* (John Wiley, 1993); Richard A. Punzo, " Managing Cross Cultural Values in Project Teams," *Proceedings of the 1996 Seminars & Symposium,* (PMI, 1996); and the *Doing Business Internationally Series,* 1996, Training Management Corporation (TMC), Princeton, NJ.

the "mental software" of multicultural members of organizations. His analysis can be summarized as follows:[87]

Out of the six dimensions of cultural differences, three dimensions—power distance, uncertainty avoidance and long-term versus short-term orientation—most affect one's thinking about organizations. The remaining two dimensions—individualism/collectivism and masculinity/femininity—help us understand the people in an organization rather than the organization itself; whereas the last dimension—attitude toward life—relates to the value system of people in different cultures. When organizing a project, one should always address four questions:

1. What is the organizational strategy?
2. Who has the power to decide what?

Table 2.4   Countries vs. Critical Cultural Dimensions

Critical Cultural Dimensions	Countries				
	Group 1 USA Canada Australia	Group 2 Germany Austria Switzerland	Group 3 Mexico Venezuela Peru	Group 4 Japan	Group 5 India Hong Kong Singapore
1) Power Distance (PD)	Moderately Low	Moderately Low	Moderately High	Moderately High	High
2) Individualistic Collectivistic (IV)	High Individualistic	Moderately Individualistic	High to Moderately Collectivistic	Moderately Collectivistic	High to Moderately Collectivistic
3) Masculine Feminine (MF)	Moderately Masculine	Moderately Masculine	Moderately to Highly Masculine	Highly Masculine	Masculine
4) Uncertainty Avoidance (UA)	Moderately Weak	Moderately Strong	Moderately Weak	Strong	Moderately Weak
5) Time Horizon (Long Term/Short Term Orientation)	Long Term	Long Term	Short Term	Long Term	Short Term
6) Attitude Towards Life: Quality vs. Quantity of life	Quantity	Quantity	Quality	More Quality than Quantity	Changing from Quality to Quantity

Adapted from Stephen D. Owens and James Reagan McLaurin, 1993, "Cultural Diversity and Projects: What the Project manager Needs to Know," *Proceedings of the 1993 Seminars & Symposium*, Upper Darby, PA: Project Management Institute, p. 233.

3. What rules or procedures will be followed to achieve desired goals and objectives?

4. What do people value the most?

The answer to the first question is influenced by the tendency of the organization to plan long term or short term; the answer to the second question is determined by the norms of power distance; the answer to the third question is influenced by external norms about uncertainty avoidance; and the answer to the fourth question is influenced by the cultural value placed on relationships (quality of life) or material things (quantity of life).

Table 2.4 shows five country groupings that are characterized *vis-a-vis* the six cultural dimensions. From this table, it can be seen how a project manager and a functional manager would deal with conflict in a different country group. For example, in the U.S., two managers are likely to meet

Team Dynamics and Cultural Diversity

face to face and reach a compromised solution without depending upon any rules or hierarchy. In the second group, represented by Germany, problems may arise because of a lack of structure, and managers would tend to rely on rules and procedures to find an acceptable solution. Countries in groups 3 and 4 would be more concerned with preserving the relationships between the parties in a conflict, but that motive would be even stronger for negotiators from countries in group 5. In Mexico and India, PDI is high and therefore the superior of the two managers would step in and force a settlement. However, in Japan, much the same approach may happen but the superior would seek input from all parties concerned and do a thorough investigation first. Decisions would likely be made by consensus.

Cultural diversity brings new solutions to an ever-changing environment, and sameness is not only uninteresting but limiting as well. Project managers must be aware of cross cultural implications and dimensions of national culture to better understand expectations of a diverse mix of project participants organized in a team to attain project goals. Project managers must learn to foster cultural synergy within their multicultural team.

Cultural synergy. The project manager can act as a catalyst to achieve synergy in a multicultural project. *Synergy* is defined as a joint or cooperative action and occurs when a diverse mix of people (project team members) work together towards a common goal. To meet global competition, project teams must aim at increasing their effectiveness by capitalizing on member's differences. The project manager can help a great deal in achieving synergy in a cross cultural project environment. Harris and Moran outlined the following skills or abilities to achieve team effectiveness in a multinational project.[88]

- Develop respect for team members
- Adapt to a new and changing environment
- Manage members with different values in their arena
- Relate more to people than to tasks
- Withhold judgment and remain objective while dealing with conflicts
- Try sincerely to understand the situation from team members viewpoint (empathy)
- Have patience and perseverance to overcome initial cultural blunders
- Be open and broad minded in accepting different cultures, languages, religions, beliefs and attitudes
- Develop understanding of political and social environments.

Managing International Projects

Learn to recognize cultural differences. Cultural diversity is a reality of life in international projects and joint ventures.

— *The Author*

International projects are more complex due to the cultural diversity of the project participants. Cultural differences combined with various factors such as currency fluctuations, political instability, economic risks, competition and pressures from national industries, governments and special interest groups can all interfere with planning and project management of international projects. Therefore, project managers must identify, distinguish and satisfy a corresponding set of project management requirements. Project managers must identify, commit, and integrate people from traditional functional organizations into a multidisciplinary and multicultural project team.

Attributes of international projects

Because of tough competition, industrial and business organizations are forced to explore new business opportunities all over the world. Consequently, many projects involve international partners and stakeholders. As more and more project managers operate in a global environment, they must recognize the unique characteristics of international projects and be sensitive to the variety of cultures with which they may interact. Here are some unique attributes within the international setting that must be considered for effectively managing international projects.[89]

Planning. Project planning will be highly influenced by political instability, currency fluctuations, local competition, pressures from national governments and local laws and regulations. Many international projects fail because of the inability of their project managers to appreciate the cross-cultural factors and comprehend and respond appropriately to foreign environments.[89] Unlike in North America, project managers in Latin America, China and Japan must spend more time in socializing, small talk, making personal contacts and attending social events, all of which may affect estimated duration of project activities.

Communication and information systems. The constraints and objectives of time, cost and performance are interpreted differently in different cultures. For example, in Western culture, time, promptness and punctuality are valued more conscientiously than in Eastern, Middle Eastern or Mediterranean cultures. Copeland and Griggs[90] pointed out that in the United States, because responsibilities are delegated and initiative is valued, the information is usually generated outside and flows in to a project manager. But in Europe and South America, authority is centralized and people don't feel responsible for keeping the project manager informed. Consequently a foreigner may not be informed of important decisions if he or she does not understand how information flows in different countries. Also, in the United States, managers are direct and straightforward; more importance is given to facts than to suggestions or to specifications than to implications. Whereas in other cultures, such as the Arab, Asian and French, the direct route is often avoided and even disliked because of the priority placed on establishing a relationship before getting down to business. Global electronic communications may use standard formats and therefore may reduce impact of cultural differences leading to different communicating styles and techniques.

Control systems. Control subsystems encompass standards, evaluations and corrective actions. Different cultural, economic, political and legal environments increase the complexity of control subsystems in the management of international projects. Also geographical distance, communication habits, language barriers, cultures and different norms influence the control subsystem.[91] A lack of understanding and appreciation of different cultural values would lead to inaccurate evaluation of information associated with project control. Managerial control is seriously influenced by criticism and how and when it is expressed. In some cultures, detailed reporting and tight controls are not accepted readily. For example in Japan, to maintain group cohesiveness, superiors tend to solve problems at the group level before taking them to upper management.[92]

Techniques and methodologies. Project management techniques and methodologies may vary in different cultures depending upon the education and training level in this area, as well as availability of project management hardware and software. Project managers must be aware of these constraints and implement only appropriate levels of scheduling, costing, modeling and programming techniques.

Organization. Authority, responsibility and accountability depend upon the nature of the project, cultural values of the participants, and management style of the organization. For example, there is more centralization and tight control for projects that are highly technical and security-sensitive. There is a tendency for more participative, management style, and group decision-making in United States and Japan than in French, Asian and Arabian cultures.[93] The meaning of responsibility, authority and accountability may vary from culture to culture. For example, project managers in the United States tend to earn respect and informal authority based on their expertise and knowledge, whereas their counterparts in other countries assume it because of their rank, status, birth and organizational position rather than merit. Consequently, project managers from Western cultures may have to deal with managers who lack expertise and are not professionally competent. Moreover, position, rank and authority are supported in many countries by codes of dress and behavior and by attitudes. Senior executives in such countries are provided with servants and chauffeurs and are not expected to mix with the masses. Although delegation, open communication and participative management

102

styles are promoted in the United States, this is not the case in other foreign countries. Consequently these organizational and operational styles significantly affect project management staffing, planning, training and implementation in international project environments.

Cultural ambiance. Cultural factors that include cultural values, attitudes, traditions, religion, belief and behavior, influence the successful management of international projects. Most problems that project managers operating in foreign countries face are caused by value orientations of different cultures.[91] According to Harris and Moran,[88] a cosmopolitan project manager sensitive to cultural differences appreciates a people's distinctness and tries to consider cross cultural factors when communicating with them. He or she avoids imposing his or her own cultural values, attitudes and viewpoints.

Human subsystem. Human subsystems that include motivation, communication, negotiations, and conflicts are more complex in international project management than in the management of domestic projects.[89] Some major differences in each subsystem are briefly described below.

Motivation. Motivation varies widely by culture and country. For example, in North America, people derive social status and self-esteem from their professional accomplishments. They are motivated to work harder to earn money. On the other hand, people in France tend to value free time and vacations more than money. In Eastern Europe, bonuses for salaried workers are used as motivating factors.[88] In Japan, society and company come first and workers are motivated by job security, bonus and fringe benefits that depend upon the overall performance of the company. In many developing countries, career opportunities and personal development are key motivators in scientific and technological areas.[94]

Communication. Communication is a dynamic verbal and non-verbal process and includes body language, dress and other non-verbal gestures. Tone of voice, choice of words and inflection can affect work relationships. Criticism or sharp disagreement with managers in the presence of others can seriously damage relationships in Arab and Latin countries. Copeland and Griggs[90] emphasize that American project managers operating in Asia, the Middle East or Africa, need to read between the lines. The context of communication is very important in understanding the information being conveyed. On the other hand, in Switzerland, Germany and Scandinavia, information is explicit.

Negotiations and Conflicts. Differences in culture, customs and legal systems make international negotiations very difficult. Interpreters are necessary to overcome language barriers. Bargaining strategies may vary in different cultures. For example in China, instead of saying "no," people use expressions like "we will look into it." Legal language—the sanctity of contracts and even the validity of certain clauses—does not always make an agreement irrevocable.[95] The successful negotiator in international project management tries to find more agreements than disagreements, manage stress, and cope with uncertainty and ambiguity. He or she sells the proposal in meaningful terms that expresses ideas clearly, benefits all parties and demonstrates cultural sensitivity, understanding and flexibility.[96]

Primary factors in cross-cultural settings

People are profiles of their cultures. To understand people, we must understand their culture.

— Anonymous

Project managers involved in both international or domestic projects face similar cultural, technological, social, bureaucratic and logical challenges. However, management of international projects poses some additional challenges because of different cultures of project participants. Communicating styles, gestures, and mannerisms may vary from culture to culture; for example a backhanded "V for Victory" sign is considered an uncourteous gesture in Australia. Managers involved in international projects, business or relations must be aware of such cross-cultural differences. Dinsmore identified some primary factors in cross-cultural settings and related these factors to the basic concepts of the project management body of knowledge (PMBOK) areas, as described by the Project Management Institute.[97] He described the factors that must be considered in order to meet goals on international projects as follows:

Functional redundancy. This refers to duplication or overlap of certain functions or activities such as human resources and communications.

Political factors. These refer to national and local politics that can significantly influence project success. Communication systems should be designed to respond appropriately to all strategic and politically related interactions.

The expatriate way of life. This refers to the expectations and habits of people transferred to the host country with different customs and living styles. PMBOK areas of communications, human resources and contracting are related to way of life.

Language and culture. This includes spoken, written and other social forms of communications systems to communicate thoughts, beliefs, attitudes and values to project participants. Obviously differences in communication systems are important here.

Additional risk factors. Rapid changes in weather, political and economic situations can cause uncertainties. Risk management techniques should be used to assess these factors.

Supply difficulties. This refers to contracting, procurement and logistic challenges. Knowledge of customs, regulations, transportation systems and negotiating techniques will help alleviate supply problems for international projects.

Local laws and regulations. Awareness and education of local laws and legislation is essential for successful management of projects in international settings, for example abstaining from drinking in Muslim countries, must be clearly communicated to project participants.

Dinsmore emphasizes that although all areas of the PMBOK are interrelated, special emphasis must be placed on management of communication, human resources, risk and contract and procurement to manage international projects successfully.

Challenges in managing international projects

To deny diversity is to deny life — with all its richness and opportunities. Thus, to be a citizen in a world of diversity, everyone should strive to be tolerant and look for the best in others.

— Anonymous

Both domestic and international projects pose tough and interesting project management challenges. However, there are some additional challenges in managing international because of different cultural backgrounds, beliefs and work attitudes of projects participants and stakeholders. Dinsmore outlined some major challenges faced by most project mangers operating in international project settings. Some of these challenges can be summarized as follows:[97]

Intercultural team building. The key to successfully managing an international project is to build an effective project team in spite of significantly different cultural backgrounds. The challenge is to align personal inputs of different project participants. Project managers must be aware of and appreciate cross cultural differences and create an intercultural environment to capitalize on these differences and optimize overall output of the project team throughout the project life cycle. Figure 2.8 shows a simplified input/output intercultural team building model that is aimed to develop and conduct a program that will help transform inputs of project participants with different cultural backgrounds into desired project outputs.[97]

Dealing with the globalization of the economy. There is an increasing trend towards globalization of economies through advances in communication, information technology, transportation and international trade agreements. Globalization between different countries presents project management challenges because of different roles and relationships between contractors, project managers, project team members and governments. For example, relationships in the United States are more formal and may at times become adversarial leading to disputes, litigation and expensive court battles. Relationships in Japan are much more cooperative and emphasize partnering and risk-sharing. Dinsmore described how knowledge and information is generated and transferred in different parts

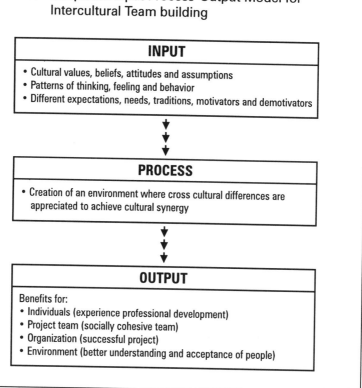

Figure 2.8 Simplified Input-Process-Output Model for Intercultural Team building

INPUT

- Cultural values, beliefs, attitudes and assumptions
- Patterns of thinking, feeling and behavior
- Different expectations, needs, traditions, motivators and demotivators

PROCESS

- Creation of an environment where cross cultural differences are appreciated to achieve cultural synergy

OUTPUT

Benefits for:
- Individuals (experience professional development)
- Project team (socially cohesive team)
- Organization (successful project)
- Environment (better understanding and acceptance of people)

Based upon: Paul C. Dinsmore and Manuel M. Benitez *Challenges in Managing International Projects,* Chapter 39 in the AMA Handbook of Project Management, edited by Paul C. Dinsmore, 1993, pp. 463–464.

of the world by using the styles commonly used in Europe, North America and Japan.[97]

It is interesting to note that globalization of project management knowledge and information is taking place through IPMA, (the International Project Management Association, based in Europe), AIPM(Australian Institute of Project Management), PMI (the Project Management Institute, based in North America) and other sister organizations such as AACE (American Association of Cost Engineers), ASQC (American Society of Quality Control), etc.

Integrating two cultures. It is a common practice in binational projects to share formal authority between two managers, one from each country. This shared authority ranges from an integrated partnership of the managers to a lead manager/backup manager situation. Conflicts may arise because of ambiguity in roles and responsibility of each country and different perceptions of situations as the project progresses through its life cycle. There is a need for open and strong communication management in such a setting because diplomatic documents are often rich in political rhetoric and poor in clear operational and technical instructions. They contain writing "between the lines" and are therefore difficult to be understood by project managers and engineers of both countries.[97]

Developing a project culture. A project culture should be developed for building an effective intercultural team and defining desirable behavior that is suitable to both project objectives and the group's culture. The development of a project culture involves identifying basic cross-cultural differences involved in the joint venture that may affect project management abilities. These may include cultural characteristics, such as technical education, language, beliefs, work ethics and attitudes, formal behavior, consensus orientation, professional project experience, group norms, social habits, traditions, norms and values and general way of life. Forming a project culture should be considered a project in itself with an objective, schedule, resources and a development plan. Basic cross cultural differences should be compared and discussed to develop a project culture with the aim of attaining a cooperative spirit, replacing "they" with "we" and creating a strong emphasis on meeting "our" project goals. The common cultural elements of both groups should be capitalized upon and desirable traits should be identified and developed through a properly designed training program.

The project culture over the project life cycle. Project culture can significantly affect project success through several phases of the life cycle. It is established during the early stages of the project. Therefore, project managers in an international setting should set the stage appropriately and create an environment to maximize the efforts of project team members as the project progresses through its life cycle. Figure 2.9 shows the typical phases of the project life cycle and appropriate project culture along with some associated issues that should not be overlooked.[97]

Self-Assessment Exercise B (see Appendix) offers a "culture quiz" to help project managers evaluate their cultural literacy.

Summary

Most people believe that they know what a team is and how it works. Management often feels frustrated that in spite of putting very competent people in a group, the output is below expectation. The groups members are equally frustrated as there is no coordination and teamwork. To achieve teamwork, it is important to understand the difference between a work group and a team and how their dynamics impact their overall performance. Project managers must understand team dynamics and the various factors that contribute to team effectiveness.

A work group is a group of people assembled to accomplish a task when responsibilities are divided and everyone works independently on

Figure 2.9 Project Culture and Project Life Cycle

Phase	Project Cultural Emphasis	Major Issues
Conceptual (Front End)	Participative	Develop "our project" spirit. Problems are easy to solve due to high enthusiasm of everyone.
Development	Cooperative	Integration should be emphasized. Emerging team leaders should be identified and motivated. Uncooperative people should be taken off project to avoid further problems.
Execution	Competitive	Different cultures may compete with each other in efficiency. Unbalanced work loads may become problems. Need stronger coordination, communication and regular follow-up meetings.
Finish (Termination)	Transfer information	Cultural integration is difficult. Project is winding down and people are leaving. Project managers must show leadership in maintaining the same efficiency and performance standards as before.

Based upon: Paul C. Dinsmore and Manuel M. Benitez *Challenges in Managing International Projects,* Chapter 39 in the AMA Handbook of Project Management, edited by Paul C. Dinsmore, 1993. pp. 463–464.

their specific tasks. Task groups could be counteracting, co-acting or interacting. A team is more than just a work group. It is a group of people who are committed to common goals, who depend on each other to do their job (work interdependently), and who produce high quality results. Teams have a common goal (task) and complimentary contributions. There are three types of interacting teams which include problem-solving teams, self-managed teams, and special purpose teams (task forces, quality circle teams, etc.).

Integrated project teams emphasize synergy. Their characteristics include a common purpose, strong commitment and sense of belonging, shared interests, high performance norms, shared accountability, pride and enjoyment in teamwork, and interdependency.

Achieving team effectiveness and influencing team behavior to inspire high performance is not easy. Team effectiveness determines the extent to which the team is successful in three dimensions: achieving project objectives and organizational goals, satisfaction and well being of team members, and team's ability to survive. There are several factors which affect team dynamics and eventually its performance. A team dynamics model has been presented that consists of four main components that influence team effectiveness. These include team context and goals (which include external environment, team goals and task characteristics); developmental sequence of team members; team composition and roles of team members (which include team size, team diversity, composition and roles of team

108

members); and major team issues (which include team norms, team cohesiveness and team leadership).

Team members move sequentially on a maturity continuum (from dependence to independence and then to interdependence). Most teams progress through five stages of team development which include - forming (testing), storming (infighting and conflict), norming (getting organized), performing (becoming productive), and finally adjourning (moving on to another project). Most project teams go through these stages of development and the time taken to progress from one stage to another may vary. Project managers must act as facilitators to move people along through all stages as quickly as possible. They must answer task and people related questions addressed at various stages.

Project managers must evaluate the team's context (external environment) in terms of technology, external competition, relationships with external stakeholders, team norms, team reward system and physical layout. They must focus on both relations-oriented as well as task-oriented goals.

Team effectiveness is highly influenced by team composition (team size and team diversity), and roles of team members. A smaller team size is normally good as long as it does not jeopardize its ability to accomplish the task. It is important to have a sufficiently broad base of knowledge and experience to explore alternatives and make rational decisions. Team diversity refers to homogenous and heterogenous teams. Homogenous teams experience higher satisfaction and better interpersonal relationships. On the other hand, heterogenous teams are characterized by diverse personal characteristics, cultural backgrounds and values of team members which may stimulate creativity, innovation and encourage team members to obtain a wide network of support and cooperation.

Roles of team members influence the team's effectiveness. Project managers must be aware of problem-solving styles and behavior roles (task-oriented, relations-oriented and self-oriented roles) of their team members and then use appropriate strategies to influence their behavior roles to increase the team's overall effectiveness.

Team norms are very powerful and it is very important that team norms are consistent with organizational goals. Team norms aid in team survival, simplify predictable desired behavior, help avoid embarrassing interpersonal problems, and emphasize on central values of the team. Project managers should be aware of how team norms develop, why and how people conform to team norms, and ensure that team norms contribute to high performance.

Team cohesiveness increases team performance only when team norms are aligned with organizational goals. Project managers may want to develop cohesive teams. They must understand major factors contributing to team effectiveness which include member similarity, member interaction, external competition and challenge, difficult entrance, team success

109

and team size. They must know the consequences of team effectiveness and develop appropriate strategy to develop team cohesiveness.

Team leadership is one of the most important factors. Effective team leaders must help in meeting both task-oriented and relations-oriented goals. They must use appropriate leadership style depending upon the situation and maturity level of team members.

Cultural diversity among team members poses interesting challenges for effective team building, especially for joint ventures and international projects. Project managers must appreciate major elements of culture (which include material culture, language, aesthetics, education, religious beliefs and attitudes, social organizations and political life). They must understand the cultural orientation model, consisting of six critical dimensions of cultural differences which include power distance; individualism/collectivism; masculinity/femininity; uncertainty avoidance; and time horizon (long-term vs. short-term); and attitude towards life, as well as five cultural variables with related orientations that include environment, action orientation, communication styles, space orientation, and thinking patterns. Project managers must evaluate the implications of cultural differences on the project management process. They must acquire abilities to meet team members on their respective cultural grounds and increase team effectiveness by fostering cultural synergy within their project team.

Currency fluctuations, political instability and competitions from national and regional governments and special interest groups can interfere with project management of international projects. Special attributes of international project, which include plans; communication and information subsystem; control systems; project management techniques, cultural ambiance and human subsystems (motivation, communication, negotiations/conflicts), must be considered. The primary factors in cross-cultural settings should be recognized and special emphasis should be placed on developing appropriate systems to manage communications, human resources, risk and contract/procurement areas of project management.

To manage international projects effectively, project managers must be sensitive to different cultures and be able to build an effective intercultural team and develop a project culture that integrates all cultures, considers the globalization of economy and is appropriate for all phases of the project life cycle.

chapter

3

Outline

About Team Building   **114**
What is team building?   114
The team building process   116
Drivers and barriers to high team performance   120

Organizing the Project Team   **122**
Setting project goals   122
Creating the team climate   123
Assembling the project team   126

Practical Guidelines for Team Building   **133**
Plan for team building   134
Negotiate for team members   134
Hold a kick-off meeting   135
Obtain commitment of team members   135
Build communication links   136
Obtain top management support   137
Utilize ongoing project team development   137
Introduce rewards and recognition   138
Manage team conflicts effectively   139
Provide good project leadership   143

Summary   **148**

If everyone is moving forward together, success takes care of itself.
— *Anonymous*

Effective
Team Building

P ROJECTS ARE ORGANIZED to accomplish complex tasks that cannot
be handled by lone individuals. As projects become, increasingly, the
building blocks of organizational strategy, multidisciplinary teams
are replacing individuals as the basic building blocks of organizations.
Project success depends upon how well participants can work together to
accomplish objectives within scope, time, cost and quality constraints.

Project managers must have the skills required to build effective project
teams. This is particularly true because most projects are organized in a
matrix fashion where the two-boss problem poses additional challenges
in obtaining real commitments from team members who may only work
for the project part time; and whose individual objectives and interests
may or may not be in line with project objectives.

Team building is a process of getting a diverse mix of individuals to
work together effectively as one unit. Team building involves integrating
both project tasks and project management process. It requires leadership
skills and a good understanding of the organization, its culture, interfaces,
authority and responsibility relationships, power structures among its
stakeholders, and motivational factors.

Effective communication is vital to effective team building and hence
to project success. This chapter emphasizes that project managers must
expedite project communications among all channels and links, minimize
communication blockers that may impede creativity and innovation and
manage project meetings effectively. ■

About Team Building

Pull together; in the mountains you must depend on each other for survival.
— Willi Unsoeld, Mountain Climber

Team building, while important for many situations, is especially crucial in a project-oriented work environment where functional specialties and support groups must be integrated to achieve complex multidisciplinary activities. To manage projects, project managers and task leaders often have to cross organizational lines and deal with people over whom they have little or no authority. Project managers in such dynamic environments must understand the interaction of organizational and behavioral variables in order to create a climate conducive to building an effective team with a diverse mix of skills and expertise. Such a team, if led and managed effectively, will have the capacity to achieve excellence and innovatively transform a set of technical objectives and requirements into specific products or services that will excel over alternatives in the market place.

What is team building?

Team building is the process of transforming a collection of individuals with different interests, backgrounds and expertise into an integrated and effective work unit. It can also be seen as a process of change. In this transformation process, the goals and energies of all team members merge and support the objectives of the team. The team building process is important for all types of projects but will vary in complexity and size depending upon the project. Typical project situations where team building is crucial include:[1]

- Establishing a new project or a program
- Improving project-client relationship
- Resolving interfunctional problems
- Integrating new project personnel for a common goal
- Preparing a bid proposal
- Working toward a major milestone
- Reorganizing a company
- Transferring technology
- Transitioning the project into a new activity phase.

Effective team building is one of the prime responsibilities of the project manager. It involves a whole spectrum of management and leadership skills required to identify, organize, commit, and integrate various task groups from functional organizations into a multidisciplinary cohesive team.

Team building is the process of planned and deliberate encouragement of effective working practices while reducing difficulties or obstacles that interfere with the team's competence and resourcefulness.[2] Though this process has been known for centuries, it becomes more challenging as vertical bureaucratic hierarchies decline and horizontally oriented teams and work units evolve. Regarding the concepts and practices of multidiscipli-

114

nary team building, many field studies have been conducted.[3,4,5,6,7,8,9] These studies have investigated workgroup dynamics and criteria for building effective, high-performing project teams and have contributed a great deal to the theoretical and practical understanding of team building and managing conflicts.

Effective team building is valid and important at all levels of management (from top executives to middle managers, first line supervisors and rank and file). The absence of teamwork at any level or between levels in any organization, will obstruct effectiveness in managing its projects and can eventually kill the organization.[10]

Benefits of team building. With the rapid changes in technology, global competition and increased size and complexities of projects, it is important to collect and transform a group of individuals with diverse backgrounds, skills, experiences and expertise into an integrated work unit. Team building develops the creative potential of everyone. Some of the benefits of team building in project management are:[11,12]

- Realistic, achievable objectives can be established for the team because those responsible for doing the work contribute to setting objectives and planning.
- Team members commit to support each other to make the team successful.
- Team members understand one another's priorities and help to support when difficulties arise.
- Communication is open. The expression of new ideas, improved methods, articulation of problems and concerns is encouraged.
- Problem solving is more effective because of broader expertise base.
- Performance feedback is more meaningful because team members understand what is expected and can monitor their performance against expectations.
- Conflict is understood as normal and viewed as an opportunity to solve problems. Through open discussion it can be resolved before it becomes destructive.
- Balance is maintained between group productivity and the satisfaction of personal team members' needs.
- Members are encouraged to test their abilities and try out ideas. This stimulates individuals to become stronger performers.
- Team members recognize the importance of disciplined work habits and conform their behavior to meet team standards.
- Learning to work effectively as a team in one unit is good preparation for working as a team with other units. It is also a good step towards self-advancement.

Outcomes of team building. Open communication is the key to an effective team building because a frank and open discussion of various issues throughout the life cycle of a project, will help reduce anxiety among team members. It will help in establishing sincere trust and mutual respect among team members, which are the foundations of building an effective team. One project leader emphasized this point:

> *There is nothing worse than being on a team when no one trusts anyone else. Such situations lead to gamesmanship and a lot of watching what any team member may say because team members do not want their own words to bounce back in their faces ...*[13]

Mutual trust and high quality of information exchanges. The more effective the project leader is in developing a strong and cohesive team membership, the stronger the trust among team members, which leads to a higher quality of information exchanges and contributions by the team members.

Effective team decision-making. Higher quality information exchanges will provide a strong data base and will help develop better decision-making processes.

Effective project control. With more trust and better information exchanges, more effective project control systems (networks, WBS) can be developed. It will also lead to constructive and timely feedback by all team members which will increase the overall performance of the project team.

The team building process

> *Collaboration operates through a process in which the successful intellectual achievements of one person arouse the intellectual passions and enthusiasm of others, and through a process in which a fact that was at first expressed by only one individual becomes a common intellectual possession instead of fading away into isolation.*
>
> — *Alexander Humboldt*

According to many management practitioners and researchers, team building and team development are some of the most critical leadership qualities that determine the performance and success of multidisciplinary projects. The outcome of a project depends upon the group efforts and how well many task specialists are coordinated and integrated in a dynamic work environment with complex organizational interfaces. Increasingly, stringent project performance requirements are mandating a high level of sustained cooperative team effort.

Team building is the process of helping a group of individuals, bound by a common purpose, to work more effectively with each other, the leader, the external stakeholders, and the whole organization. To understand the process of team building, it is useful to look at models that explain team building and team development and some characteristics of an effective project team.[12]

Factors influencing team success. There are several factors that characterize the project team and its final performance. Figure 3.1 shows a simple model to analyze these factors. According to this model, team characteristics are influenced by three factors: environmental factors (working

116

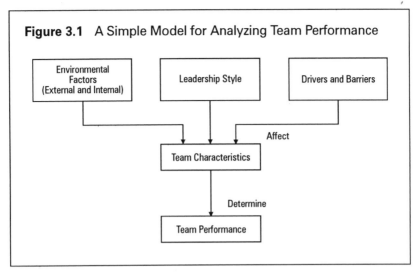

Figure 3.1 A Simple Model for Analyzing Team Performance

Adapted from: David I. Cleland, *Project Management—Strategic Design and Implementation* TPR (Tab PRofessional and Reference Books) Division of TAB Books Inc., Blue Ridge Summit, PA 1990, pp. 302. By permission of the publisher.

conditions, organizational climate, job content and resources), leadership style, and the drivers and barriers towards team performance.[1]

All these factors are interrelated with each other. However, a systems approach may allow project managers and management practitioners to break down the complexity of the team building process and analyze its components. It can help in formulating a team building strategy by identifying the drivers and barriers and to motivating the human resources to achieve their maximum potential under the influence of managerial, organizational, and other environmental factors.

Team building model. Becoming familiar with this model can increase the problem-solving capacity of the project team. Immediate problems can be resolved and the team can learn how to deal with new problems as they arise. This learning experience helps a project team anticipate and minimize or avoid problems. When a project team has "learned how to learn," it can be more effective and efficient than a team that simply reacts to internal and external events. There are some indications when teams require a proper team building approach. The following team characteristics indicate the need for more team building:[2,7]

- There is excessive "wheel-spinning" within the team.
- Team performance is dropping but no one knows why.
- Action items decided are not followed.
- Objectives are unclear or team members are not committed to those objectives.
- The team leader encounters detrimental surprises and destructive conflicts.
- Team members are unresponsive to the needs of the team or the project.

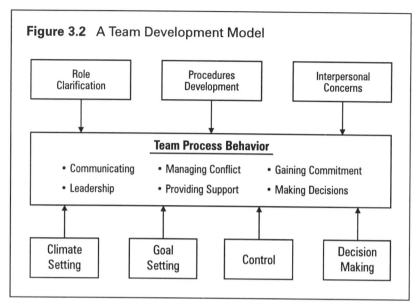

Figure 3.2 A Team Development Model

Role Clarification

Procedures Development

Interpersonal Concerns

Team Process Behavior

- Communicating
- Leadership
- Managing Conflict
- Providing Support
- Gaining Commitment
- Making Decisions

Climate Setting

Goal Setting

Control

Decision Making

Adapted from: D.L. Wilemon, et al., *A Model for Developing High Performance Project Teams,* PMI Seminar/Symposium, Houston, Texas, Oct. 17–19, 1983, pp. 111–H1.1 to 111–H12.

- Team meetings are unproductive, full of conflict, and demoralizing.
- Team members work independently and avoid needed cooperation.
- Problem-solving activities like constructive conflict are avoided.
- Quality problems, cost overruns and schedule delays are common.

Task and process activities are major components of a team building model.[12] Project managers must analyze task and process activities and develop a strategy to implement these activities in the process of building a project team.

Task activities are related to establishing goals, defining and negotiating roles and procedures. Seven major task activities are: staffing of team members, setting a climate for team development, setting goals, clarifying roles and responsibilities, developing procedures, making decisions, and controlling the project (monitoring and taking corrective actions).[12]

Process activities refer to interpersonal activities necessary to accomplish tasks. For example, the tasks of establishing goals and defining roles require a process activity of intensive communication among team members. Other major process activities used in team development are: resolving conflicts, listening, providing psychological support, exerting power, encouraging participation and involvement, gaining commitment, providing appropriate rewards and recognition, creating environment for self-development, building mutual trust and respect.

Wilemon and Thamhain discussed in detail these task and process activities. Figure 3.2 shows a typical team development model.[12]

118

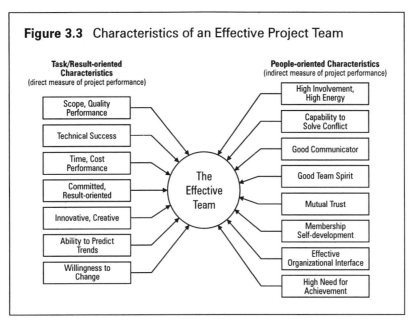

Figure 3.3 Characteristics of an Effective Project Team

Task/Result-oriented Characteristics (direct measure of project performance)

- Scope, Quality Performance
- Technical Success
- Time, Cost Performance
- Committed, Result-oriented
- Innovative, Creative
- Ability to Predict Trends
- Willingness to Change

The Effective Team

People-oriented Characteristics (indirect measure of project performance)

- High Involvement, High Energy
- Capability to Solve Conflict
- Good Communicator
- Good Team Spirit
- Mutual Trust
- Membership Self-development
- Effective Organizational Interface
- High Need for Achievement

Adapted from: David I. Cleland, *Project Management—Strategic Design and Implementation* TPR (Tab PRofessional and Reference Books) Division of TAB Books Inc., Blue Ridge Summit, PA 1990, pp. 304. By permission of the publisher.

Once the project team is built, it is important to evaluate its effectiveness. Two basic questions should be addressed in this regard: *How will team performance be measured?* and *Is team building an ongoing process?*

Measuring team performance is very important. The performance of a successful team is measured by three factors: technical success according to agreed on project objectives, performance on project schedule (finished on time), and performance on budget (finished within financial constraints).[1]

High-performance teams are characterized not only by these task- and results-oriented outcomes, but also have specific job- and people-related qualities that represent indirect measures of project performance (see Figure 3.3). Some of these qualities include innovative or creative behavior, personal goals that are congruent with those of the project, interdependence among members, conflict resolution skills (and the wisdom to encourage constructive conflict), effective communication, an orientation toward change, and high levels of trust, achievement needs, morale, and energy.[1]

Team building as an ongoing process is crucial to project success. While team building is essential during the front end of a project, it is a never-ending process. It must be kept alive. The project manager must continually monitor team functioning and performance to evaluate if any corrective actions are needed to prevent or correct various team problems. Following are some of the major factors that may provide good clues to potential team dysfunction:[7]

- Noticeable changes in performance levels for the team and/or individual team members, which can be symptoms of problems such as conflict, unclear objectives, poor work integration and communication.
- Changing energy levels because of stress, changing work environment, and other factors, which can be dealt with by reviewing and adjusting project objectives and plans if necessary.
- Verbal and non-verbal clues from team members. In general, regular meetings to focus on "what are we doing well as a team" and "where do we need more attention" help to evaluate the impact of special technology development, change in client behavior, progress with regard to schedule, etc.).

Team building helps to blend the talents of key project personnel to meet project goals and challenges like a well-trained sports team. It maximizes the strengths of team members and provide opportunity to learn new things and share experiences. Project managers must understand team dynamics, and the process of building a team to increase their own performance and that of their teams. In a team, everyone gets a feel for what other team members will do in a given situation. Special results occur when people in a project environment work together as a team and help each other win.

Drivers and barriers to high team performance

The team motto should be to rub out another's mistake instead of rubbing it in.
— Anonymous

In a project environment there are generally certain drivers and barriers that influence the performance of project teams. A better understanding of these drivers and barriers can help in developing an environment conducive to effective teamwork.

Drivers to effective team building represent positive factors associated with the project environment that enhance effectiveness of the project team and increase its performance. Studies of workgroup dynamics show significant correlations and interdependencies between team performance and work environmental factors.[7,14] These studies indicate that building effective teams to achieve high team performance involves four primary factors: managerial leadership, job content, personal goals and objectives, work environment and organizational support.[7,14]

The six drivers that have a strong positive correlation to project team performance are:[1,7,14]

1. Professionally interesting and challenging work, which demonstrates confidence in people

2. Recognition of accomplishment which provides positive reinforcement

3. Experienced technical management personnel, which improves integration and interface management

4. Proper technical direction and leadership, which reduces mistakes and inspires high performance

5. Qualified project team personnel, which ensures quality results

6. Professional growth potential, which motivates team members.

These six drivers positively affect the tangible and direct performance of the project team in terms of its technical success regarding schedule and budget performance. But they are also positively associated with tangible and indirect measures of team performance such as commitment to creativity, quality, and change-orientation, mutual trust, effective communication and high achievement needs.

Barriers to effective team building include negative factors such as insufficient resources and unclear directions that reduce the effectiveness of the project team and its performance. These factors must be analyzed and appropriate action taken to minimize their impact and develop an environment to encourage teamwork. The six major barriers to effective project team building and high team performance are:[1,7,14]

1. Unclear project objectives and changing goals and priorities, which create confusion

2. Lack of team definition, structure, and environment. which lead to poor teamwork

3. Communication problems, which lead to destructive conflicts

4. Power struggle and conflict in terms of roles, personnel selection, which lead to lack of cooperation

5. Lack of commitment from team members, which leads to poor quality

6. Uninvolved, unsupportive upper management.

In addition to these barriers, Wilemon and Thamhain identified some other barriers to effective team building. For example:

- Differing outlooks, interests, and judgments of team members
- Dynamic project environment
- Credibility of project leader
- Role conflicts
- Lack of appropriate rewards and recognition
- Insufficient resources.

They analyzed these major barriers to team building efforts and suggested some remedial actions to minimize or eliminate them.[7] For an organization to be successful and manage its projects effectively, barriers to team performance must be eliminated by paying special attention to the human aspects of team management. Project managers must foster a work environment conducive to innovative and creative work where people find professional challenges, get proper recognition and opportunities for personal and professional growth. Such an environment will also lower communication barriers, reduce conflict, and encourage team members to be more proactive in managing change and complex project requirements. Project managers must concentrate on minimizing barriers and reinforcing the drivers to teamwork in order to achieve human synergy and obtain increased commitment and ownership of team members to project objectives.

Organizing the Project Team

Everyone has to work together; if we can't get everybody working hard toward common goals, nothing is going to happen.
— *Harold K. Sperlich, President, Chrysler Corp.*

Most individuals appreciate an opportunity to belong to a really successful team. Creating such a project team is one of the most rewarded activities for project managers or project leaders. After understanding the basic concepts of a project team and its characteristics; ingredients, benefits, process, outcomes, drivers, and barriers of team building, it is important to develop a practical approach to and ideas for building a successful project team by using the principles and concepts discussed earlier. The success of this process depends upon choosing the right leader and team members, and obtaining their commitment to the project.

Setting project goals

Validate your goals by asking, "Will this help me become my very best?"
— *Anonymous*

Before the team building process can begin, it is important to define the technical contents or specifications of the project along with its constraints in terms of time, budget, resources, organizational, political etc. Overall goals and objectives must be defined right at the front end. Cleland has identified the major segments of a typical project management system that must be defined before the size and type of the project team can be identified. They include:[1]

- Scope and quality of the work (requirements, statement of work, work breakdown structure, list of deliverables)
- Timing (master schedule, milestones, network, critical path analysis
- Resources (budget and resource plan)
- Strategy (risk assessment, contract/procurement strategy, justification)
- Responsibilities (task matrix, project charter, work packages).

Regardless of how vague and preliminary these project segments and goals are at the beginning, the initial description (with the information available) will help in assembling an appropriate project team with a proper mix of skills and experience. Without a precise statement of goals, projects will not get very far. Therefore goal setting processes must clearly establish the goals of the tasks to be accomplished. Some important characteristics of good goals are that they should be *SMART*:

- Specific (to avoid assumptions and provide focus)
- Measurable (helps in monitoring progress)
- Attainable (optimistic but realistic goals provide challenges)
- Rewardable (what gets rewarded gets done)

122

- Time-based (should have clearly associated milestones).

Project managers must ensure that there is a common, shared perception among the team members about the goals. This will help avoid the typical problems in this process, such as:

- Goal ambiguity (refers to lack of clarity and specificity in goals)
- Goal conflict (conflict between goals of individual team member, team leader, client and organization etc.)
- Goal overload (unrealistic goals can discourage the project team resulting in loss of its self-confidence)
- Goal complexity (unmeasurable and complex goals lead to lack of self-satisfaction)

Certain practical steps and ideas for setting goals are outlined in Figure 3.4, while Table 3.1 shows suggestions to assist in the goal clarification process.

The core team should be formed prior to finalizing the project plan, goals and contractual agreements that must be followed and implemented. This will provide the project team members with an opportunity to participate in the formulation of strategies, trade-off discussions and customer negotiations, thereby leading to technical confidence, acceptance and commitment by all parties involved in meeting project goals.

Creating the team climate

Life does not require us to be the biggest or the best, it asks only that we try.

— Anonymous

After project goals are set and the major segments of the project management system are defined, the project team leader must set a climate conducive to maximizing the output of the project team and encourage the creative potential of everyone involved.

Setting an appropriate climate refers to establishing an environment within which team spirit can blossom. A few common barriers to setting such a climate are:

- Fear of change (by the team leader and team members)
- Fear of exposure/risk (new ideas may fail)
- Hidden agenda or hidden feelings (caused by lack of open communication)
- Non-productive use of time (caused by lack of commitment to project goals)
- Discouragement of new ideas—"Didn't we already try something like this last year?"

As a first step, project team leaders must themselves believe in and be committed to the project, and then prepare an overall plan to minimize the above-mentioned barriers. They must try to sell the concept of team building to top management and project team members. To achieve this, some of the main points that should be stresses are: the importance and benefits of team building, the how and why of the team building process,

Effective Team Building

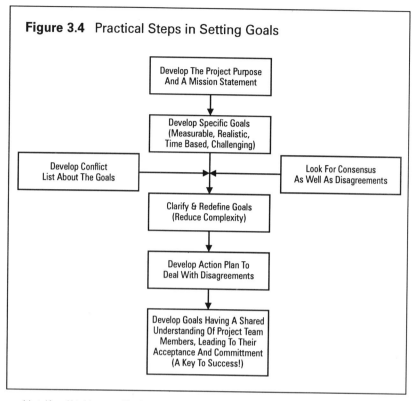

Figure 3.4 Practical Steps in Setting Goals

Develop The Project Purpose And A Mission Statement

Develop Specific Goals (Measurable, Realistic, Time Based, Challenging)

Develop Conflict List About The Goals

Look For Consensus As Well As Disagreements

Clarify & Redefine Goals (Reduce Complexity)

Develop Action Plan To Deal With Disagreements

Develop Goals Having A Shared Understanding Of Project Team Members, Leading To Their Acceptance And Commitment (A Key To Success!)

Adapted from: Materials presented in a David Wilemon workshop, Oct. 1984, Philadelphia, PA.

the amount of time and personal involvement that will be required, how the team environment provides challenges, satisfaction, professional development, growth, and—last but not least—fun.

Because of tight project schedule constraints, project managers may not get to do everything they would like to do for effective team building (special training, offsite meetings and retreats, etc.), but nevertheless they must encourage open communication, participation and an overall management philosophy that will create a "real" team environment. Such managers display at least some of the following traits:[2]

- They are accessible, open, honest and reliable.
- They practice what they preach.
- They manage by walking around.
- They encourage open discussions and innovation.
- They delegate effectively where appropriate, giving opportunity to team members.
- They participate in social gatherings to improve informal relationships.

Table 3.1 Suggestions to Assist in the Goal Clarification Process

Goal Clarification with Individual Team Members
- Discuss overall project goals
- Develop specific goals with team members
- Document agreements
- Circulate agreements
- Monitor progress

Goal Clarification with Functional Support Groups
- Communicate to reach agreement on goals
- Document agreements
- Circulate agreements
- Follow-up on additional issues which need clarifying or negotiating
- Monitor deviation from goals

Goal Clarification with Client
- Review proposed contract (or signed contract if in effect) and other relevant project documentation
- Develop an understanding of the client's goals
- Meet with the client and test the understanding
- Work on any differences which exist
- Confirm goals
- Follow-up on additional agreements
- Monitor deviations from goals

Source: D.L. Wilemon, et al., 1993, "A Model for Developing High Performance Project Teams," *Proceedings of the 1983 Seminar/Symposium.* Project Management Institute, pp. III H1 to III H12.

- They provide training opportunities that encourages professional development.

The team member roles. Project teams consist of a variety of individuals. They are bound to have different personalities, communication styles, decision-making approaches, and influence on others. In general, team members may play either constructive or destructive roles in terms of their contributions to the project team effort. People who play constructive roles are highly valuable assets to the project team, whereas the project manager must deal diplomatically with those who tend to play destructive roles that contaminate the team spirit. See the discussion of group roles in Chapter 2 for a full description of constructive and destructive roles.

People function in more than one of these roles at different times. Generally, most people want to be good team players and contribute to team efforts. However, project managers should be aware of those who play destructive team roles. For example, the role of a devil's advocate is valid and very useful in generating new ideas and creativity in problem solving but if overdone, it can seriously impede team building and the project effort. Effective project managers must try to know their team members well (both formally and informally) and emphasize the values of mutual respect, synergy, and commitment to help each other win—key ingredients of a good team climate and effective team building.

Assembling the project team

Warm working relationships and commitment to help each other win are vital to successful project teams.

Assembling the project team includes getting their commitment. Every precaution must be taken to avoid any lack of technical skills, interpersonal conflicts or incompatibility among members. Project leaders must ensure that the efforts of all team members are integrated and lead to innovative results. This section describes how to select the right team members, clarify their roles and responsibilities, and get their commitment to the project.[15]

Selecting the team members. This crucial step starts the project off on the right foot. Typically, project team selection should start while developing the work breakdown structure because at that time, the skills required to execute the project become apparent. Project managers should try to fill the project requirements from permanently assigned staff. However, if there are skills that are not available from permanent staff, they should identify other sources of personnel with those skills, and negotiate with their supervisors (functional managers) to get their commitment according to overall priority of the project. Sometimes special support and decisions are needed from senior management. But in most cases, the project manager's negotiating skills combined with interpersonal skills and general influence can obtain the required resources. Figure 3.5 shows the basic steps in assembling a project team.[15]

What to look for in prospective team members. The importance of choosing the right people as project team members from the collection of potential members can hardly be overemphasized. It is the first principle and vital step towards team success. There are a variety of objective or technical criteria that should be used in choosing the team members, including technical ability, estimating proficiency, project management skills, experience as a task leader on other projects, attitude towards projects in general and this project in particular.

The project team leader should try to evaluate potential team members by getting information from fellow project managers regarding personal attributes and prior experience with similar projects. The project manager

126

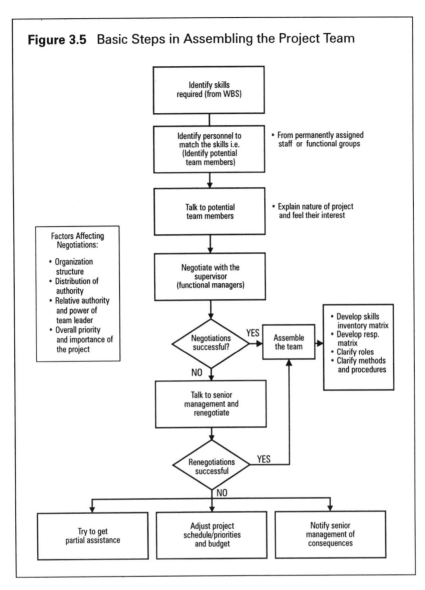

Figure 3.5 Basic Steps in Assembling the Project Team

should then talk to potential team members before negotiating to have them join the project. There are three key questions that the project manager needs to answer in determining the potential effectiveness of a prospective team member.[15]

- Would I want this individual to work for me?
- Would I want this individual as one of my peers?
- Would I want to work for this individual?

Table 3.2 shows a checklist for selecting the right team members. Sometimes, of course, the project manager does not have the option of selecting the team members. Nevertheless, the ideas presented in the checklist may be helpful and should be used whenever possible.

Clarifying roles and responsibilities. Once goals, breakdown structure, and suitable team members have been clearly identified and an agreement reached, the next phase is to define their roles and responsibilities. Unless roles are clearly defined, nothing much will occur except frustration and conflict. For instance in goal setting, it is important to look at the expectations of others. Others may have diverse views on the roles and responsibilities of the team and its members. These conflicting views need to be identified and resolved at the very beginning of a project. Some of the key questions related to role clarification are:[16]

- Who is responsible for what?
- What skills are needed?
- What skills do we have within the team?
- How much freedom do team members have in defining their roles?
- How are work assignments/responsibilities allocated?
- Where do roles within the team conflict?
- How do we deal with conflicts over roles?

Some of the common statements you will hear people make that are symptomatic of various role-related problems are:[16]

"My responsibilities are not clear" or "I'm not clear about how much authority I have." (Role ambiguity: roles and responsibilities have not been adequately defined.)

"My role is to design this equipment as specified, not to satisfy promises made by the marketing department" or "My role as a project manager is not to compromise quality just to balance the books." (Role conflict: the person has two roles that seem incompatible.)

"I can not do all that is required of a project engineer!" and "Do you really expect us to be able to accomplish all of the different demands that have been made on us?" indicate role overload.

For a more thorough discussion of the types of roles problems, see Volume 2 of this series, *Human Resource Skills for the Project Manager*.

Communicating clear role messages. Communicating clear role messages helps project managers identify what they want others to do and helps the recipient understand their expectations. It forces clarification of roles and gets things started off on the right foot, the project manager may say, for example, "This is what I want you to do by next Friday..." or "What do you need from me to help you complete the test reports on time?"

The criteria for communicating clear role messages can be summarized as:
- A role message must clarify the deadline.

128

Table 3.2 Checklist for Selecting the Right Team Member

TASK	YES	NO
1. Is she/he technically competent?	❏	❏
2. Does she/he have an up-to-date knowledge and skills?	❏	❏
3. Do his/ her knowledge/skills complement those of other team members rather than duplicate them?	❏	❏
4. Is she/he motivated to seek excellence in results and methods of working together?	❏	❏
5. Does his/her track record really bear out the scores given above?	❏	❏
6. Does he/she have project management knowledge in terms of integration and interface management?	❏	❏

TEAM		
7. Will she/he work closely with others in decision making and problem solving without rubbing people the wrong way?	❏	❏
8. Is she/he an effective communicator, especially a good listener?	❏	❏
9. Is he/she willing to do extra work to help their meeting objectives?	❏	❏
10. Is she/he flexible enough to adopt different roles within the group?	❏	❏
11. Can she/he influence other through assertiveness rather than being aggressive?	❏	❏
12. Will she/he contribute to group morale rather than dropping it?	❏	❏
13. Does he/she help others to participate by encouraging to present new ideas?	❏	❏

INDIVIDUAL		
14. Has she/he a sense of humor and a degree of tolerance for others?	❏	❏
15. Does she/he have an ambition to achieve more?	❏	❏
16. Does he/she understand that she/he cannot do it alone?	❏	❏
17. Is he/she committed to meet team goals, not just his/hers own only?	❏	❏
18. Has she/he integrity?	❏	❏
19. Does she/he have realistic perception of his/her strengths and weaknesses?	❏	❏
20. Can she/he cope with stress effectively?	❏	❏

Source: John Adair. 1986. *Effective Team Building*. Grower Publishing Co. Ltd., England, pp. 133. By permission of the publisher.

Effective Team Building

- A role message asks if the team members need any help to finish the task on time and if so, ask them to clarify that in detail.
- To be sure messages were understood, develop an accountability control sheet.

Project managers must clarify the roles and responsibilities of all team members and also their own expectations in terms of meeting schedules, budgets and performance standards.

Negotiating roles and responsibilities. Often, the roles and responsibilities of all team members do not match their original expectations and desires. In such case, these may have to be negotiated with the team members, their supervisors and sometimes with senior management. Figure 3.6 shows a typical role negotiation process. Following are some tips on negotiating roles successfully:[16]

- A role negotiation practice session can be held. This helps team members learn the rules in a non-threatening environment.
- Typically, role messages should be developed before the role negotiation team meeting.
- Circulate them at the meeting.
- Seek clarification on ambiguous points.
- Negotiate differences. A "no" is not acceptable. A "no" kills the negotiation and avoids the issue.
- One outcome can be that you agree to work on the conflict at a later date. Be specific as to date and time.

Getting commitment from team members. In order to obtain commitment from team members, it is important to define and document their contributions to the team. A skill inventory matrix and a responsibility matrix can be used as tools to gain commitment of team members.

Skill inventory matrix. Every project requires a variety of skills to accomplish various tasks. At project start up, it is important to match people, skills and tasks. As the project progresses, project managers may need to split assignments, add staff to existing assignments, or trade assignments. In order to achieve this, project managers must know or find out who on the project team possesses which skills. A skill inventory matrix showing skills or areas of expertise along the columns and the team members along the rows should be developed. It will create a useful overview of team members and skills from which to assign tasks. Figure 3.7 shows a typical Skills Inventory Matrix for a software development project to illustrate the concept.[15]

Responsibility matrix. This refers to a process for defining who on the project team is most qualified to perform which task. This matrix should document a performance contract between the project manager, the project team members, and their superiors. It is an important mechanism for obtaining individual commitment, or buy-in, and for graphically depicting respective responsibilities.[15]

130

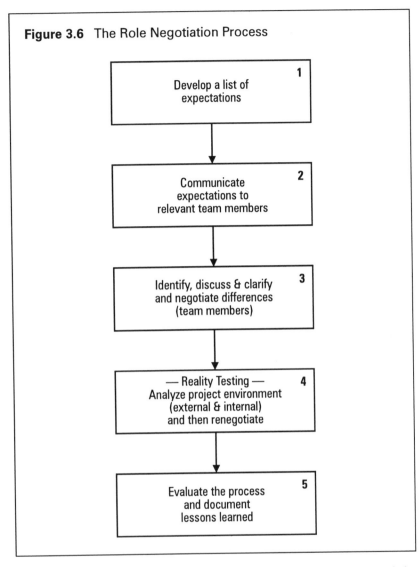

Figure 3.6 The Role Negotiation Process

> **1** Develop a list of expectations

> **2** Communicate expectations to relevant team members

> **3** Identify, discuss & clarify and negotiate differences (team members)

> **4** — Reality Testing — Analyze project environment (external & internal) and then renegotiate

> **5** Evaluate the process and document lessons learned

To develop this matrix, list the tasks in the left hand column, and the names of job titles of project team members on the top. Now match the tasks to the team members by indicating the person with prime responsibility (P) and having a support role (S). Each task requires one and only one person with a prime responsibility but several supporting members may be assigned. The team member with prime responsibility has ultimate responsibility and accountability for ensuring that the task is done at the expected level of quality, on time, and within budget. The members in a supporting capacity are chosen because they can also contribute their

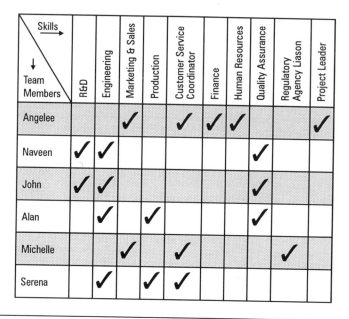

Figure 3.7 Skills Inventory Matrix by Area of Expertise

Team Members	R&D	Engineering	Marketing & Sales	Production	Customer Service Coordinator	Finance	Human Resources	Quality Assurance	Regulatory Agency Liason	Project Leader
Angelee			✓		✓	✓	✓			✓
Naveen	✓	✓						✓		
John	✓	✓						✓		
Alan		✓		✓				✓		
Michelle			✓		✓				✓	
Serena		✓		✓	✓					

skills to accomplish that task. Five rules of thumb to be followed when preparing a responsibility matrix are:[15]

1. Assign staff because they have the correct skills, not because they have time available.

2. Do not assign too many people to one task.

3. Obtain input and commitment of team members: "ask" don't "tell."

4. Consider who is good at what, who wants to do what, who can or cannot work together, and who likes to create versus maintain.

5. From the perspective of the project, consider what skills are needed, what skills are available, and, if someone left a task, whether his or her work could be redistributed.

Figure 3.8 shows a typical Responsibility Matrix for a software development project to illustrate the concept to develop this matrix.[15] Ideally, the project manager should have had some exposure to these areas of responsibility. This background, coupled with intuition, interpersonal skills, psychology, and a bit of luck, can make the task of assigning responsibilities both challenging and rewarding.

Project success depends upon how well the leader and members of the project team perform their roles and responsibilities. Because of a diverse mix of team members with different backgrounds, norms and expectations, there are bound to be few problems and conflicts. However, these

132

Figure 3.8 Responsibility Matrix

Project Name Develop a new Product	Prepared by: Naveen V.	Page 1 of 1	Legend: P = Prime S = Support
Project Manager: Naveen V.			

Task ID	Task	Angelee V.	Naveen V.	John R.	Alan S.	Michelle M.	Serena V.
A	Marketing Research	P		S	S	S	S
B	Develop prototype	S	S	P	S		S
C	Tests & approval to manufacture	S	P	S	S	S	S
D	Engineering design	S	S		P		S
E	Procure material		S		P	S	S
F	Set up manufacturing facilities	S	S	S	P		S
G	Manufacture	S	S		S		P
H	Test & ship	S	S		S		P
I	Advertising & sales	P	S	S	S	S	S
J	Project evaluation	P	S		S	S	S

problems can be resolved and their impacts can be minimized if there is a true team spirit and team environment. The project leaders must themselves be fully committed to accomplish project objectives through teamwork. Top management must involve the project manager in selecting project team members whenever possible. Project managers must ensure that tasks assigned to the team members match their interests and offer professional challenges and opportunities. They must give positive reinforcement for high performance.

Praise and rewards should be given immediately following successful efforts and project managers should be specific about the tasks or assignments about which the team members are being recognized.[17] Project managers must involve team members in developing plans and making decisions in order to gain their acceptance and hence their commitment to implement those plans successfully. They must clarify the roles and responsibilities of team members and their own expectations to minimize conflicts and achieve human synergy.

Practical Guidelines for Team Building

I could not have done it without the boys.

— *Baseball legend Casey Stengel*
(after winning his ninth American League Pennant in ten years)

Before getting into techniques of effective team building, project managers must take into account three important factors that determine the need for effective teams:[7,17]

- In an organization, there are several technical specialists/experts whose talents must be integrated into a large task—a project.

- More organizational members today want to be involved in their total work environment.
- Teamwork leads to synergy and creativity.

Global competition, complicated environmental interfaces, and rapidly advancing technology also encourage the development of effective teams. What's different about projects? What should be done to integrate team building into the life cycle of a project? Following are ten guidelines which project managers can use for effective team building.[18]

Plan for team building

If you fail to plan, you plan to fail.

— Anonymous

A project plan is the first and the foremost thing that the project managers must develop to launch a project on the right foot. The project plan, which addresses the *what* (project goals and objectives), *how* (project procedures), *when* (schedule), and *who* (project roles), becomes the basis for team building.

Each portion of the project plan should be developed carefully with the aim of providing as much positive impact as possible on the team building process. For example:[18]

Project goals and objectives must be well developed because they are used to define team goals and objectives. Project managers must try to align both sets of objectives in terms of consistency and compatibility. Sometimes team members have their own goals and objectives. Therefore, project team objectives should be defined in a way that reinforces team member's efforts to attain their personal goals as well as team's goals.

Project procedures and controls should be planned and implemented to encourage team effort. Project monitoring and control tools and procedures should strengthen the team environment and cohesiveness.

Project schedules should be developed with active participation of team members to gain wider acceptance and hence their commitment. Often teams work best under pressure but not if the schedules are totally unrealistic.

Project roles must be defined and developed to assist in selecting the right team members for each job assignment. Project managers must be aware of which tasks should be assigned to *team players* and which ones will be best done by *loners*. They must utilize a highly technical specialist to optimize his/her contribution to a project.

Negotiate for team members

Negotiation is the exchange of ideas for the purpose of influencing behavior …Wishes are converted into reality through the water of bargaining.

— Anonymous

Selecting the right team members is crucial to effective team building. Project managers must try to match interests and technical skills while nego-

134

tiating with functional managers for team members. Unfortunately, project managers rarely have the luxury of selecting their own team members. Instead, often, even in a projectized organizational structure, project managers inherit some of the team members and new hires may not prove to be the best choices. This problem is even compounded in a matrix structure, because personnel are assigned to the project teams by functional or line managers based upon who can be spared at that time. However, it must be recognized that compromises made in selecting the team members will lead to difficulties in building an effective project team. Therefore, project managers should do everything they can to influence this selection process in their favor.

Hold a kick-off meeting

A kick-off meeting is crucial to team building process because it helps start the project on the right foot. It can initiate active team building process. Since it is at the kick-off meeting that project participants are brought together for the first time, project managers should get everyone involved and build a unity of purpose for accomplishing project objectives.

A kick-off meeting can be organized as an informal meeting or a social event to answer any concerns the team members may have and to develop a team spirit. A kick-off meeting should have all or most of the following objectives:[18]

- Get team members to meet each other
- Establish working relationship and channels of communication with emphasis on "openness"
- Explain team objectives and their significance to projects as well as organizational objectives
- Review project plans, status, and problems
- Establish individual and group responsibilities, authorities, and accountabilities
- Obtain individual and group commitment
- Convey top management's commitment to support team approach and team building process.

Project managers must plan and conduct a project kick-off meeting carefully. It is important that team members get to know the project manager and his/her expectations and leadership style. Also, it is even more important that team members get to know each other to achieve cohesiveness. One of the most important objectives of a project kick-off meeting is to obtain commitment of team members because commitments made publicly almost assure their fulfillment.

Obtain commitment of team members

Project managers must obtain commitment from project team members in terms of their time commitment, role commitment and priority commitment. It is necessary but often a frustrating process. Sometimes, the lack of commitment by some team members can be attributed to uncertainties whether or not they will stay with the project on a long-term basis. Level of commitment may vary from very little to complete dedication.

Project managers can best obtain commitments from team members by involving them actively in the project. Involve them early in the project life cycle (e.g., in preparing project plan, bids and preparing schedules and budgets) and give them interesting, challenging assignments, those that contribute to their professional growth and bring them into the mainstream of the project.

Obtaining commitment of team members is a slow process but it is absolutely essential for building an effective project team.

Build communication links

Openness eliminates barriers to effective communication.

— The Author

Good communication links within and outside the project organization are essential in achieving teamwork. Project managers must recognize both formal and informal communication links in a project. Three basic channels and links of communication in a project environment are *upward communication* (vertically or diagonally) with top management and client, *downward communication* (vertically or diagonally) with team members and contractors, and *lateral communication* (horizontally) between the project manager and his or her peers.[19]

Upward communication links help management assess priorities and take corrective actions to effectively meet project objectives. Downward communication contains pertinent information on projects that include: scope, quality, schedule, budget, structure, implementation plans and evaluation/feedback systems. Also, it may include organizational policies and procedures, project objectives and constraints and any other relevant information useful to team members. Lateral communication is essential to succeed in a highly competitive environment where management by projects is likely to be the most effective style of managing organization. It requires diplomacy, experience and mutual respect.

Building and maintaining all these communication links is the key to effective team building. Project managers must encourage the openness in communication and expedite the process of communication to ensure that project participants understand the intent and real meaning of the information being transferred. They should create an environment by making sure that the right people interact in a timely manner, participate in meetings and disseminate the information promptly and accurately.

For a more thorough discussion of communication, see Volume 2 of this series, *Human Resource Skills for the Project Manager.*

Obtain top management support

Top management, which may include the project director, project champions or sponsors, must emphasize the importance of team building as means to reach organizational success. They must demonstrate their commitment to team building by providing extra training and resources in this area and conducting team building exercises at various levels in the organization. Special team building events and activities should be sponsored by top management. Unfortunately, because of tight project schedules, there may not be plenty of time available for special exercises on team building. Therefore, team building should be integrated into the normal day-to-day project activities. It should be recognized as an effective, practical and standard approach for managing any project in the organization.

Utilize ongoing project team development

Team building is not a one-shot process. It is a major step in the right direction but it must be recognized as an ongoing process throughout the project life cycle. One major concern is to keep up the momentum and morale of the project, particularly during long projects. The project team's effort cannot be allowed to deviate away from project objectives. There are many conditions that pose challenges in maintaining strong team environment, for example:[18]

- New members joining the project team later
- Emphasis may change as project enters a new phase and key members of that team may change completely (e.g., from R&D to design or from development to manufacturing)
- Project manager may be replaced because of change in project emphasis
- Client representative may be changed or transferred

The impact of such changes depends upon their timing. The earlier the changes are implemented in the project life cycle, the less negative will be their impact. However, changes in a project environment are inevitable and to manage them effectively, a continued or a renewed team building effort must be applied.

Team building should be made an important part of every project activity, particularly meetings, one to one or group counseling sessions, informal conferences with team members, celebrations and organizational events. Project managers will have a wide variety of meetings and interactions with project team members during the life of a project during which they can take the opportunity to use techniques that foster team spirit.

They should avail every possible opportunity to discuss the importance of team effort and emphasize its importance in personal and organizational interfaces. Every meeting should be a *team meeting*—not the *project manager's meeting* and the team members should be the principal participants. Here are some recommendations to get team members more actively involved and promote teamwork:[18]

- Introduce new team members.
- Recognize team members for their special contributions to project performance.
- Keep the team members informed on latest project developments—both good news and bad.
- Keep the team informed on management strategies (especially as related to the project).
- Keep the team informed on client and customer actions and thinking.
- Bring in special outside speakers to provide training in team building.
- Provide exposure for team members by giving them major roles in every meeting.
- Get project and team recognized by having the media and senior management members attend selected project meetings.

One of the most important skills of project managers in developing a team environment involves handling project team problems in meetings. In case of cost overruns, delays in schedules, technical difficulties and poor quality, project managers should discuss these as team issues without accusations or finger-pointing. The entire team should be encouraged to work collaboratively and resolve these issues and problems with no uninvolved bystanders on the sidelines.[18] Everyone should work interdependently, which will apply peer pressure to be more productive and innovative.

Introduce rewards and recognition

Be alert for opportunities to recognize your people and show praise and appreciation for their efforts.

— The Author

People feel motivated if they feel that they are valued in the organization and this value is demonstrated by the rewards given to them. Generally, money is viewed by most as a very important aspect of any reward system. However, in a team environment, wide ranges in the pay structure can sometimes demotivate people. Team building may have some problems if team members feel that there is too much inequity in pay.

Generally, most project team members are motivated by an opportunity to grow, accomplish, and apply their professional skills to meet new challenges. In addition to money, there are other "perks" that can be included into the total team reward package. Some types of rewards that are often seen as components of a reward system:[18]

- Private office with a secretary
- Assigned parking space
- Reimbursement for after hours education
- Opportunity to attend conferences and seminars
- Stock purchase options
- Special holidays and vacation benefits.

The list is endless and project managers should use their creativity in developing an appropriate reward package. Team rewards are effective motivators, and therefore if possible, project managers should try to budget funds for team incentives such as team building exercises, professional training, and paid retreats. Public recognition of good performance leads to positive reinforcement. A good rule for project managers is to give the team all possible glory during the life cycle of the project rather than after the project is handed over to the client and the closing ceremony becomes mainly a political event.

Manage team conflicts effectively

The test of the first-rate intelligence is the ability to hold two opposed ideas in the mind at the same time, and still retain the ability to function.
— F. Scott Fitzgerald

Conflicts are inevitable in a project environment. When project team members interact during the course of completing their tasks and responsibilities, there is always a potential for conflict. In fact, it is virtually impossible for people with diverse backgrounds, skills, and norms to work together as a team to meet project objectives without conflict.

In handling conflict in a team environment, it will help the project manager to remember that:[19]

Conflict is natural. Project teams are expected to be dynamic, vibrant and high performing. Because of their high diversity in terms of backgrounds, expertise and interests among team members, conflict is natural and actually improves creativity.

Openness resolves conflict. Open discussions in a team can sharpen the differences, present additional alternatives, and provide necessary checks and balances.

Conflict resolution must focus on issues, not personalities. People should not be confused with their issues. In spite of any dislike on a personal level, each team member should focus on the pros and cons of the issues rather than on personalities.

Conflict forces a search for alternatives. In a true team environment, project team members do not blame others for a problem or a failure. Normally, project teams are primarily interested in finding solutions and therefore their motivation is *"Since the present situation is not satisfactory, what else would we prefer as an alternative?"*

Conflict resolution is present-oriented. An effective team should not consider past events, disagreements or behaviors of team members that may have taken place either within or outside the team. What matters is the *present* circumstances and what is being said *now*.

Conflict is a team issue. Any disagreements among team members can affect the effectiveness of whole team and therefore these should be considered as team issues. The whole team should help the members involved in resolving their differences instead of leaving them on their own.

Even a rather minor conflict can almost instantly destroy a team spirit that may have taken a long time to develop. Therefore, managing team conflicts promptly and effectively is one of the prime responsibilities of the project managers.

Conflict resolution basics for project managers. There are several important issues that project managers should be aware of about managing team conflicts effectively, which are briefly covered here. For a more thorough discussion of conflict, please see Volume 2 of this series, *Human Resource Skills for the Project Manager.*

Competition versus conflict. Competition within a team should not be confused with negative conflict. Competition can be regarded as a desirable asset, and therefore should be encouraged. Competition is useful because it enhances the energy and the incentives needed to stimulate creativity, innovation and high performance. Competition brings out the best individual efforts and in fact is the key to superior teamwork. The project manager must be very cautious in encouraging a healthy team competition, while at the same time ensure that it does not lead to negative (destructive) conflict.

Team conflict avoidance. Project managers should use careful planning and try to resolve conflict at early stages. Most project team problems are caused by either personality clashes (people problems) or disagreement over project aspects (with respect to resources, schedules, technical opinions, etc.).

Personality clashes should be dealt with before they become serious problems. Project managers should select the team members carefully and emphasize the importance of being a good team player. However, this is not always easy because some project activities may require specialized technical skills of people who are by nature loners and don't fit in a team. Project managers must define their roles clearly so that they can work independently.

Disagreements over project aspects can be caused by lack of clarity in roles and relationships between team members, competition over resources and different technical opinions and ideas to meet project budgets and schedules. Such potential conflicts can be avoided if project managers take the following precautions that should be a part of internal team building:[18]

- Keep team members informed of project objectives, plans, status and all decisions.
- Define task assignments clearly by avoiding duplication and overlapping.
- Make task assignments challenging and interesting.
- Involve team members in establishing objectives, preparing plans and making decisions with respect to shifts in priorities, schedules, and budgets.
- Get top management involved and committed to teamwork.

In a nutshell, all these ideas emphasize keeping the communication links working to keep the conflict to minimum.

140 ————————————————————————

Dealing with outside conflict. In a matrix structure, project managers are dependent upon functional managers, support personnel and other project stakeholders. They must negotiate resources with functional managers for various project tasks. Functional managers often view project managers as "body snatchers" and are not always sympathetic to project urgency.

Also, project managers are the ones who initiate and establish frequent contacts with the world outside the project (external stakeholders) and with functional managers and support personnel (internal stakeholders).[18] Wilemon and Thamhain conducted a study involving a survey of about 100 project managers and identified seven sources of conflict that were ranked as follows:[20]

1. Schedules (task uncertainty and information requirements)
2. Priorities (goal incompatibility and differences in time horizon)
3. Human resources (staffing and resource allocation)
4. Technical issues (technical opinions and performance tradeoffs)
5. Administrative problems (managerial and administrative issues outlining how the project will be managed: may include role uncertainty, authority and responsibility of each project participant, and reporting relationships)
6. Personality (interpersonal disagreements)
7. Cost.

The predominant sources and intensities of conflict vary over the life cycle of the project.[20]

The work of Thamhain and Wilemon was later confirmed by other investigators working in a variety of project environments.[21,22] Posner's work moved the rankings of conflict over costs from seventh to second place and conflict over administrative problems from fifth to last position. Table 3.3 compares the research findings of these two studies.[22]

Conflicts are possible between project team members and support personnel outside the project. These conflicts may start with minor disagreements that can be disastrous if not managed immediately. As a "team spirit" develops and project team becomes more cohesive, it tends to adopt a "we" attitude and may consider others including administrative and support personnel, functional managers, etc., as "they." Some of this attitude is useful for effective team building but too much may lead to conflict. This is especially true when the project team starts to blame "them" for every project problem, which leads to even further conflict.[18]

Conflict resolution. The success of project managers in team building and managing a project often depends a great deal on their ability to resolve conflict. Different project managers may have different conflict resolution styles. While there is no "right" way to settle a conflict, it is important to understand the principal conflict resolution modes and be able to choose among them appropriately. The choice of an appropriate style for resolving conflict depends upon a broad range of factors such as:[23]

Effective Team Building

Table 3.3 Conflict Source Ranking by Phase of the Project Life Cycle

Thamhain & Wilemon (1975)	Posner (1986)
Conceptual/Initiation Phase	
1. Priorities	1. Schedules
2. Administrative procedures	2. Cost/Budget
3. Schedules	3. Priorities
4. Human resources	4. Human resources
5. Cost/Budget	5. Technical Issues/ Performance tradeoffs
6. Technical Issues/ Performance tradeoffs	6. Personality
7. Personality	7. Administrative procedures
Development/Planning Phase	
1. Priorities	1. Human resources
2. Schedules	2. Priorities
3. Administrative procedures	3. Schedules
4. Technical Issues/ Performance tradeoffs	4. Technical Issues/ Performance tradeoffs
5. Human resources	5. Cost/Budget
6. Personality/ Performance tradeoffs	6. Personality
7. Cost/Budget	7. Administrative procedures
Execution/Implementation Phase	
1. Schedules	1. Schedules
2. Technical Issues/ Performance tradeoffs	2. Priorities
3. Human resources	3. Cost/Budget
4. Priorities	4. Technical Issues/ Performance tradeoffs
5. Administrative procedures	5. Human resources
6. Cost/Budget, Personality	6. Administrative procedures
Phaseout	
1. Schedules	1. Schedules
2. Personality	2. Cost/Budget
3. Human resources	3. Personality
4. Priorities	4. Priorities
5. Cost/Budget	5. Human resources
6. Technical Issues/ Performance tradeoffs	6. Administrative procedures
7. Administrative procedures	7. Technical Issues/ Performance tradeoffs

- The relative importance and intensity of the conflict
- The time pressure for resolving the conflict
- The position taken by players involved
- Motivation to resolve conflict on a long-term or a short-term basis.

Conflict management possibilities are also dependent upon the ratio of assertiveness to cooperation among the parties involved in the conflict, as well as on the type of conflict being handled. Conflict resolution techniques range from the power-based "steamroller" approach to a more defensive, diplomatic and tactical approach. Intermediate views suggest variations of avoidance, give-and-take negotiation, collaboration and problem solving,[26] representing just a few of the six general techniques for resolving conflict:[23]

1. Withdrawing/Avoiding
2. Smoothing/Accommodating
3. Compromising
4. Forcing
5. Collaborating
6. Confronting/Problem Solving.

Blake and Mouton[24] combined the fifth and sixth techniques into one which is sometimes also referred to as "negotiating." Table 3.4 summarizes these six interpersonal conflict resolution techniques.[23]

Project managers must use an appropriate style for managing conflict because it can have a significant impact on success in team building and overall management of the project. For instance, forcing and withdrawal techniques, when used to resolve conflicts with support personnel, functional managers and assigned personnel, are least effective, while confrontation, compromise, and smoothing tend to work well. Problem solving and collaborating tends to be very effective in managing conflicts with clients, top management and regulatory agencies.

Provide good project leadership

The difference between a successful person and others is not a lack of strength, not a lack of knowledge, but rather in a lack of will.
— *Vincent J. Lombardi*

The overall success of project managers depends upon the quality of leadership provided to their project teams. Effective teamwork is the by-product of good leadership. During one of the workshops that I facilitated, one participant made the point, "There is nothing worse than being on a team where communication is not open, no one trusts anyone else, and there is no team leadership." There is an ample body of literature on communication, teamwork, and leadership. However, it is still not very clear what project leadership is and how it relates to project management. Verma and Wideman dealt with this issue in addressing the question, *Is it leadership or*

Table 3.4 Conflict Management Styles

Style	Description	Effect
Withdrawing/ Avoiding	Retreats from an actual or potential conflict situation	Does not solve the problem
Smoothing/ Accommodating	Emphasizes areas of agreement rather than areas of difference	Provides only short-term solution
Compromising	Searches for and bargains for solutions that bring some degree of satisfaction to all parties	Does provide definitive resolution
Forcing	Pushes one viewpoint at the expense of others; offers only win-lose solutions	Hard feelings may come back in other forms
Collaborating	Incorporates multiple viewpoints and insights from differing perspectives; leads to consensus and commitment	Provides long-term resolution
Confronting/Problem Solving	Treats conflict as a problem to be solved by examining alternatives; requires give-and-take attitude and open dialogue	Provides ultimate resolution

management that is most needed for managing project successfully in the next century?[25] Some pertinent issues about project leadership include:

- What is leadership?
- Is it different than managership?
- What is the most effective way to provide leadership to obtain the best teamwork?

About project leadership. There has been a spate of publications on leadership and team building by authors such as Batten, Bennis, Covey, Depree, Dilenschneider, McLean, Fisher, and others.[26] Most of these authors agree that vision is a primary ingredient of leadership. Batten defines leadership as "development of a clear and complete system of expectations in order to identify, evoke, and use the strengths of all resources in the organization, the most important of which is people.[27] John Naisbit probably comes closer to a definition of a leader with his description: "An ability to attract followers ... a clear destination, and ... a timetable."[28] With these at-

144

Table 3.5 Leader or Manager?

Leaders Focus On:	Managers Focus On:
Vision	Objectives
Selling what and why	Telling how and when
Longer range	Shorter range
People	Organization and structure
Democracy	Autocracy
Enabling	Restraining
Developing	Maintaining
Challenging	Conforming
Originating	Imitating
Innovating	Administrating
Directing	Controlling
Policy	Procedures
Flexibility	Consistency
Risk (opportunity)	Risk (avoidance)
Top line	Bottom line
Good Leaders	**Good Managers**
do the right things	*do things right*

Source: Vijay K. Verma and R. M. Wideman. 1994. Project Manager to Project Leader? and the Rocky Road Between. *Proceedings of the 25th Annual Seminar/Symposium*. Upper Darby, PA: Project Management Institute, pp. 627–633.

tributes in mind, leadership in a project context can be defined in the following simple, yet comprehensive, distillation of leadership thought.

Project leadership is an ability to get things done well through others. It requires:

- A vision of the destination (*project goal*)
- A clear, compelling reason to get there (*to inspire commitment*)
- A set of directions and a realistic timetable (*project plan covering schedules, budget, etc.*)
- A capacity to attract a willing team and make it work (*developing and fostering teamwork*).

Pinto synthesized various leadership studies and indicated the following points about the nature of project leadership:[29]

- Effective project leaders must be good communicators.
- Project leaders are flexible in responding to ambiguous or uncertain situations with a minimum of stress.
- Successful project leaders work well with and through their project team.

- Good project leaders are skilled at various influence tactics by using the art of persuasion and influence.

He pointed out that examining the traits of successful leaders is valuable but not sufficient. One key to understanding leadership behavior is to focus on what leaders *do* rather than on who they are.[29]

According to Robert Townsend, leaders come in all ages, shapes, sizes and conditions. Some are poor administrators, some are not overly bright. True leaders can be recognized, because some how or other, their people consistently turn in superior performances.[30] Leadership in a project environment can be best described by a piece of project management folklore: Leadership is getting people who don't work for you to do things for the project to meet project objectives.[18] This emphasizes the use of more informal power than formal power.

Leader versus manager. Is there a difference between a project leader and a project manager? Careful analysis of the roles of project managers and project leaders reveals that the distinction between their styles can be attributed to how and what they focus on. Leaders focus on "doing the right things" (effectiveness) while managers focus on "doing the things right" (efficiency). The respective positions of leaders and managers on a number of issues are shown in Table 3.5.[25, 26]

Successful project management requires both project leadership and project management skills. Collectively project leadership and project managership may be called project *stewardship*, which implies holding something in trust for another. Project stewardship refers to a willingness to be fully accountable for meeting project objectives and for giving a higher degree of importance to project objectives than to self-interest. It entails holding people accountable without harshly exacting compliance from them.

Leadership and the project life cycle. Do project leaders need different skills and leadership styles in different phases of the project life cycle? Both project leadership and managership are important to project success. Leadership emphasizes communicating the vision and then motivating and inspiring project participants to higher performance, whereas managership focuses on getting things done. Can the two be reconciled? Verma and Wideman addressed this issue and indicated major attributes and leadership blends needed during various phases of the project life cycle.[25]

Leadership styles. There are several leadership styles that project managers exhibit. Some project managers have a preferred leadership style while others fit their style to the situation. Leadership styles can be described in terms of four possible extremes of leadership:[18]

Autocratic project managers make most decisions themselves and do not encourage active participation from team members.

Consultative autocrat project managers solicit intensive information from project team members but keep all decision-making power to themselves.

146

Consensus managers throw open the problem to the team for input and discussion. They often encourage the team to reach consensus in making relevant decisions.

Shareholder managers should not be confused with the shared leadership concept because managers using the shareholder management style do not encourage effective communication information exchange among team members even though the team is given ultimate authority for the final decision. It is a poor management style.

According to Slevin, the key to successful leadership is knowing what your dominant style is and being able to modify that style depending upon the contingencies of the various leadership situations.[31] Slevin has developed a leadership model and a diagnostic tool (The Jerrel/Slevin Management Institute) to provide feedback to managers on their management style.[32]

Shared leadership. The concept of shared leadership is a very effective one that project managers should use for successful team building and providing effective project leadership. More than participatory management, shared leadership involves encouraging project teams to assume leadership roles and then letting them take over as much of leadership role as they will accept. Project managers must be prepared to give up some of their formal authority. Moreover, by sharing some of their authority with the project team, they become like a member of the project team and the team members assume more of the leadership role depending upon their expertise during specific phases of the project life cycle. It motivates and encourages team members to participate in preparing project plans, resolving project problems and making decisions. Project managers gain wider acceptance and hence commitment of team members to meet project objectives as team members accept responsibilities and feel accountable for the success or failure of the project. Shared leadership even reduces workload for project managers while team members actually take an increased ownership of project tasks, which usually leads to high performance and quality. It is the most effective route to achieve team commitment and true teamwork.

Successful project managers tend to solve problems collectively through team effort rather than on a one-to-one basis. In this context, to be an effective project manager, it is essential to become a coach, a facilitator, a developer, a team builder.[18,33] Coach is perhaps the best analogy for a project manager. Just as the success of a sports team depends upon the ability of its coach to make individual players work together as a team, project success depends upon project manager to create a real team environment and make the project team members work together and help each other win. Like team coaches, project managers can plan, organize and direct the project activities, but they will not be able to inspire high performance and achieve human synergy unless there is shared leadership with the team members.

Leadership challenges. Sometimes, during the early stages of a project, the leadership role of the project manager may be challenged. Some technical experts on the project team may question the credibility of the project leader, especially in leading technical problems or issues. Such challenges are often temporary but can significantly retard the team building process.[21] The management and leadership performance of the project manager is closely watched by the project team. Sometimes they may have too high an expectation. However, this is a very critical time for project managers. They must acquire a balanced combination of technical, human and conceptual skills. They must be able to analyze the situations and interact openly and honestly with their team members. They must recognize that their performance is based upon how well they can get work done through the project team. Therefore, they must use proper human skills and recognize team members for their strengths and high performance.

TEAM BUILDING INVOLVES a whole spectrum of management skills to commit and integrate efforts of various team members. It involves a combination of human skills with special emphasis on communication, conflict management, negotiation, and leadership. Project managers must capitalize on drivers to effective team building and minimize the negative impact of barriers to effective team building. They must provide challenging assignment to team members, recognize them properly for high performance. They must acquire strong management support and commitment to team building. Above all, teamwork should be made a part of an organizational culture. Figure 3.9 shows major elements of teamwork in a nutshell.

Summary

It is to the advantage of any project leader to have a positive attitude towards team building. One of the most important developments in the project management area is the widespread application of project teams to a variety of complex tasks. A strong project team is the nucleus of a successful project. When the concept of team building is understood and applied at all levels, it becomes much easier to transform groups into teams throughout the organization. Building effective project teams is one of the prime responsibilities of project managers.

Team building involves a whole spectrum of management skills required to identify, commit and integrate various task groups from traditional functional organizations into a multidisciplinary task management system. Team building is the process of helping a group of individuals, bound by a common sense of purpose, to work interdependently with each other, the leader, external stakeholders and the whole organization. Outcomes of team building include mutual trust and high quality of information exchange, better decision-making and effective project control. The team building model consists of *task* activities (establish goals, define and nego-

Figure 3.9 Teamwork in a Nutshell

T — Trust

E — Encouragement/Effective Communication

A — Action orientation

M — Milestones (well defined and agreed upon)

W — Work interdependently

O — Organized (project structure and personally)

R — Resources availability/
Recognition for results

K — Knowledge mix

tiate roles and procedures) and *process* activities (interpersonal activities with emphasis on communication, conflict management, motivation and leadership). Although the process of team building can entail frustrations and requires energy from all team members, the rewards are great.

In addition to technical guidance and management expertise, project managers must provide an appropriate atmosphere conducive to teamwork and give their full enthusiasm and support. They must be committed to building a strong project team and encourage the creative potential of all team members. Project managers must try to identify any problems early in the life of a project and deal with them effectively by maximizing the impact of drivers and minimizing the impact of barriers to effective team building.

Team building is also one of the most critical leadership skills. It determines the level of performance and success in a project environment. Special care should be given to selecting team members, clarifying their roles and responsibilities, and getting their commitment by developing with them a skill inventory matrix and a responsibility matrix. Project management must emphasize the importance of teamwork, trust, and confidence among team members. This will not only help meet project objectives within the given constraints but will make work fun by increasing the long-term morale of team members and increasing their productivity.

Effective team building is crucial to project success. It is not a one-shot event, it is an ongoing process. Project managers can use ten guidelines for effective team building and developing a strategy to manage projects successfully, which include: plan for team building (in terms of project goals, plans, procedures and controls); negotiate for team members (to get the best mix); hold a kick-off meeting (to start project on the right foot); obtain commitment of team members (by involving them right from the start); build communication links; obtain top management support (in terms of resources); utilize ongoing project team development (throughout the project life cycle); introduce rewards and recognition (individual and team plus monetary and others); manage team conflicts effectively (inside and outside the project team); and provide good project leadership (with emphasis on shared leadership).

Outline

Developing a Project Team for Success   154
Coordinating team efforts   154
Appropriate use of power and authority   155
Developing problem-solving abilities   157

Developing a Team Communication Plan   159
Modes of communication behavior   160
Communication channels and links   162
Listening—The key element of team communication   163
Building effective team communications   167

Effective Team Decision-Making   171
About team decision-making   172
Rational decision-making process   175
Decision styles in a team environment   179
Guidelines for effective team decision-making   180

Managing Project Teams During the Project   182
Changing project team members according to project life cycle   182
External factors affecting team performance   183
Team management   186

Summary   189

Everyone has to work together; if we can't get everyone working toward a common goal, nothing is going to happen.

Harold K. Sperlich, President, Chrysler Corp.

Developing Effective Project Teams

THE SUCCESS OF a project team depends upon its team leaders' ability to effectively manage and influence the diverse mix of personnel. Because of the multidisciplinary and interdependent nature of project teams, project managers must learn team-building skills in order to integrate the efforts of all project participants. They must understand the dynamics and the process of team development. They must create an environment where all team members are personally and professionally satisfied, are involved and have mutual trust. They must be able to create a clear, compelling vision towards which team members work together with unity of purpose. They must build commitment for that vision through motivating, communicating effectively, encouraging genuine participation in decision-making, and managing the team throughout the project life cycle.

Effective project teams are characterized by clear, well-understood priorities, mutual understanding, and commitment to help each other win. It is important to understand that project team members normally progress through a developmental sequence in team building.

This chapter deals with coordinating team efforts, developing a team communication plan, using power and authority appropriately, and motivating each other. It describes pros and cons of team decision-making, rational decision-making in a team environment, various decision styles and guidelines for effective team decision-making. Various styles of team management and the importance of changing team members, as necessary, according to the project life cycle are presented. Various external factors that may affect team performance are described, along with strategies and guidelines to minimize their negative impact. Project teams can be managed successfully throughout the project life cycle provided that project managers know their team members well and use an appropriate team management style depending upon the situation. ■

Developing a Project Team for Success

United we stand, divided we fall.

— Watchword of the American Revolution

A strong project team is the backbone of a project. As team members deal with difficult issues of time, cost and performance constraints, project managers need to provide their technical guidance, management and leadership skills and above all their positive attitude, enthusiasm and support. Generally, there are not many project problems that cannot be resolved by a capable team through utilizing its collective knowledge and collaborative skills.[1]

Wilemon and Thamhain[1] suggested some team symptoms that may indicate that more effort should be spent in developing project teams. Some of such major indicators are:

- Excessive "wheel-spinning" within the team
- Objectives unclear or not accepted by the team members
- Decisions not implemented in due course
- Team meetings unproductive, full of conflict and demoralizing
- Destructive surprises encountered by the team leader
- Poor motivation and apathy
- Team performance going down but no one knows why
- Schedule delays, poor quality, and cost overruns
- Team members not responsive to the needs of the team or of the project
- Team members withdraw, confine themselves to their own areas of responsibility
- Team members avoid raising issues that stimulate problem-solving activity and encourage collaboration.

Although this list does not cover all possible indicators, it gives a good idea how to recognize the need for more team building and team development.

It is relatively easy to establish a degree of teamwork or cooperation between a group of people but it is much harder to develop a high-performance project team. Several important factors must be understood and implemented in order to develop a strong project team.

Coordinating team efforts

Project teams normally consist of a group of individuals, with a diverse mix of skills and backgrounds, who must be integrated into one work unit. A very high degree of coordination is required to ensure an overall increase in team productivity and to integrate all interfaces throughout the project life cycle. The following are some of the major techniques for building a solid foundation for coordinating the work efforts of a project team.[2]

Build a broad-based team. Choose the best people for your team: Those who are known to get the job done and are good team players. Unfortunately, project managers sometimes do not have such choices but are told who is assigned to their project.

154

Establish a formal leader. A single person must be officially designated to manage the project and given the appropriate degree of responsibility and authority to go with it.

Build and maintain team spirit. Team spirit is one of the most important aids to productivity. Everyone knows the joy and energy that comes from being on a winning team. A winning team is more than the sum of its parts; good team spirit enables common people to do uncommonly good things. Project managers themselves must be enthusiastic and make everyone aware that their own success depends on everyone else succeeding. Positive attitude, enthusiasm, support, and confidence are powerful stimulants to productive team members.

Elicit management support. Typically, project team members are assigned by their direct supervisors or functional managers for the duration of the project or for the time required to perform specific tasks. The project manager must obtain their full commitment to the project by using persuasive, motivational and leadership techniques. He or she must convince each team member that the project is an essential part of their job. It is easier to convince the team members if their supervisors (functional managers) are also convinced and if the project manager has a say in the team member's performance appraisal.

Keep team members informed. Project team members become frustrated if the game plan is changed without their knowledge. Project managers need the respect of their teams and this can be achieved by establishing open communication channels so that the project manager and project team members can exchange information in a timely and accurate manner.

Figure 4.1 shows main elements of a good team environment.

Appropriate use of power and authority

Most project managers are highly motivated to deliver a high-quality end product or service but may have limited authority and power to manage team members and other resources. Project managers must try to acquire and exercise a balance of informal and formal authority and power. For example, in a matrix project structure where team members are from various functional departments, one source of formal power and authority a project manager may have is associated with the performance appraisal of project team members. However, this is only as effective as the degree of influence acknowledged by the functional managers in the matter of raises and promotions for team members allocated to the project. Some organizations have a policy that outlines how the project manager provides performance information to the direct superior or manager of particular team members. Some of the essential elements of this process are:[2]

- Project team members should know (from the start of an assignment) that their functional manager or supervisor will obtain and use performance appraisal information from the project manager.

Developing Effective Project Teams

Figure 4.1 Main Elements of a Good Team Environment

E — Emphasize teamwork

N — Needs are addressed

V — Value team member's contributions

I — Involvement (genuine) in goal setting & decision making

R — Recognize/reward good performance

O — Open communication

N — Negative criticisms discouraged

M — Motivation through challenges & self development

E — Encourage creativity & innovation

N — Negotiate to achieve win/win

T — Time management/timeline

- The assignment must be for a sufficient number of person-hours to warrant initiating this appraisal process.
- Inputs from project managers should be obtained when the performance of the team member is fresh in their mind rather than at the end of the appraisal period.
- The functional manager should use this information to do an overall performance appraisal of their people working on the project.

Project managers must identify and clarify some key power needs required to manage the project. This can help them later to avoid getting frustrated and will also give them some bargaining power when they may actually need it. Project managers can also gain power, in a project environment, through the use of the following strategies:

Influencing is a strategy of shared power and relying on interpersonal skills to get others to cooperate for common goals. Team members can be influenced by using the following guidelines:[2]

- Walk your talk and follow through your commitments.
- Be consistent in terms of what you ask for in order to build and maintain reliability.
- Clarify about how a decision will be made.

156

- Use a flexible interpersonal style, i.e., adjust to the person you are with, especially your vocal tone and non-verbal behaviors.
- Build your power base (ability to influence) appropriately.
- Apply your power skillfully and cautiously.

Negotiating is a strategy of trading for power. As a first step in negotiating, project managers must analyze the situation. The following skills and behaviors are useful in negotiating successfully.

- Differentiate between wants and needs—both theirs and yours.
- Ask high, and offer low—but don't be ridiculous.
- When you make a concession, act as if you are yielding something of value; don't just give in.
- Always make sure both parties feel as if they have won. This is win-win negotiating. Never let the other party leave feeling as if he or she has been taken.

Using coercion is a strategy of power imposition. It implies that project managers may need to turn to formal organizational lines of authority to *issue* orders and get compliance. Coercion is generally the least practical and most politically expensive strategy to use. Sometimes it is necessary, but project managers should use it only as a last resort, not as their first move.[2]

Each of the three strategies has been presented in its pure form for simplicity. In reality, they are mixed together according to the personal style of the project manager and the needs of the situation. The more the project manager uses and mixes these strategies appropriately, the more successful he or she is likely to be in motivating others.

Developing problem-solving abilities

Soloists are inspiring in opera and perhaps even in small entrepreneurial ventures, but there is no place for them in large corporations.
    — Norman R. Augustine, chairman and CEO, Martin Marietta Corp.

One of the main advantages of using a team concept in managing projects is that it broadens the knowledge base. In project teams a diverse mix of people with differing expertise, skills and experiences interact with each other and work together to develop more options than any one member could do on his or her own. It enhances the problem-solving ability of the team by encouraging everyone to participate in developing solutions. Team members "buy in" in this process, as well as in the outcome of this process, increases their commitment to meet team objectives.

Effective problem solving requires the intellectual efforts of most team members to analyze the situation and identify problems, constraints, and solutions. The thinking process leading to problem solving has two main components: analytical ability and innovative or creative ability.[3]

In most teams, it is relatively easier to find people with analytical skills who love to study problems and diagnose their causes. However, it is not so easy to find people who can quickly come up with innovative and imaginative solutions to problems. Truly creative people are rare indeed; and a growing number of complex projects are creating even a greater demand for such people. Project managers cannot rely on high IQ while selecting their team members, because IQ is primarily a measure of analytical ability and does not necessarily ensure creativity.

Project managers are under pressure to find immediately effective solutions to project problems. They cannot afford to depend on a single individual "genius" to provide innovative spark to the whole project team. Also, technical specialists may tend to solve problems or suggest solutions within their own disciplinary context that may lead to suboptimum solutions, because most project problems are of a multidisciplinary nature and may need an analysis of external environment as well. Therefore, project managers must create an environment where all problems are solved through a team effort.

However, there is considerable controversy regarding whether creativity is essentially a trait of the individual or whether teams can be really creative. Another issue is whether or not creativity is a skill that can be learned through team-building exercises and other relevant training. Generally, true innovations are created by an individual alone; therefore the ability of teams to come up with innovative and creative solutions is questionable.[3] However, an effective team leader can direct the efforts of the whole team towards a creative solution if the team leader understands the dynamics of a team and has good team-building skills.

Here are some ways that project managers can enhance the creativity of the team problem-solving process.

Keep the team size small. This encourages full participation from all team members and allows them enough time to explain and evaluate each other's ideas. A team of five to nine members is generally most effective.

Plan meetings thoroughly. The team leader should define major issues to be addressed by the team at the problem-solving meeting and invite all team members to come prepared with ideas and possible solutions. Individuals are better at generating ideas and teams are better at evaluating ideas.

Encourage team member participation. Use a round robin approach to get everyone's input. List ideas on a flip chart. During this process, encourage questions to clarify the ideas and diffuse negative criticism or attempts to evaluate ideas. Innovative ideas can come from anyone.

Emphasize that ideas are owned by the team rather than by the originator. Ideas, once tabled, belong to the whole project team. The originator should answer questions to clarify the idea, but not be put on the spot to defend the idea.

Rephrase criticism in a positive way. Creative problem solving is generated only if there is a freedom to express ideas and if management has a reasonable tolerance for failure. Even weak ideas should not be shot down immediately. For example, instead of saying "It has been tried before and it did not work" or "It is too expensive and difficult to implement." A positive way could be "What is new in this version compared to the previous one?" or "Has our situation changed enough to retry this idea?" Positive criticisms keep alive the process of idea generation.

Invite positive remarks from negative people. Encourage people who are negative or lukewarm about the suggested ideas to come up with advantages and strength of those ideas. This reduces defensiveness, opens new horizons, broadens thinking, and encourages people to look for way to make things work rather than focusing on why things won't work. Encourage people to look for solutions rather than problems.

Lead by example, by not defending your own ideas. Project leaders may tend to over-defend their ideas. They should remind the team members that all ideas (including their own) are the team's. However, they should offer to clarify the issues involved, if necessary. If this is done assertively, other team members will tend to follow. Set an example by not being overprotective of your own ideas.

Since project objectives are met through teamwork, project managers should concentrate on encouraging team creativity. Usually problem solving capabilities of a project team depend upon team climate, team motivation, and team leadership. [3] Effective project managers can achieve these conditions by encouraging team members to express and discuss their ideas freely with others, encouraging people to try new ideas by demonstrating a tolerance for failure, and stimulating cross-fertilization of ideas from discipline to discipline. In a team environment, there is a higher potential for creativity and innovation because of broader knowledge base and a diversity of experience. Open discussions, constructive criticisms, management's tolerance for failure, team approach, and mutual support will increase the chances of synergistically building on a tentative or weak idea to make it a winner. This leads to creative solutions, effective problem solving, high performance, and personal satisfaction. Above all, it makes the whole process become fun for all team members.

Developing a Team Communication Plan

Effective communication builds trust, partnership and collaboration. This is what creates synergy in teams.

— *The Author*

Communication is the key to effective team building. All project managers must understand the concepts and goals of communication, barriers to successful communication and suggested remedial actions, modes of communication behavior, roles and relationships between different communication channels in a project environment, importance of verbal/nonverbal

Developing Effective Project Teams

communication (with special emphasis on listening); and build effective team communications using practical ideas.

Project managers need to define their goals for team communication when the teams are formed and determine the forms of communication to be used in managing the project (meetings, telephone calls, written status reports, electronic mail or some combination of these.)

- *Written reports* must define the content, level of detail and the format for the reports. To be effective, these reports must satisfy the needs of the audience.
- *Meetings* are generally used to coordinate project activities. Common questions as to how, when and why meetings take place must be addressed. Strategies should be formulated to get the most out of project team meetings.
- *Formal or informal communications* must be planned in view of how frequently project objectives and all communications associated with the project are reviewed.

The project manager must try to facilitate communications by responding to the information needs of the people associated with the project and of the organization and keeping the appropriate parties in all directions (top, bottom and lateral) well informed. Figure 4.2 shows a typical example of such information needs.[4]

The power of effective communication for project team members cannot be overstated because it leads to several important outcomes for the project:

- Clearer sense of team roles and expectations
- Increased team productivity and quality of work
- Better team collaboration and problem solving
- Improved working relationships among team members
- Increased job satisfaction
- Greater sense of personal achievement
- Reduction in destructive conflicts.

High commitment is achieved by understanding modes of communication behaviors, identifying and expediting communication channels and links in a project, and building effective team communications.

Modes of communication behavior

Effective communication among team members is vital to achieve collaboration and support. The working relationships among team members and their effectiveness as a team is influenced by the way they members communicate with one another both with words and with non-verbal cues. In other words, communication involves not only *what* is said but also *how* it is said. Good communication gives clear directions and messages that enhances harmony and performance. To build trust and credibility, communication must consist of two messages:[5]

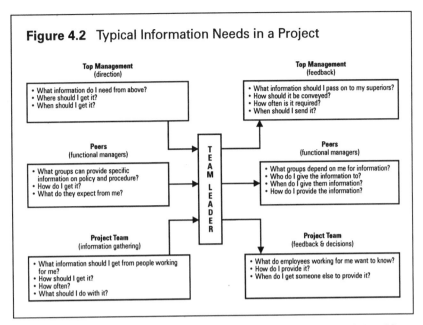

Figure 4.2 Typical Information Needs in a Project

Top Management (direction)
- What information do I need from above?
- Where should I get it?
- When should I get it?

Top Management (feedback)
- What information should I pass on to my superiors?
- How should it be conveyed?
- How often is it required?
- When should I send it?

Peers (functional managers)
- What groups can provide specific information on policy and procedure?
- How do I get it?
- What do they expect from me?

Peers (functional managers)
- What groups depend on me for information?
- Who do I give the information to?
- When do I give them information?
- How do I provide the information?

TEAM LEADER

Project Team (information gathering)
- What information should I get from people working for me?
- How should I get it?
- How often?
- What should I do with it?

Project Team (feedback & decisions)
- What do employees working for me want to know?
- How do I provide it?
- When do I get someone else to provide it?

Source: Robert B. Maddux, *Team Building: An Exercise in Leadership*, Crisp Publications, Inc., Los Altos, California, p. 47. By permission of the publisher.

- What you see is what is there.
- What you hear is what is meant.

It is important that all team members feel free in expressing their needs, wants and ideas in a manner that is acceptable to others, which can be done only by being assertive. Assertiveness is one of the most important skills to achieve effective team communication and should not be confused with aggressiveness. In the spectrum of communication modes, the four dominant modes are aggressiveness, assertiveness, responsiveness, and non-assertiveness, with aggressiveness and non-assertiveness being the two undesirable extremes.[5]

Assertive communicators state positively the meaning of people's statements and avoid common communication problems that create resentment, anger, stress, and defensiveness. Generally assertive communicators:[5]

- Express their needs, wants and ideas to their teams in a positive manner without threatening their team members in any way.
- Believe that all team members will cooperate in looking for agreements and solutions.
- Express their anger or dissatisfaction without hesitation.
- Act to change undesirable conditions or persuade others to change them.
- Focus on issues rather than on positions and personalities when dealing with conflicts.
- Feel full control over their own feelings and perceptions.

Developing Effective Project Teams

- Receive trust and respect from other team members.
- Listen empathetically to others.
- Convey their assertiveness in terms of words, vocal tones and body language. [5]

Responsive communicators focus primarily on others rather than themselves. They recognize strengths of others and are prepared to address joint concerns *before* their own. The main characteristics of responsive communicators are different than those of assertive communicators in terms of how they deal with information, feelings of others and change. Responsive communicators:[5]

- Seek information by inviting others to describe the situation as they see it.
- Seek to know feelings of others by asking others how they feel and acknowledging their viewpoint (without necessarily agreeing).
- Seek change in themselves, for instance by trying to be more helpful to others and to the team.
- Define the advantages of the change for themselves by emphasizing a win/win situation if the desired change is made). [5]

A combination of assertive and responsive communication behavior is the best for team communications because it leads to win/win negotiations, *effective* problem solving and conflict management. It acknowledges the rights and feelings of all parties involved, creates a comfortable environment to express ideas, and recognizes that each person has needs, wants, resources, and strengths. The assertive-responsive approach can be used to find an outcome that is acceptable to everyone.[5]

Communication channels and links

Along with the significant informal communication that takes place in a project environment, the project manager must recognize and understand the project's formal communication channels. The traditional project organization chart depicts the relationship between people and jobs and shows the formal channels of communication between them.

Three basic channels of communication exist in a project environment.[6]

Upward communication (vertically or diagonally with managers and officers) primarily contains information that higher management (project director or sponsor) needs to evaluate the overall performance of the projects for which they are responsible, or to refine organizational strategy. Project managers may use the "by exception" format for project status reports, production reports, shipping reports and customer concerns. This feedback helps top management assess priorities and make organizational modifications to effectively meet project goals and objectives and be more successful in the future.

Downward communication (vertically or diagonally) provides direction and control for project team members and other employees. It contains job-related information focusing on:

- What actions are required (scope definition)
- To what standard (quality)
- When the activities should be performed (schedule)
- How the activities should be done (implementation)
- How the progress will be measured (evaluation and feedback).

Downward communication may include statements of organizational philosophy, policies, project objectives, schedules, budgets and constraints, position descriptions and other written information relating to the importance, rationale and interrelationships and interactions of various departments projects, and jobs in an organization.

Lateral communication (horizontally) flows between the project manager and his or her peers: functional managers, line/staff personnel, other project managers, contractors, subcontractors, clients, service/support personnel and other project stakeholders. It involves negotiating resources, schedules, and budgets and coordinating activities with contractors, regulatory agencies and clients, as well as developing plans for future operating periods.

Lateral communication is vital to the success of a project and is also the most important factor for survival and growth in a highly competitive and turbulent environment where management by projects is likely to be the most effective style of managing organizations. It requires diplomacy and experience. If managed properly, it creates a harmonious, cooperative environment based on trust and respect for one another. When poorly managed, however, it may lead to conflict, unconstructive finger-pointing and failure to meet project objectives.

IN A PROJECT ENVIRONMENT, project managers communicate with the client, project sponsor or project director (for requirements, guidance and funding); with the top management (for organizational support); functional managers (for resources); and project team members, contractors, subcontractors, etc., (for project management). They should expedite the communication process to reduce ambiguity and the probability of making wrong assumptions and interpretations that can lead to conflict, delays and other unpleasant results. Figure 4.3 shows the typical communication links of a project manager along with the function of each link.[6]

Listening—The key element of team communications

Listen actively, opportunity knocks softly.

— Anonymous

Listening is the communication skill that project managers and team members most need to develop and use. One of the most important components of communication, listening involves paying attention, not interrupting, not changing the subject, and not taking over. While listening, you should try to make every team member with whom you interact feel that what he or she is saying is very important for you at that moment.

Figure 4.3 Communication Channels and Links

	Relationship	Provides	Expects	Skills
A	Top Management/ Client/Sponsor	Status and warnings	Organizational support, feedback, decisions, requirements, funding	Problem solving, system setup and reporting
B	Functional Managers, Other Project Managers	Planning and coordination	Technical support and cooperation	Negotiating and contracting
C	Project team members, Contractors, Subcontractors, Subordinates	Leadership direction and control	Quality and conformance to requirements	Planning, team building, and coordination
D	External Stakeholders: Regulatory Agencies, Public Press	Ongoing information	Feedback and support	Public relations and interfacing

Source: R. Max Wideman. 1994. Personal communication.

Remember that each communication may have a significant impact on some aspect of your project. *Therefore, don't miss that vital message: listen actively and effectively.*

Guidelines for effective listening. Effective listeners are effective receivers and are often very effective communicators. (However, sometimes a good listener may be a poor speaker or vice versa because of shyness or other personal habits.) They are equally aware, in addition to the verbal

Table 4.1 What Makes a Good Listener

The Poor Listener...	The Good Listener...
Always interrupts	Does not interrupt
Is impatient	Waits until the end, then asks questions
Makes hasty judgments	Asks for clarification
Shows disinterest (poor posture, wandering eyes)	Pays close attention
Doesn't try to understand	Verifies understanding by repeating what was said
Doesn't respond	Gives feedback: smiles, nods, or frowns
Mentally prepares an argument to "win"	Avoids arguing and its negative effects on relationship
Reacts to person, loses temper	Responds to idea, not to person
Fidgets with pen, paper clips	Gets rid of distractions
Goes off the subject	Concentrates on both the words and the feeling behind them; stays on track

component of communication, of the influence of vocal tones, facial expressions and other nonverbal components including body language, eye contact, gestures and mannerisms, empathy, dress, surroundings, symbols, interpersonal space. They empathize with the speaker, ask questions to clarify the message, and give frequent feedback so that the sender can evaluate the accuracy of his or her message. The characteristics of poor and good listeners are summarized in Table 4.1.[7]

Effective listening, within a project team, requires paying attention to the task, relationship and environment dimensions of communication (see Figure 4.4).[6] It requires every team member to be genuinely concerned for each other as a person, be neutral on all subjects, and take an objective approach. It requires patience, which means that no one should make decisions for the other party, but help them to verbalize their own decisions. Developing mutual trust and respect makes both parties feel comfortable in talking and listening. All team members must identify and overcome the barriers to effective listening that exist within their own project team. The following practical guidelines for effective listening will help build trust and good relationships and hence enhance team performance. These guidelines emphasize patience, empathy, and creating a permissive and appropriate environment.[8]

Stop talking! Decision makers who do not listen have less information upon which to base decisions—and you cannot listen while you are talking.

Figure 4.4 Main Elements of Listening

L — **Look** (observe vocal tones and body language)

I — **Involvement and Interest** (take interest in the other person as a human being)

S — **Summarize** (paraphrase to confirm and verify real meaning of the message)

T — **Territory** (manage the space appropriately; lean forward to reduce distance)

E — **Empathy** (listen "between the words" to understand feelings)

N — **Nod** (to show that you understand)

As Polonius said in Shakespeare's *Hamlet*, "Give every man thine ear, but few thy voice."

Show the speaker that you are ready to listen. Put the speaker at ease by creating a "permissive" communication-friendly environment. Some elements of such an environment are:

Silence. A space in the conversation, even if uncomfortable, should be tolerated. It encourages others to talk by signaling that you are ready to listen, and are waiting patiently to hear what they have to say.

Few distractions. Shut the door, put the phone on hold, and refrain from impatient mannerisms such as doodling, tapping pencils, shuffling papers, opening mail. These communicate lack of time and/or respect for the speaker.

A receptive attitude. Make an effort to empathize with the speaker's point of view. Listen for the total meaning, not just for points of opposition. Use one ear to listen for the meaning of the words, and the other to "hear" the feelings behind them. Allow plenty of time for the communication to take place—if it runs over, end it in a manner sensitive to the speaker's feelings, not by interrupting, walking away or repeatedly checking your watch.

Ask questions to encourage further communication and the development of a point. This proves to the speaker that you are paying attention.

And, above all, hold your temper. An angry person takes things the wrong way. Suspend judgment while listening in order to avoid putting the speaker on the defensive. Don't argue—even if you win, you lose by impairing the relationship.

166

LISTENING IS AN IMPORTANT PART of project communication. Through effective listening, project managers, as well as team members, are able to identify problem areas, prepare better negotiation and conflict management strategies, make decisions, and resolve problems among clients, project team members, and other stakeholders. Effective listeners are also effective communicators because they really become involved in the communication process. Effective listening develops a better appreciation of what the other person is thinking and feeling because giving and asking for feedback clarifies meaning. Failure to listen effectively not only creates problems but also affects business relationships.

Building effective team communications

Practice empathy. Try to see things from the other person's point of view.
— Anonymous

The communication skills of project managers are challenged by lack of authority, overlapping areas of responsibility, and potential conflict with and among project team members. Yet effective communication within the project team and between the project manager, team members and all external stakeholders is essential for team building and a smoothly functioning project team. Openness in communication is a gateway to real teamwork and high performance.[9] It improves working relationships among project team members and creates mutual trust.

Communication involves more than just writing a memo, sending an electronic mail or speaking to someone on phone or face to face. It involves understanding, good working relationships and trust. Project managers should not assume that there is an effective team communication just because people are talking to each other. Openness in communication is a gateway to real teamwork and high performance.[9] Because the needs of project team members may change as the project progresses through its life cycle, there are six possible areas of action that a project manager should use to enhance project communications and team building throughout the project life cycle.[3]

Be an effective communicator. Project managers are engaged for most of their working hours in some form of communication: conferences, meetings, writing memos, reading reports, and talking with team members, top management, functional managers, customers, clients, contractors, subcontractors, suppliers, etc. At least one-half of their communication time will be with project team members and therefore this time must be managed effectively. Being a good communicator does not mean you need to be eloquent public speakers, accurate technical writers, or spellbinders, but they must recognize the importance of:[3]

- Interpersonal communication between team members
- Human relations factors in the success of communication flow and team building

Developing Effective Project Teams

- Harmony, cohesiveness and mutual trust in enhancing communication among team members
- Cultural differences, which must be appreciated in order to avoid communication breakdowns.

Project managers must recognize that communication is a two-way street. They should not just give orders, and the project team members must understand, participate and accept project plans to achieve teamwork. Feedback is essential in both directions for team building and continuous team effort.

Be a communication expeditor. Successful project managers expedite all channels and link of project communications. They establish both formal (reporting and responsibility) and informal communication channels. Effective informal communication within and outside the project team enhances good interpersonal relationships and smooth working project team.

In order to develop effective project teams, its members must be willing and able to communicate in ways that reflect openness, trust, and respect. Effective team communication practices include:[5]

Sharing information without withholding or rationing information that could be useful to other team members. Information should be viewed as a tool to empower the whole team—not any one member.

Providing feedback is very important in a team environment. Team members need to know if their individual performance is contributing to team's performance or not. Feedback should be given in a timely manner without putting people down or given conflicting or hidden messages.

Encouraging participation is what gets everyone working together and committed to meeting team goals. Active participation from project team members leads to innovation, creativity, effective problem solving, and better decision-making. Some team members may ask questions or disagree with team decisions in order to ask for clarification of some issues or highlight something that no one may have considered yet. Supportive behavior from other team members will lead to wider acceptance of plans and decisions and hence increased commitment to implement them.

Project managers can never be sure of real communication within project team. Project managers must create a conducive environment and expedite communications among team members especially during early stages of the team-building process when team members do not feel free to talk with each other. They should make sure that the right people communicate to each other as effectively as possible.

Minimize communication blockers. Too many good ideas are suppressed by negative attitudes before being considered seriously. Negative thinkers prefer to come up with several reasons why something will not work, rather than figure out ways to make it work. People who overdo the "devil's advocate" role are more likely to develop this inclination and act as communication blockers, seriously impeding the process of team building. They respond negatively to any innovative ideas. The following types of responses, characteristic of negative thinking, are considered "idea killers":[3]

- It will never work.
- It has been done before.
- The boss won't approve it.
- That's interesting, but ...
- It will never fly.
- It costs too much.
- Let's be realistic.
- It will take ages.
- The customer will not agree.

Sometimes there are too many such communication blockers in a project team, and their way of thinking cannot be changed. In such circumstances, project managers should try to find team members who are less sensitive, have positive attitude and commitment to teamwork, and who will not be discouraged by such negative comments.

Use a tight matrix. A "tight matrix" refers to bringing together all team members in one location or close proximity. This is an organizational option to improve communication and teamwork in a matrix. Normally, most project personnel work on project activities in their own functional departments and only go to the project site or office when attending meetings or conferences. Bringing them together to work in the same area can be extremely effective in facilitating effective communications, timely input and feedback, and rapid team building. The tight matrix enhances teamwork by decreasing outside distractions and focusing the efforts of the entire team on the same problems.

Unfortunately, a tight matrix is not practical for some projects where team members can work more effectively in their own disciplinary environment. This is particularly true of scientists, engineers, and other technical specialists who need to use special facilities, equipment, and support from their own discipline. Part-time people may not be able to adjust to a tight matrix. In addition, both functional managers and top management may oppose the idea of moving people temporarily from their departments to work on projects.[3]

The concept of the tight matrix has been used very effectively in construction, new product development, public works, and in other similar projects. It facilitates *concurrent engineering* by having the designers with their drafting boards and computers, working next to the manufacturing engineers. Concurrent engineering helps ensure that the project is designed in such a manner that it is also cost effective to manufacture. A tight matrix may not be a solution for all team-building problems but it certainly facilitates communication and teamwork.

Developing Effective Project Teams

Have a war room. The "war room" creates an environment to strengthen communication and teamwork. The term was used by project managers in defense and aerospace industries to refer to an office or conference room where the project or any members of the project team can get together for any purpose. It can also be referred to as the control room or the project information room. For very small projects, it can be the project manager's office, whereas large projects may require a large conference room.

The war room can be used at any time by any group of project team members. It should display project artifacts, models, records, and almost anything that conveys the feelings of teamwork and indicates outcomes of working together. This room can also be used for displaying organization charts, sample specifications, up-to-date wall charts of technical performance, schedule, and cost status. If considered appropriate, the project implementation manual (showing policies and procedures), list of vendors and contractors can also be stored in the war room. With an effective use of the war room, no one can use the excuse that they did not know what was going on.

Manage project meetings effectively. Meetings have become a way of life in project management, providing a means to exchange and share messages, ideas and information. Project managers and team members spend an appreciable amount of time in meetings. The effectiveness of these meetings depends upon the emphasis a project manager places on communication and the success in achieving it. Many project managers feel that cohesive team effort can only be built and maintained through meetings, *meetings and more meetings.*

On average, a project manager spends approximately eight years of his or her lifetime in meetings.[10] Therefore, in a project environment, where schedules are normally tight, it is important to develop specific ways to make team meetings more focused and productive. This can be done by ensuring that both leaders and participants play their roles properly. Following are some commonsense ideas that can be used to make team meetings more productive:

The leader's role is to set expectations, stay focused and on track, and increase participation. Participation increases acceptance and hence commitment, or "buy-in."

The participant's role is to be prepared, look confident and interested, and speak up without monopolizing the discussion.

The role of humor is both to raise and to *indicate* the level of morale. If morale is low, humor will go underground and project participants will become cynical snipers. Humor should be healthy; that is, not sarcastic or directed at any particular team member. Avoid humor based on ethnic or gender bias at all times. The type of jokes published by *Reader's Digest* provide a guideline.[10]

170

Managers dislike meetings—especially if they are called by someone else. Undoubtedly, well-run project meetings provide an effective focus to manage the *project* successfully; but sometimes, project managers can resolve important issues and problems by working individually with the team members by telephone, personal discussion, or a brief ad hoc meeting.

It is not certain how cost-effective meetings are as a way of managing communications in a project environment. Unfortunately, many meetings are unproductive, poorly conceived and badly run. They may dampen inspiration and enthusiasm. They may do nothing towards achieving teamwork and only serve as a forum for furthering the personal aspirations of some aggressive participants. Meetings require a great deal of time and effort and therefore should only be called when necessary. Therefore, it is important to understand when and how many meetings are necessary, and how to run project meetings effectively.[3]

In order to build effective team communication, project managers must ensure that all project meetings hold the interest and attention of all participants. Project managers must remember that good project meetings don't end with communication at the meeting itself. They must then get team members to follow through on their promises by obtaining their commitments to the outcome. There is an extensive literature on "dos and don'ts" for conducting effective meetings. Project managers can increase the interest, participation and level of commitments by using the techniques shown in Figure 4.5 to create a GREAT meeting; that is, one that enhances team building and makes team members more effective and productive.[6]

Effective communication is the key to high team performance. It can be achieved by creating open communication environment, clarifying roles and responsibilities of all team members and encouraging genuine participation of all team members in planning, team activities, and decision-making.[2,3]

Effective Team Decision-Making

A decision is a judgment. It is a choice between alternatives but rarely a choice between right and wrong.

— *Peter F. Drucker*

According to Peter Drucker, Japanese managers encourage active participation from team members, which often leads to well accepted and better quality decisions. They have developed a systematic and standardized approach to decision-making that emphasizes consensus. However, their approach or process of making decisions is very different from that used by their counterparts in North America and Europe.[11]

Figure 4.5   Main Elements of a Great Meeting

G   **Goals** for the meeting should be SMART: Specific, Measurable, Achievable, Results-oriented and Timely.

R   **Roles and Rules:** roles should be rotated among project team members, so that everyone gets an opportunity to show leadership. Ground-rules for discussion should be agreed upon beforehand.

E   **Expectations** should be clearly defined.

A   **Agendas** should be distributed in advance.

T   **Time** is money so be sensitive to the team member's scheduling needs. Keep it brief; begin and end meetings on time.

About team decision-making

Making decisions and solving problems are some of the most important elements of project management. Decisions cover a large spectrum of problems including all the whats, whens, whos, wheres, whys, and hows that may come up during any phase of the project life cycle. Whether making small or large decisions, good project management requires asking and answering the following questions:

- What has to be done and where? (scope)
- Why should it be done? (justification)
- How well must it be done? (quality)
- When is it required and in what sequence? (schedule)
- How much will it cost? (budget/cost)
- What are uncertainties? (risk)
- Who should do the job? (human resources)
- How to organize people to work in teams (communication/interpersonal skills)
- How shall we know? (information dissemination/communication). [12]

Project managers are expected to be good decision makers because they have the responsibility for decisions associated with the traditional and basic functions of management which involve planning, organizing, leading, monitoring and controlling.

All project activities focus on decision-making in one way or another. Development of project plans at the outset requires decision-making about the future. Expediting efforts require decisions based on cost benefit analysis. Data gathering and evaluation of alternatives affects the deci-

172

sions on progress. Negotiation and ongoing problem solving require decisions on compromise. [7]

Clearly, the project team's mission is to make sound, logical decisions based on the best information available and which will lead to the best solutions.

Why and when team decision-making? With increased complexity of projects characterized by multiple disciplines, technological uncertainties, international interactions, complex financing arrangements and multiproject environments, it is very unreasonable to expect one person to know everything that is going on. One person does not have the expertise to make decisions that may have a critical impact on the project and hence on the whole organization. Information from varied sources becomes essential and team decision-making becomes more effective.

Team decision-making is also a practical technique for obtaining broad-based commitment from team members. However, sometimes it is used when there is a lack of agreement on the decision criteria, and when a project manager feels that he/she has or can manipulate the team's solution to important decisions. Some project managers may make the decisions themselves and implement them. However, by manipulating the project team, they may give the impression of democracy and achieve increased commitment to the decisions outcome from those who participated in it. Whenever such a participation and involvement of the team members is just "lip service," it does not lead to effective results in the long run.

Advantages and disadvantages of team decision-making. Decisions can be made individually, by team members, or the project team as a group; each has its own strengths and weaknesses. Neither approach is ideal for all situations. However, teams offer several major advantages over individuals making decisions.[13] Two heads are better than one; and decisions made by teams incorporate more complete information and knowledge. This additional input brings a greater quantity and diversity of ideas into decision-making.

In addition, team-based decisions lead to increased acceptance of the solution because of team involvement in the process. Team decision-making encourages participation in the process which increases the commitment and motivation to carry out the decision thus facilitating its implementation.

Also, because team decision-making follows a democratic approach, this makes the resulting decisions more legitimate than those made autocratically and arbitrarily by a single person (project manager, client or anyone else).

However, team decision-making does have some drawbacks. Because it is time consuming it may lead to inefficiencies. And the pressures to conform inherent in groups may lead to a desire to be accepted, squashing

Developing Effective Project Teams

any overt disagreements even if conflicting viewpoints could be logical and worth considering.

The ambiguous nature of responsibility in teams, where no single person is responsible and all team members share the responsibility, works well if decisions lead to a successful outcome. But if not, it can result in finger-pointing and back-stabbing.

Despite the benefits of team decision-making, its inappropriate use may waste project resources because the time of the team members could have used more effectively on other project activities. It can create boredom and reduce motivation. Moreover, inappropriate use of individual team member's decisions can result in inaccuracies, poor coordination, lower acceptance, lower quality and less creativity.[14]

Continuum of team decisions. A project team or a task group gains more autonomy as it deals with important decisions. Moreover, these types of decisions are cumulative in nature; that is, a project team that can decide on additional tasks to be undertaken, will generally be able to decide when it will work and which methods to use to accomplish those tasks. Teams can generally expand their decision-making abilities along a continuum of increasingly responsible choices, as shown below, if they are given room to grow by management:

1. Team members have almost no ability to influence decisions about functions of the team.

2. Team members individually decide their roles and how they will fulfill their obligations.

3. Team decides on internal leadership, depending on the task at hand.

4. Team decides on recruitment and selection of new members.

5. Team decides how to accomplish tasks.

6. Team decides its work schedule and holidays.

7. Team decides what additional responsibilities to undertake.

8. Team can influence quantitative goals.

9. Team can influence long term and qualitative goals.[15]

Elements of decision situations. Before discussing rational team decision-making, it is important to understand the elements of decision situations to be recognized and evaluated. According to Wilson and Alexis, there are six elements of the decision situation.[16]

The state of nature refers to those external and internal environmental factors that influence the decision makers.

The decision makers themselves; the individuals or project teams who actually select an alternative. Ernest Dale identified the four following different orientations of weak decision makers.[17]

- Receptive decision makers rely heavily on suggestions from other people and basically like others to make decisions for them.

- Exploitive decision makers take ideas from others and normally extend no credit for the ideas to anyone but themselves.

- Hoarding decision makers preserve the status quo as much as possible and emphasize maintaining their present position.
- Marketing decision makers make decisions that will enhance their value and therefore are conscious of what others think of their decisions.

Ideal decision makers emphasize reason and good judgment and do not possess these undesirable decision-making qualities.

The goals to be served. Decision makers are always seeking to attain the project objectives that should help converge towards organizational objectives.

The relevant alternatives. There should be at least two relevant alternatives that are feasible and can be implemented to solve an existing problem. Otherwise, there's no decision to be made.

The ordering of alternatives. The decision makers must outline criteria, process and mechanism to rank alternatives. The process could be subjective (based on past experience) or objective (based on rate of progress or earned value analysis).

The choice of alternatives. The alternative chosen must maximize the benefits to project goals.

Rational decision-making process

As human beings, we are endowed with freedom of choice and we cannot shuffle off our responsibility upon the shoulders of God or nature. We must shoulder it ourselves. It is up to us.

— *Arnold J. Toynbee*

A decision is choosing one alternative from a set of available alternatives. The decision-making process refers to a step-by-step approach that a decision maker may use to actually choose this alternative. The best decision-making process is the one that works within the context in question. In decision-making, being right is not enough; whether the solution will work or not is the true test.

Personal qualities for effective decision-making. Decision-making is one of the most important skills the project managers should have. It is both an art and a science. There are four basic qualities of a good decision maker.[13]

Judgment. Humans are not computers. It is not always possible to perfectly assimilate and evaluate all the information. While most project managers demonstrate sound judgment in their decisions, errors still occur. Project managers should try to get accurate, timely and relevant information to support their decision.

Experience. In general, experience is most valuable for routine and programmed decisions (during the implementation phase of conventional construction projects for example) and least valuable for non-routine and non-programmed decisions (such as front-end planning and commissioning phases). Experience also tends to increase with the level in the organization.

Developing Effective Project Teams

Experience becomes a key factor in estimating contingencies and dealing with project stakeholders.

Creativity. Creativity is the ability to uncover a solution no one else saw and identify truly unique alternatives. In a project environment, creativity in decision-making is needed not only in technical aspects but also in integration and interface management when dealing with clients, team members, top management, functional managers and external shareholders. However, the value of creativity is reduced by overemphasis on short-term goals and lack of encouragement to try out new ideas. Unfortunately, in such cases, creativity may not be sought because of human and organizational constraints. Visible problems may be emphasized and only the solutions that are "good enough" (generally in the short term) are implemented. Creativity is generally encouraged and nurtured in an organizational climate or culture that supports innovation and tolerance for risk or in situations when the visible, obvious and safe alternatives are not acceptable.

Quantitative skills. As with creativity, quantitative skills are meaningful when the decision makers seek optimum solutions. Quantitative tools can improve the quality of decision-making but are still not widely used in managing projects. The reason is that project managers are seeking immediate rather than optimum solutions, and generally it is hard to validate the assumptions used in quantitative models. The use of quantitative tools tends to increase with the size, complexity and number of variables in the project and/or the organization. Some of the common quantitative tools are linear programming (for manufacturing projects), queuing theory (which balances the costs and benefits of waiting in line against the cost of maintaining that line), probability theory (to reduce risk), inventory models (to minimize the cost of carrying inventory for new products and marketing projects), break- even analysis (addressing financial aspects of the project), and network analysis (for scheduling and control).

Rational decision-making model. Once the decision is made to actively involve project team members in making decisions, project managers need to think of an appropriate decision-making model or process. The project team's mission is to make good decisions leading to the best solutions. Some project managers like to make decisions by using a step-by-step game plan while others favor a less structured yet still disciplined approach that requires maintaining a healthy debate and exploring new ideas until full consensus is reached. Rational decision-making can be illustrated by a six-phase model[18] that assumes that the project team has achieved the performing stage of group development discussed earlier. The six phases can be briefly described as follows:[18]

Phase I: Problem Definition. In this phase the project team should fully explore, clarify and define the problem. They must identify symptoms and causes, generate and collect information (from internal and external sources), define and clarify the project goals (which could be a problem in

176 ───────────────────────────────

itself), determine the relative priority of solving the problem (to properly allocate resources).

Phase II: Problem Solution Generation. Phase II requires prolonging the new idea generating process by brainstorming solution activities and discouraging premature decisions. In complex project environments, generating more new ideas and alternatives generally leads to better solutions. However, some project teams tend to be more solution-oriented than idea-oriented and consequently they take a shortcut, choosing a solution before they have generated enough ideas.

Phase III: Ideas to Action. In this phase, the team members define the criteria and then evaluate the alternatives according to that criteria by analyzing their pros and cons and selecting the best solution. All alternatives or options should be considered until everyone agrees on a solution. Project managers can initiate and use this phase effectively to resolve technical problems or come up with ideas to save time and costs through the life cycle of the project—as long as the process itself does not delay the project!

Phase IV: Solution Action Planning. Once the solution is selected, the project team plans to implement the solution by involving the key participants in order to get their acceptance of and commitment to making the solution work. The project manager creates an environment that encourages the project team to plan and organize resources, anticipate implementation problems and work out solutions together. Getting the commitment of the team members to the chosen solution is the key to a successful outcome.

Phase V: Solution Evaluation Planning. This refers to a postmortem analysis. This phase, if used constructively, offers the greatest potential for group learning in problem solving. The project team should avoid finger pointing and instead focus on extracting the lessons or mistakes that must be avoided in future projects. Determining what kind of evaluation information is needed, who will obtain it and when it should be collected, combined with honest and open discussion will offer the maximum learning opportunity.

Phase VI: Evaluation of the Outcome and the Process. In this extension of Phase V the project team should focus on how well the problem was solved or project goals were achieved. It may lead to redefining the problem, generating more alternatives, and reviewing the assessment procedure and/or modifying the implementation plan. As suggested in the group development stages discussed earlier, open and constructive evaluation of the product and process increases the maturity level of the team members.

Team decision-making rarely proceeds as smoothly as suggested in the six phase model. Problem solving groups often jump around and skip phases. However the decision-making process, discussed in this section, should lead to rational, high-quality and well-accepted decisions. Rational decision-making models assume that the project team members have sufficient technical knowledge and expertise, a reasonable level of maturity and above all an attitude to participate actively and constructively by generating and supporting new ideas. This process is particularly vital in improving the effectiveness of interacting task groups, in multidisciplinary projects or in a multiproject environment.

Decision styles in a team environment

The decision-making style depends upon several factors, which are discussed below along with the four basic decision styles, and how decision styles are related to the types of the problem. The first question must be: Which of the four styles to choose?

Four decision styles. According to Roskin's model[19] there are four basic decision styles normally used by project managers: command, consultation, consensus, and coin flip (random).

Command style. If quality is more important than acceptance, then a "command" style (where a project manager makes the decision individually) is appropriate, provided the project manager has in-depth knowledge and experience about the situation. Unpleasant or tough decisions are often made this way.

Consultation style. When quality and acceptance are both important, the project manager should use a "consultation" style that allows for some involvement of team members but allows project managers to maintain control over the final decision. In this style, team members are free to express their opinions but the project manager makes the final decision.

Consensus style. If acceptance is more important than quality, then a "consensus" style (where all team members are involved and reach an agreement) is practical. Most Japanese institutions make decisions by consensus. Consensus is achieved only when every team member can honestly say:[20]

• "I believe that you understand my point of view."
• "I believe that I understand your point of view."
• "I will support this decision whether I prefer it or not, because it was arrived at in an open and fair manner."

Advantages and disadvantages of consensus style. Decisions made through consensus have both advantages and disadvantages. Some of the advantages are that project managers can focus "several heads" on making a decision. Also, team members are more likely to be committed to implement a decision if they helped make it.

The disadvantages of consensus style are that discussions may become quite lengthy and hence costly. And some project teams may never reach real consensus and may have to use voting system, in which case it is bet-

178

ter to use odd number of voting members to avoid deadlocks (useful when deciding on successful bidders to award various contracts).

Despite its drawbacks, decision-making by consensus is highly effective. Negotiated agreement reached by consensus pays off in terms of increased productivity because of involvement in the decision-making process of the parties who will ultimately perform the tasks. This process, according to Ouchi,[20] also breeds trust and loyalty, which are intimately connected with productivity. The corresponding American model, which shares such managerial traits as intimacy, loyalty, and trust, has been dubbed as the "type Z" organization.[20]

In summary, Japanese decision-making and the corresponding American model used at companies like Hewlett Packard, 3M, and Proctor and Gamble, are based on the proposition that generalized commitment is necessary to reach the highest productivity levels. Commitment in turn comes from participant involvement obtained through consensus decision-making.

Coin flip style. If neither quality nor acceptance are important, then a "flip of the coin" is as good as anything.

Factors affecting decision styles. The Rick Roskin model allows project managers to decide when they should make decisions individually or when and how they should use project teams. According to this model, there are four major factors that affect the decision style.[15]

Time Constraints. When time is critical, decisions are made individually in a command style.

Trust. The level of trust between the project managers and their peers and team members (those affected by the decision). In case of a high level of trust, project managers should use the consultation style. However, in case of high trust, sometimes if decisions are made in a command style, they will be accepted as long as it is not overdone.

Quality. The need for making the "right" or the "best" decision. This is more important when the level of trust is low. Also, if the quality of the decision is critical (design criteria, safety factors, etc.) then the project managers should keep some control over it themselves otherwise they may adversely influence the decision-making process.

Acceptance. The importance of gaining acceptance and commitment to the decision. If the acceptance of project team members is critical, then they must be involved in making it, to gain their commitment to implement the decisions.

The project manager weighs each of the above four factors in turn and decides whether the decisions should be made individually, after consulting with others, or as a team.

Developing Effective Project Teams

Guidelines for effective team decision-making

The decision-making process is complex by nature because of the need to generate, evaluate and select an alternative under somewhat unknown conditions. Therefore there is no "best" process of making decisions. "Will it work?" is the true test of decisions and the processes used to reach them. See Figure 4.6 for some guidelines.

Focus on goals to be served. The goals to be attained are the most important elements of a decision-making situation. The decision should contribute towards meeting the project goals and objectives. As discussed earlier, goals should be specific, clear, time-based, measurable and realistic, but challenging.

Follow the rational decision-making process. Follow a step-by-step game plan to make decisions in a team that meet the criteria of effectiveness and efficiency with emphasis on accuracy, speed, creativity, and degree of acceptance (which helps gain the commitment of team members).

A rational and well-documented decision-making process is logical. It can also motivate team members because it emphasizes their active participation and therefore they feel that they are "in it all the way."

Study the environmental factors. To make a sound, rational decision, it is important to study both the external and internal environment. Decision makers should not overlook important and relevant environmental factors that may influence them.[21]

Develop personal qualities. Project managers must acquire and help team members develop basic personal qualities—judgment, experience, creativity, and knowledge of quantitative tools, which can help make a quality decision.

Stimulate team creativity. Creativity is the key to effective decision-making. Project managers must encourage new ideas and creativity in solving problems and making quality decisions leading to optimum outcomes. Two approaches for stimulating team creativity are:[15]

Nominal Group Technique (NGT). Group members pool their judgment and then determine a satisfactory solution. NGT emphasizes idea generation, increases attention to each idea (by recording and clarifying ideas) and a greater likelihood of balanced participation and presentation by each group member. NGT may be most effective when there are certain barriers or problems in a team, such as a few dominating members.[15]

Electronic Brainstorming (EB). Brainstorming is a group process in which team members express as many ideas in a given time period (20-60 minutes) and then the project manager compiles and evaluates those ideas. However, in face-to-face brainstorming groups, some team members may be prevented from producing ideas because someone else is talking or they may exercise self-censorship because of lack of confidence.

180

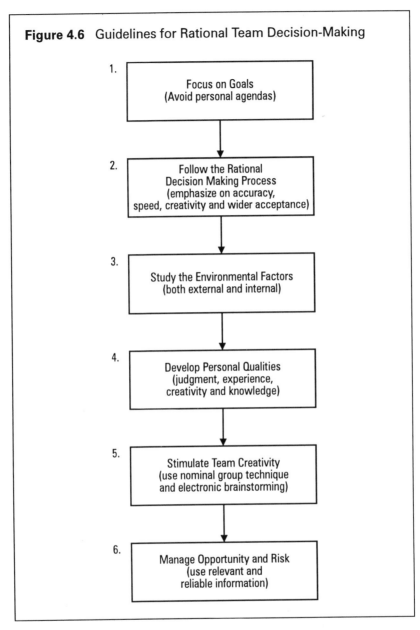

Figure 4.6 Guidelines for Rational Team Decision-Making

1. Focus on Goals
(Avoid personal agendas)

2. Follow the Rational
Decision Making Process
(emphasize on accuracy,
speed, creativity and wider acceptance)

3. Study the Environmental Factors
(both external and internal)

4. Develop Personal Qualities
(judgment, experience,
creativity and knowledge)

5. Stimulate Team Creativity
(use nominal group technique
and electronic brainstorming)

6. Manage Opportunity and Risk
(use relevant and
reliable information)

Electronic brainstorming involves the use of computer technology to facilitate the entry and automatic dissemination of ideas in real time to all members in a team, each of whom may be stimulated to generate other ideas. The team uses a software tool called "Electronic Brainstorming" and every team member has a terminal networked with other team members.

Developing Effective Project Teams

Every time any individual enters an idea, a random set of the group's ideas are presented on the individual's screen. The individual can continue to see new random sets if he or she wishes.[22] Preliminary research indicates that electronic brainstorming produces significantly more non-redundant ideas than ordinary face-to-face brainstorming. It maintains privacy because members do not know the originator of ideas, which leads to more free idea generation. There is no need to fear "sounding like a fool" to fellow team members or project manager in the spontaneous generation of ideas.[23]

Manage opportunity and risk. Results of alternatives are always somewhat uncertain and therefore most decisions made in a project environment have both opportunity and risk associated with them. It is important to identify and evaluate the tradeoffs and manage accordingly. The degree of opportunity/risk depends upon the quality of information available to make the decision. For example, the lower the quality of information related to the outcome of an alternative, the more uncertain the situation is and the higher will be the risk and the lower the opportunity.

THE STUDY OF TEAM decision-making concepts, techniques, decision-making model, and styles can help both the project manager or leader and the team members, become more effective in making decisions in a project environment. Sometimes good decisions are made individually by the project manager, sometimes by a process of consultation; and sometimes with the full consensus of everyone directly concerned. When each of these methods is most appropriate depends upon the situation.

Managing Project Teams During the Project

Hold yourself responsible for a higher standard than anybody else expects of you. Never excuse yourself.

— *Henry Ward Beecher*

As the project progresses, several external factors may come into play that affect the team's performance. Teams that were self-managing and well-focused earlier may start acting more like committees. The membership of the project team may have to be changed by adding or phasing out certain team members as needed to meet project requirements throughout the life cycle of a project. The project manager must be able to identify and analyze the impact of changing membership of the project team and of external factors and minimize their impact to meet the project objectives within the constraints of scope, quality, time and costly.

Changing project team members according to project life cycle

Since projects are dynamic, the composition of the project team is subject to change to suit the project life cycle. Even though members of the project team (such as the project manager, client representative, key technical area managers etc.) may remain with the project throughout its life cycle, other members (such as consultants, contractors and external shareholders) should be added or phased out depending upon project requirements. Figure 4.7 shows the typical phases and main actions to be done during each phase of a large and complex project. To manage project teams effectively, it is vital to have some mix of appropriate resources from conceptual and front-end planning through to implementation and termination. The project manager must review the project scope and upcoming milestones in terms of special resources, specific type of study or information (legal, environmental, economic impact or special regulations and by-laws, etc.) and add or phase out the team members as required. This must be done in consultation with the client representative and senior management or project sponsor. Incoming members should be properly informed of project goals and their role and responsibility.

Also, the outgoing members, as a human courtesy, should be appreciated for their efforts and contribution to the project so that they continue feeling proud of their affiliation with the project. This will not only motivate existing team members, but will also reinforce outgoing members positively and they will then be more willing to help with the project in the future, if needed. This appreciation can be shown by giving appropriate rewards and recognition, such as formal letters of appreciation with copies to their supervisors and top management, awards, and/or economic rewards.

Sometimes project managers may prefer to give these rewards and recognition at the completion of the project along with the whole project team. This helps reinforce a positive team spirit that is valuable for the organization and enable successful completion of future projects.

External factors affecting team performance

Project teams are made of a diverse mix of personnel with special expertise, norms, individual expectations and personal goals. Several external factors may arise that will undoubtedly have an effect on the team's performance. Here are just a few of the factors that should be evaluated on an on-going basis, and corrective actions taken to minimize negative impact.[2]

Poor performers. All projects are not blessed with superstars. Typically, most project teams are made up of average or even poor performers. Poor performers are not only non-productive, but they also distract and drag down good performers around them. Project managers must use their skills to get rid of poor performance and increase the productivity of average performers by using the following steps:[2]

- Determine if poor performers are competent. Assign them the tasks that match their level of ability.
- Use performance feedback and counseling if poor performers are aware that they are perceived as such, otherwise talk to them, give them the

Figure 4.7 Project Phases and Actions for a Large and Complex Project

	1. Concept or Initiation (1–2 Years)	2. Review & Fund Feas. Study (0.5–1 Year)	3. Project Definition or Feasibility Study (1–1.5 Years)	4. Review & Full Funding (0.5–1.5 Year)	5. Organize (2–3 months)	Design Development, & Production	6. Install & Commission (1–2 Years)	7. Achieve Full Potential (3–10 Years)
Phases					← 3–5 Years →			
Actions	• Identify need (gather user support) • Establish technical feasibility • Establish goals, estimate resources • Economic impact studies (for political support) • Motivate international interest	• Technical and other reviews and decision to fund feasibility study	• Engineering feasibility study • Prototyping • Concept designs • Better cost estimates & schedules • International commitments • Industrial capacity • Economic impact & spin-offs study	• Reviews and decision for full funding	• Overall project management approach • Overall plans & schedules • Define scope WBS and resources • Build up project teams & design teams • Evaluate prototyping requirements	• Major work assoc. with design development construction & fabrication • Procure major components • Assemble & acceptance tests for major components • Site preparation for installation and commission	• Installation of major parts of research facility is completed, followed by commissioning • Test the system & commission for reliable operation	• Peripheral facilities installed & commissioned • Upgrade as necessary to achieve full potential (can take 3–10 years)

Source: Vijay K. Verma. Organizing a feasibility study for a world class research faculty. *Proceedings of the 1989 Seminar/Symposium*, Drexel Hill, PA: Project Management Institute, p. 338.

warning and clarify your expectations that they must meet to stay on the team.

• If neither reassignment nor counseling helps, then try to get them off the project if politically possible. Otherwise just isolate them to avoid any negative influence on other team members.

Turnover. Turnover during the project can cause a negative impact on the team because of the extra time and effort needed to orient the new team member. The degree of impact depends upon who has left the team and the time in the project life cycle when turnover takes place (the later it is, the more impact it will have).

A functional manager should be required to give ample notice of replacements to the project manager in order to allow time for proper evaluation and solution. If the project manager disagrees with the replacement, he or she must talk to senior management before the actual transfer, because reversal of an implemented decision is often difficult and sometimes impossible. In general, circumstances change and turnover is inevitable. However, project managers can cope with this by requesting a contingency to deal with added time and cost needed to assimilate the new team member. The key issue here is not just the relative expertise of the original team member and the replacement, but the commitment, mo-

184

tivation, and the sense of ownership of the project plan. Three guidelines that can help cope with the turnover are:

- If the project manager or client is moved, the impact is significant, so plan properly.
- Reevaluate the turnover immediately and renegotiate the budget and schedule accordingly.
- If possible, try to accomplish any turnover early in the project.

Adding human resources. Adding people to the team will impact team productivity. Although adding a small number of human resources may reduce the duration of some specific activity/ies, such a direct relationship is not always true. There is a law of diminishing returns that occurs because of additional communication channels that must be established and maintained because of additional resources.[24] It can be represented by the formula:

$$I = \frac{E(E-1)}{2}$$ where I = Number of interfaces or communication channels that must be established.

E = Number of people on the project team.

The number of interactions is quite important because it can have a significant impact on the token number of person-hours required to perform the task. Therefore, beyond a certain point, the introduction of additional resources is non-productive rather than productive.

Effect of overtime. In a project environment, overtime can have a very critical effect. There are two major viewpoints concerning overtime.[2] One is that overtime is effective only when it is required for short intervals. The other view is that overtime is ineffective.

The first philosophy implies that project team members would be willing to spend overtime if they know its importance and they can see an end to it. When overtime becomes a routine practice, it is no longer effective and productive but adds to the project cost unnecessarily. F.L. Harrison has suggested that a person who works six days at twelve hours per day (72 person-hours), is approximately 88 percent productive, giving only 63.4 effective hours; and a person who works seven days at twelve hours per day (84 person-hours) is approximately 77 percent productive, giving thereby only 64.7 effective hours.[25]

Some project managers may not agree with these above estimated percentages of productivity, but they will agree with the premise that people who work too much consecutive overtime show diminished productivity.

On a project, change is a way of life and changes in circumstances impact the performance of the project team as a whole. However, project managers must try to anticipate problems and be prepared to adjust their overall plan to minimize negative impact and maintain or increase the per-

Developing Effective Project Teams

formance of their team. These factors should be kept in mind while managing the team throughout the project.

Team management

Real leaders are ordinary people with extraordinary results.

— Anonymous

Teamwork is the by-product of good project leadership. Good leadership makes everybody's work more effective and therefore more rewarding. Project team leaders must foster an environment where team members are involved, have job satisfaction and mutual trust. They must stimulate the drivers and minimize the barriers in order to develop effective project teams having a high degree of mutual trust and willingness to share information readily and openly among team members. In order to accomplish this, project managers should be aware of the various styles of team management and use them flexibly according to the situation.

Team management styles. Several management styles may be applied in a project environment. These styles basically depend upon how much authority the project managers are willing to share with team members and whether they focus more on tasks or people. Most project managers use one or more of four main styles:[26]

The autocratic style. Autocrats do not delegate responsibility and authority and team members are not involved actively in making decisions. This may work for low achievers, but only for a short time. This style does not build team players nor encourage strong ties, trust and confidence among the team members. It may cause team members to become dependent on their project managers.

The bureaucratic style. This is management "by the book" and is typified by the project manager's reliance on rules, regulations, policies and procedures. This style does little to stimulate creativity and motivate team members. A bureaucratic project manager is perceived generally as a watchdog.

The democratic style. This style uses a more modern "we" approach. These project managers tend to delegate and encourage active participation by team members in problem solving, decision-making, conflict resolution and innovations. These project managers attempt to build a strong team spirit and to foster mutual trust, respect, and interdependence between themselves (mainly as coaches) and the members of the team, as well as among the team members and their peers. This style is also known as consultative or participative style. This style of management is quite effective in a project environment and also in managing changes throughout the life cycle of the projects. Cooperation and team spirit are strongly promoted, leading to a high morale. Team members appreciate the trust, freedom and confidence expressed in them by their project manager and they tend to understand and appreciate the contribution of their peers to a greater degree.

Spectator style. This style is characterized by treating everyone as an individual. The real team concept is either played down or non-existent. These project managers make themselves available for consultation with a strong open-door policy. They do not interfere with day-to-day activities but give a significant freedom to their team members. They continually provide necessary management and administrative support as needed to meet project objectives. Team members working with such managers are mostly on their own, self-motivated, and high achievers. They strongly feel the need to prove themselves to their project managers and their peers. Consequently, they need constant reassurances and feedback that their performance is high and that they are appreciated by the project team members, team leader, top management and the client.

Each of the four styles can have a negative or a positive impact on the team members depending upon their characteristics and the situation. Like a firearm, the management style can contribute to winning prizes or inflicting injuries.

The amount of formal authority that the project manager may decide to share with the other members of the team will determine the management style of the project manager. But the decision to share authority is not totally in the hands of the project manager. The sharing of decision-making is also influenced by senior management, client/owner, and the experience and confidence of the project manager and the team members.

Project managers should also be aware of some other management style models, such as: the dimensional model of managerial behavior developed by Lefton et al.,[27] and the managerial grid developed by Blake and Mouton.[28]

The management style of project managers may vary according to the project phases, depending upon their primary strategy for managing the project. However, their daily behavior may vary considerably according to the situation, the experience level and self-confidence of the team members and their assessment of what is at stake, demands from clients, and economic factors. Each interpersonal relationship is unique because the project manager, team members and senior management members have different perspectives regarding their expectations and behaviors changing continuously. Project managers must custom tailor their approach in motivating and managing different individuals in their project teams depending upon the particular situation and circumstances.

The dimensional model of managerial behavior. This model developed by Lefton et al.,[27] presents four aspects of management styles: dominance,

Developing Effective Project Teams

Figure 4.8 Dimensional Model of Management Behavior

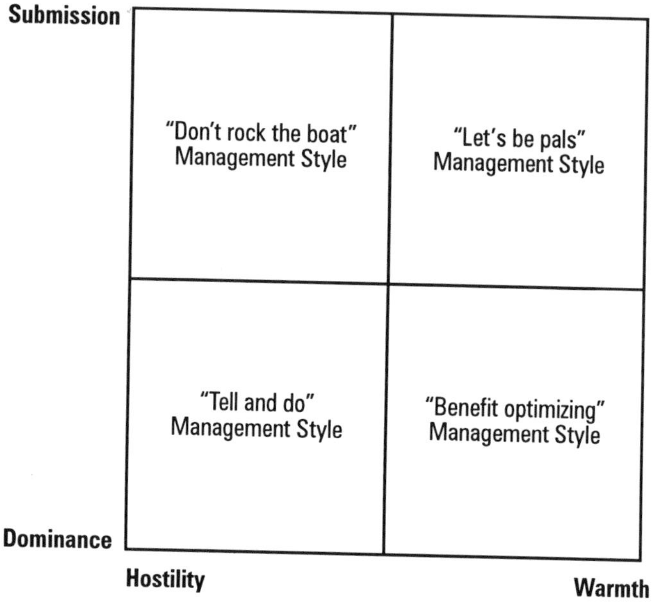

Submission

"Don't rock the boat" Management Style	"Let's be pals" Management Style
"Tell and do" Management Style	"Benefit optimizing" Management Style

Dominance

Hostility　　　　　　　　　　　　　　Warmth

Adapted from: R.E. Lefton, V.R. Buzzotta, and Mannie Sherberg, *Dimensional Management Strategies,* (St. Lewis: Psychological Associates, 1978), pp. 6–11. By permission of the publisher.

submission, hostility, and warmth. These four aspects form a matrix as shown Figure 4.8.

According to the above model, a manager's style depends upon his/her primary strategy. However, the daily behavior of a project manager may vary significantly according to the situation, experience level, self-confidence and economic factors. Therefore the project managers must be capable of custom tailoring their approach in dealing with each individual on the project team.

The Managerial Grid. The Managerial Grid developed by Blake and Mouton[28] is an often-cited concept and popular training theme for identifying managerial traits. It is a matrix that is used to show the relationship between the manager's concern for final output or work results, on the horizontal axis, and the manager's concern for people (team members and peers) on the vertical axis. The resulting grid, as shown in Figure 4.9 shows a graphic display of management style ranging from the authoritarian who is mainly concerned with production to the "nice person" who manages in the "country club management" mode, and is so wrapped up

Managing the Project Team

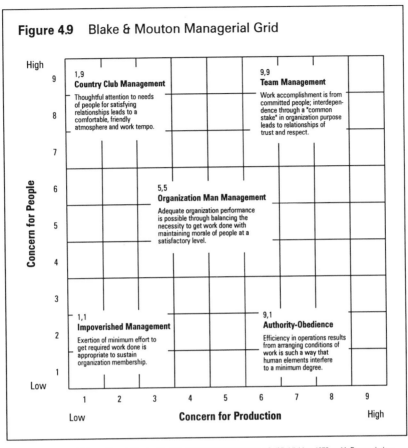

Figure 4.9   Blake & Mouton Managerial Grid

High

9 | **1,9**
Country Club Management
Thoughtful attention to needs of people for satisfying relationships leads to a comfortable, friendly atmosphere and work tempo.

8

9,9
Team Management
Work accomplishment is from committed people; interdependence through a "common stake" in organization purpose leads to relationships of trust and respect.

7

6 | **5,5**
Organization Man Management
Adequate organization performance is possible through balancing the necessity to get work done with maintaining morale of people at a satisfactory level.

5

Concern for People

4

3

2 | **1,1**
Impoverished Management
Exertion of minimum effort to get required work done is appropriate to sustain organization membership.

9,1
Authority-Obedience
Efficiency in operations results from arranging conditions of work is such a way that human elements interfere to a minimum degree.

1

Low

    1   2   3   4   5   6   7   8   9
Low   **Concern for Production**   High

Source: Robert R. Blake and Jane S. Mouton, *The New Managerial Grid*, Houston: Gulf Publishing, 1978, p. 11. By permission of the publisher.

with concern for people that production is neglected. Impoverished management refers to poor concern for both production and people.

Blake and Mouton identified five management styles based on their relative concerns for production versus people that are uniquely positioned on the managerial grid.

Self-Assessment Exercise C (see Appendix) will help gauge an organization's readiness for teams, while Exercise D measures team effectiveness.

Summary

Team development involves a whole spectrum of management skills in integrating the efforts of a diverse mix of project participants from traditional functional organizations. Project managers must enhance their skills in developing cohesive and high performing project teams. Effective team development is also one of the most critical leadership qualities that determines the overall performance and success in a project environment. Final effectiveness of team building and team development depends upon the quality of facilitation provided throughout the process.

In addition to technical directions and management expertise, project managers must coordinate team efforts. They must build a broad-based team, establish a formal leader depending upon the project phase, build and maintain a team spirit, elicit management support and keep the team members informed. They should use their power and authority wisely with more emphasis on influencing and negotiating rather than on using coercion. They should also enhance creativity in problem-solving abilities of the project team by keeping team size small, planning problem solving meetings properly, seeking active and genuine participation from team members, supporting ideas, and making problem solving a "team" issue.

Effective communication is the key to effective project team. They must know the importance of verbal and non-verbal components of communications. Project managers must understand the process of interpersonal communication, barriers to effective communication, and appropriate remedial actions, different communication channels in a project environment. They must know when and how to use written reports and project meetings. Above all, project managers must develop effective listening skills to earn the trust and respect of project team members that is vital for creating a real team spirit.

A project team communication plan has many benefits. Project managers will have fewer forgotten tasks if they remember to involve the right people early enough for project planning. Also, through effective communication, they are likely to reduce the number of wrenches thrown at the project midstream. Perhaps the strongest benefits are on the human side of the equation: You are likely to achieve greater buy-in and commitment to the project, and you may even reduce the impact of difficult people as well.

Effective communication within the project team and between the project manager, team members and all external stakeholders is vital for team building and for project success. Project managers must encourage open communication because openness is a gateway to real teamwork and high performance. It improves cohesiveness, working relationships among project team members, and enhances mutual trust. Six possible actions that a project manager should use to enhance project communications and team building include: communicating effectively, expediting communications through all channels and links, minimizing communication blockers (idea killers), using a tight matrix and war room, and managing project meetings effectively.

As the project teams mature, they want more autonomy in making decisions that affect them in terms of their roles, working relationships and overall contributions to the project. There are both advantages and disadvantages in making team decisions. On one hand, team decision-making offers more information, knowledge, and increased acceptance; but on the other hand, it may take more time and lead to ambiguous responsibility. It is important to recognize and evaluate major elements of decision-making situations.

Rational team decision-making processes should lead to rational, high quality and well accepted decisions. Such processes require project teams to acquire four basic qualities that include—judgment, experience, creativity and quantitative skills, and then follow a six-phase model, described in this chapter, to gain better acceptance of decisions made and hence stronger commitment of team members to implement the decisions.

Project managers may use anyone of the four basic decision styles—command, consultation, consensus and coin flip. The choice of decision style depends upon the situation, type of problem, and importance of time constraints, level of trust among team members, and quality versus acceptance of the decision.

Project managers can use six guidelines for effective team decision-making, which include focusing on project goals; following the rational decision-making process; studying environmental factors; developing personal qualities; stimulating team creativity through nominal group technique and electronic brain storming; and managing opportunity and risk.

Project managers must recognize the need to change the project team by adding or subtracting the team members to suit the phases in the project life cycle. They must analyze and evaluate the external factors affecting team performance: poor performers, turnover, effect of overtime and adding human resources. It must be recognized that the impact of turnover depends upon who has left the project team and at what stage. The project managers must try to minimize the negative effects of external factors and not let the project teams become committees to develop effective project teams and avoid unnecessary bureaucracy.

Project managers must make efforts to know their team members well in terms of their goals, career plans and growth aspirations. They must be flexible enough to use an appropriate team management style (according to the situation) in order to optimize overall team performance. In most cases, since project team members are generally self-motivated and keen to get a variety of project experiences, project managers should encourage their involvement in planning and decision-making and use more of a participative/democratic management style where leadership is shared between the team members and the project manager.

Developing Effective Project Teams

Outline

5

Managing Communication Challenges   194
    Creating openness in communication   194
    Enhancing performance through effective communication   196
    P=Priority   196
    A=Agreement   197
    R=Recognition   198
    C=Confront   198
    S=Sandwich approach   200

Developing Trust and Motivation   201
    Developing trust within the project team   201
    Team motivation   204

Managing Team Morale   208

Team Leadership   216
    What leadership is and what it is not   216
    The keys to leadership   217
    Common leadership styles   220
    Roles and responsibilities of leaders   221

Summary   223

Through team work, ordinary people can produce extra-ordinary results. They can lift things that come into their hands a little higher, a little further on toward the heights of excellence.
— Henry Ford

Inspiring High Team Performance

TODAY, MOST PROJECTS require a diverse mix of individuals who must be integrated into an effective unit—a project team. This requires special skill, attitude and commitment to shape those individuals into an effective team. It takes even more to make them a high-performing, winning team, especially on international projects.

Inspired performance comes from inspired people. To inspire team members for high team performance, project managers must create an environment in which everyone feels valued and committed to manage their tasks and interpersonal concerns and increase overall team performance. Inspiring high team performance involves effective team building, team development, motivating, and leading team members while also providing them with opportunities to develop and grow. Developing project teams for high performance involves emphasizing not only cost, schedule and quality parameters, but also the human interactions and feelings that arise during the project. Open communication, development of trust and high team morale must be reinforced to inspire high team performance. When full participation of team members is encouraged, it leads to their acceptance to project plans, decisions and strategies, and hence their commitment to meet project objectives. It creates a psychological bond between the project plans and those who generate them. ■

Managing Communication Challenges

Effective communication builds trust, partnership and collaboration and creates synergy in teams.

— Anonymous

Communication is complex. It involves formal or informal communication among project participants conducted in verbal, nonverbal or written form. It consists of any behavior that results in an exchange of meaning. Effective communication is vital to project success. The ability of project managers to effectively obtain and disseminate relevant project information directly affects team performance in terms of coordination and integration of effort. The communication skills of project managers are challenged because of overlapping areas of responsibility, lack of authority, delegation problems, project organizational structures and conflicts with and among various participants on the project. Yet openness in communication is a gateway to top performance.[1] It creates mutual trust that makes it easier to resolve conflicts in a constructive manner.

Creating openness in communication

Openness generates right questions and answers. It helps make right decisions.

— The Author

Normally a message communicated in a project consists of a task and relationship component. Ineffective and negative messages lead to interpersonal and task problems. Many of these problems can be prevented or handled more easily in an atmosphere of open communication

Project leaders can create open or closed communication by setting examples. They should encourage open communication in a project team because it leads to effective problem solving and decision-making and hence to higher performance. Openness in a project environment can be created in several ways. For example, the project manager can encourage task openness by repeating and summarizing the main points to confirm understanding and clarify the meanings and intentions of the message. For example:[1]

- Let me see if I understand what you are saying ...
- So the problem appears to be ...
- If I heard you correctly, the key parts of our agreement are ...
- The three main issues I think you are identifying are ...
- If I understand you correctly, you want ... Is that right?
- Help me understand why ... it is important.

Similarly, the door to open communication can be slammed shut by an "idea killer" phrase. Team members should be discouraged from closing communication by discouraging new ideas, as in:[1]

- It will never work.
- It has been done before and it does not work.
- Your approach will create more problems.

194

- It's not my problem.
- It will cost a fortune.
- Let's be realistic.
- The boss won't like it.
- That sounds interesting, but …
- I don't like it, do it again and see if you can get it right the next time.
- Excuse me while I answer this telephone call.

Create partnership and openness by respecting other people's opinions and ideas and showing your sincere commitment to support and work together as a team to resolve project problems. This can be done by saying:
- I like your idea …
- What you want to do is …
- How can I help you?
- What you need from me is …
- How can we solve the problem together?
- How can we create a better solution by partnering on this or putting our efforts together?
- Let's look into it, you can count on me for full support.[1]

And, since "actions speak louder than words," you must also create an environment that encourages openness by modeling open communication in your behavior, for example:[1]
- Sit next to the person you are communicating with, not across the desk or table (it diffuses the sense of inequality in status/power).
- Take turns speaking rather than interrupting the other person.
- Ask meaningful questions. It helps to develop further points of discussion.
- Create a permissive environment that helps the other person feel free to talk.
- Listen genuinely and attentively (as discussed in Chapter 4).
- Focus on mutual interests, not differing positions.
- Make decisions through a persuasion and consensus approach.
- Ask for feedback and give specific feedback in a timely manner.
- Go easy on argument and criticism.
- Avoid putting other person on the defensive.
- Empathize with talker; try to see the other person's point of view.
- Remove distractions; minimize noise, telephone interruptions, interruption by others, etc.
- Do not doodle, tap or shuffle papers.
- Be patient. Allow sufficient time, don't finish sentences for others and don't walk away.

Highly effective teams emphasize creating an environment of open communication. The key to open and effective communication is to create both task and relationship openness. Project leaders must set an example for openness and then facilitate the development of openness in communication as a key element of teamwork.

Inspiring High Team Performance

Enhancing performance through effective communication

Effective communication is the first step to inspire high performance.

— Anonymous

Effective communication is essential in any organization or interpersonal endeavor. Projects often fail when project participants fail to decipher and transmit appropriate information in a timely manner. The major components of communication in a project team environment are recognizing recognize good performance and confronting ineffective performance.

In the first case, the project managers should praise and give proper rewards and recognition to project participants for the job well done. This not only makes people feel happy and satisfied, but also acts as a positive reinforcement that encourages repetition of similar behavior. On the other hand, confronting a poor performer can be difficult and tricky. However, poor performance must be identified as early as possible and the poor performers given the necessary help to turn around the situation and achieve effective performance. A model that may help the manager with this task can be described by five key words represented by the acronym PARCS. This model consists of five steps, which must be followed in order, laying a foundation and building on it (see Figure 5.1).[1]

P = Priority

Have one clear priority. High-performing teams are characterized by clear, well-understood priorities. They allow sufficient opportunities to discuss and clarify team objectives. Project team members individually must understand their own priorities in relationship to project objectives and how to accomplish them. In order to achieve top performance, it is important that people are very clear about their top priority and that they use this priority as a decision tool to perform various tasks. The team may create its own No. 1 priority or carry out a No. 1 priority developed somewhere else in the organization.

In order to accept and take ownership of the top priority, project participants must define roles, boundaries and working relationships.[1]

The *roles* played by team members need to be clarified in relation to the priority by asking questions such as: How can we do our jobs according to the priority? What can we do or not do versus what we did before?

Boundaries refer to the conditions or boundaries associated with the project team such as: What are the boundaries that unite us as a team? What does it look like when we are or are not working well together? What do we do when we need to expand or change boundaries?

Working relationships reflect our feelings and perceptions about working together and can be defined by asking such questions as: What is the relationship between the work done by different team members? With whom should agreements be made about expectations to work together? and How should we raise issues of poor performance?

196 ———————————————————————

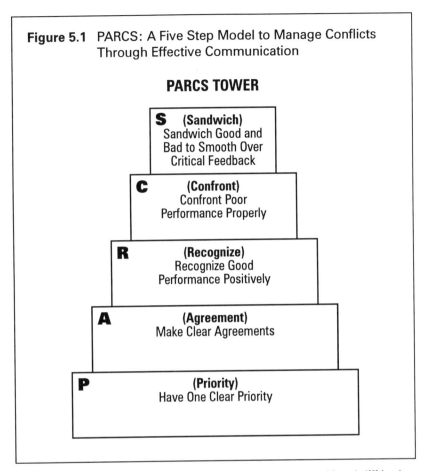

Figure 5.1 PARCS: A Five Step Model to Manage Conflicts Through Effective Communication

PARCS TOWER

S (Sandwich)
Sandwich Good and
Bad to Smooth Over
Critical Feedback

C (Confront)
Confront Poor
Performance Properly

R (Recognize)
Recognize Good
Performance Positively

A (Agreement)
Make Clear Agreements

P (Priority)
Have One Clear Priority

Source: J. Kostner and C. Strbiak, "Inspiring People and Performance," materials presented in a workshop at the 1993 Annual Seminars & Symposium of the Project Management Institute. By permission of the authors.

A = Agreement

Make Clear Agreements. Vague and poorly understood agreements lead to misunderstanding, conflicts and poor working relationships. Conflict can be reduced by taking time and create a clear, unambiguous understanding of project's main issues and how the team will work together to resolve these issues. This can be facilitated through open communication and willingness to work together. All project team members should strive to achieve customer satisfaction, focusing on the final results or deliverables by continually planning, implementing and evaluating the ideas as a team. Also to make clear agreements, it is important to follow a SMART approach: clarify *Scope*, *Motivate* the team to meet project objectives, and agree on the *Attributes* of quality standards, on what *Resources* will be needed to do the work, and on the *Timeline,* or schedule

Inspiring High Team Performance

with a plan to monitor and follow up on it. This approach, if followed properly, can help reduce conflicts in a project environment. It should be used to make clear agreements, preferably be in written form and approved by both parties, before starting the project in full swing.

R = Recognition

Recognize good performance. Recognition and praise for good performance is essential to achieve high performance. High achievers in project teams are self-motivated and willing to accept challenging assignments provided they get proper recognition for their efforts. When someone shows a good performance, the project manager must recognize it. Recognition should be given immediately or as soon as possible and the managers should be specific about the jobs and/or assignments that people are being praised for. Recognition and positive feedback should be given at every opportunity. Project managers should use positive feedback model to recognize good performance that emphasizes the power of positive words and results, focusing on agreements rather than disagreements and then reinforcing the effort, relating it to team priority and communicating success to other project participants.[1]

C = Confront

Confront poor performance without raising defensiveness. Conflicts are inevitable in projects. Both long- and short-term team performance is profoundly affected by the ways in which the project team handles conflicts. To achieve high team performance, it is critical to recognize as well as raise performance issues without putting poor performers on the defensive. The key to this is to be neutral, stay with the facts and wait for a response. Key factors that must be kept in mind in order to stay neutral are:[1]

Use "I" statements. No one likes to be criticized especially if it is a negative criticism. One should avoid accusing others by using "I" statements in their opening statements and emphasize the essence of expectations and observations. "I" statements make it easier to focus on the facts:

Poor: "You are very slow!" This accuses the recipient and shows that you have drawn a conclusion.

Neutral: "I just checked my mailbox and couldn't find the cost estimates for the project." By using *I* instead of *you*, you can state a fact that you have observed.

The use of "I" statements tends to soften the issue and the recipient is likely to react positively. Therefore, use "I" phrases to help you stay neutral, and then:

- State a fact as briefly as possible (preferably in one or two statements).
- Wait for a response. Many people feel uncomfortable when there is silence and will offer their explanation about the situation.

Be specific. Sometimes minor project problems, when addressed in a vague manner, become serious. It is important to be very specific because

198

then the team members can think together and come up with a solution. For example:

Vague: "Jack, I know you have done it before, but I don't think that it is going to work in this project."

Specific: "Jack, I noticed that you have changed assembly procedures." Jack knows exactly the issue at hand and he is not likely to be over-defensive.

Be non-judgmental. Staying neutral is vital to raising a poor performance issue. One should not pass judgment because it puts people on the defensive, it may not be correct, and it may cause hurt feelings. For example, what should a project manager say to a team member who comes late to work?

Poor: "You're late." The team member may have had a car problem or could have been involved in an accident. Or the team member may have come in very early and then left to go to a contractor's site.

Neutral: "I came by to discuss this with you at nine o'clock but I guess you weren't in yet." The team member knows exactly what you are talking about and he or she is not put on the defensive.

In communication it is not only what people say that's important but how it is said. Try to modify the message and its tone in a way that will help you stay neutral and assertive, rather than blaming and aggressive.

Be non-punishing. Sometimes people in project teams can address conflict in a punishing manner, like a parent may do to a child. People can punish through words or phrases used in conflict. Here are some of the common punishing phrases people use when communicating verbally:

- You don't trust me.
- You don't respect me.
- That was a really silly idea of yours.
- You are unreliable.

Sometimes people can also punish by the nonverbal communication they use in a conflict situation. For example they may:

- Withdraw or ignore the other person
- Keep quiet but show anger
- Smile as if making fun or indicating the person doesn't know what he or she is talking about
- Smile in a way that shows disagreement.

People normally react negatively to someone if they feel they have been punished verbally or nonverbally.

Stick to facts. In raising poor performance concerns, it is important to state facts in a short and simple manner. Staying with the facts can be difficult. Often people tend to editorialize and fill in missing pieces with their assumptions and opinions. When raising a performance issue, everyone working on the project should leave off any information that is irrelevant or is not essential to raise the issue.

Be as neutral/positive as possible in order to stay neutral. The neutral way promotes harmony. However, cultural differences regarding the use of 'I' statements and the following recommendations about staying neutral should not be overlooked.[1]

- Don't ask a question that has an obvious answer (shows sarcasm)
- Don't use "you" as the subject
- Don't editorialize with your own opinions
- Don't state conclusions. Instead, use phrases like these to help one stay neutral:

> "I just received a phone call from client's representative XYZ. He stated ... "

> "It has just been brought to my attention that ... "

> "I just learned that ... "

> "The manager of department X called and told me that ... "

S = Sandwich Approach

"Sandwich" good and bad messages. Some people believe that conflict can be diffused by sandwiching the negative message with positive messages. There are two kinds of sandwiches that are commonly used in conflict situations. First there's the "Deluxe Sandwich Approach"—saying something positive, negative and then positive. For example:

John, I was glad to get a positive feedback from our client about the training manual you had written for them. However, I am not pleased with the way you handled the planning session with the other customer in which you tried to put their organization down. I strongly feel that you are a good facilitator and will do better next time.

Then there's the "Open Faced Sandwich Approach"—saying something positive first and then stating the negative part of the message.[1] For example:

Bill, I am really impressed with the format and the back up information you have generated for estimating the project cost. But I wish you could learn better presentation and human skills in implementing project plans.

Both sandwich approaches are commonly used in a project environment. However, it should be recognized that the degree of effectiveness depends upon the situation and the personalities involved. Therefore, project managers must assess the situations themselves and use this concept appropriately.

While most people react positively to the "sandwich" approach, it is important that the positive feedback be sincere and genuine and emphasize how to improve in the future. Team members may react negatively if they perceive the positive portion of the message is phony, simply a set-up for the criticism to follow. Criticism should always be aimed at improving performance by supporting team members in their efforts.

200

Effective communication is vital to high team performance. Project managers must encourage task and relationship openness, set clear priorities, goals and agreements, create a permissive environment, create partnership openness by respecting each other's opinions and ideas, and encourage innovations and creativity. They must recognize good performance and confront poor performance without raising defensiveness by following the model presented above.

Developing Trust and Motivation

The chief lesson I have learned in a long life is that the only way to make people trustworthy is to trust them.
— *Henry Stinson, U.S. Secretary of War during World War II*

The project team is a group of individuals selected for their skills and capabilities to perform the project task. However to be successful, the project team must be managed effectively, i.e., individual efforts must be integrated. In addition, these individuals must work together to produce the innovative results as conceptualized in the project plan.

Project managers must create an environment where team members are professionally satisfied, are involved, motivated, and have mutual trust. It is important that project team members are open, flexible, and supportive. They must be able to trust each other and help each other win. This section deals with the importance of trust and motivation and how these can be enhanced in the project team environment.

Developing trust within the project team

Trust is a pillar of high performance teams. Building trust is a gradual process that requires constant management action.[2] Project managers must recognize that trust leads to open communication and hence to real teamwork in solving problems, making decisions and optimizing team's output. Project team members will share their problems with other team members and their project manager only if there is a true sense of trust between them; otherwise, it is common for project participants to convey only the information that they believe others want to hear. Some organizations discourage sharing problems by "shooting the messenger." To be really effective and to achieve high team performance, project managers must build trust by knowing their team members better in terms of who they are and what their problems might be. They must dig beyond surface indicators such as reports, schedules and budgets.

To enhance trust within the project team, project managers must find out how effectively the team is working together and what are the interpersonal, organizational and technical problems. They must show and express confidence in their team members and be completely open about why and how important decisions are made.[3] Such actions demonstrate that the project managers value their team members. They must get to the heart of the issues and talk about what is really going on in the project team. They must take time to become familiar with team problems in order to solve them. Such actions demonstrate that the project manager cares for the project team and therefore fosters the development of trust in interpersonal relationships.

Trust is also necessary to ensure successful leadership.[3] Following are some ideas that can be used by the project managers to develop trust within the project teams.[4]

- Model the desirable level of trust on the team.
- Be consistent in words and actions. Project managers must "walk their talk." It demonstrates their integrity. Generally team members trust their project managers to act in a predictable manner.
- Encourage friendly working relationships among team members. Friendship leads to trust. People that like one another normally develop mutual trust and rapport.
- Ask direct questions about trust, such as "How much do we trust each other?" or "What can we do to improve our level of trust?"
- Create an environment that encourages interaction. Ensure that all team members have the opportunity to participate, listen and contribute.
- Encourage genuine respect for each other positively. The team environment should demonstrate genuine consideration for all team members. Interruptions, domination in meetings, and personal attacks should be discouraged.
- Use win/win negotiation strategies. It shows openness and willingness to compromise that leads to development of trust.
- Support the discussion of sensitive topics. Project managers should not shut out sensitive issues and people who bring up such issues should be supported.
- Reward excellent performance and confront poor performance. This will ensure accountability for performance. If a project manager is unable to confront poor performance, it demotivates others, and team members feel you are not doing your job effectively.
- Be open about issues that affect the team. This shows care on the part of project manager. A project team in charge of its own destiny builds commitment.

Table 5.1 summarizes ten key factors for developing trust within the project team.[1]

Trust is very important in a project environment. Because of the diverse mix of team members from cross-functional departments, there is a significant level of informality in a project environment. Project teams in such environments can produce high performance through mutual trust, rapport and open communication. It should be emphasized that trust is very delicate and should not be tinkered with because once trust is bro-

202

Table 5.1 Ten Key Factors for Developing Trust

TRUST IS A KEY TO HIGH PERFORMANCE GUIDELINES

1. Model the desirable level of trust
2. Walk the talk
3. Encourage business relationships and interaction
4. Address questions to enhance trust
5. Demonstrate genuine respect and consideration
6. Use win/win strategies
7. Support sensitive issues
8. Reward excellent performance and use positive reinforcement
9. Confront poor performance without raising defensiveness
10. Be open about issues that affect team performance

ken, it is hard to win it back. However, one must try to regain it by using the following strategies:

- Communicate openly to establish how and why it happened.
- Give up ego and try to see things from other person's point of view.
- Admit your mistakes (to err is human).
- Try to find out how the situation can be mended.

The risk of managing a project with lack of trust is very high. Therefore, every effort should be made by the project managers and all project participants to develop mutual trust because it leads to effective communication, better working relationships, win/win negotiating and effective conflict resolution.

Team motivation

There is no exercise better for the heart than reaching out and lifting people up.
— *Anonymous*

Project teams are comprised of team members with diverse backgrounds, norms, expectations and individual objectives. The overall success of the project depends upon the level of motivation that determines the commitment level of the project team. Motivating in a project environment means creation of an environment to meet project objectives while gaining maximum self-satisfaction about what people value the most. Project managers must themselves be motivated and also must be able to motivate their project team and other project stakeholders to achieve high performance. This section deals with team motivation and highlights major driving and restraining forces in motivating the project team.

About team motivation. Project success is dependent upon the combined performance and productivity of team members. Most project team members want job satisfaction, a challenge in work (in which they can take pride), a sense of accomplishment, achievement and growth while getting enough financial compensation and other rewards and recognitions they feel are important. It is well recognized that satisfied project team members will generally do their best and produce quality results. Therefore, project managers must understand the dynamics of change, and human behavior, and continually motivate their project team members. Most project team members feel that few things are more satisfying in life than belonging to a really successful team. General theories of motivation as discussed in Volume 2 of this series, *Human Resource Skills for Project Managers,* are valid and applicable to team motivation as well.

Project managers can stimulate creativity in team members by using a combination of project management techniques, total quality management approach, and motivational tools. However, the overall project climate and leadership can influence overall team motivation more than motivating team members as individuals only. Project managers must be aware of the values in which winning teams believe, so that special attention can be focused on creating an atmosphere conducive to motivate project team members and nurture these values. Some of these values are:

- *Pride* in performance
- *Loyalty* to the success of the organization
- *Teamwork* through cooperation with other members
- *Self-discipline* and *accountability* for behavior
- *Dedication* through a willingness to work hard
- *Trust* through building honest relationships with other members
- *Credibility* by being consistently accurate and honest
- *Dependability* by being there when needed, especially in the tough times.

Driving and restraining forces. Throughout the project life cycle, there will always be driving forces that push the project towards success and some restraining forces that may induce failure. In a steady state environment, the driving and restraining forces are well balanced. The formal analysis of these forces is commonly referred to as force field analysis[5] and can be used to monitor the project and project team's performance, effectiveness of team building, and measure the sensitivity of proposed changes. Dugan[6] *et al.,* conducted studies in force field analysis and obtained information in several areas. Personal drives, motivation and leadership were found to be very important in all project life cycle phases because they provide the strongest driving forces, and represented important attributes of the project manager and the team members. Lack of these factors was found to increase the restraining forces leading to project problems and failure. Table 5.2 shows the driving and restraining forces that may influence team motivation:[6]

204

Table 5.2 Driving and Restraining Forces in Team Motivation

DRIVING FORCES

- Good interpersonal relations
- Expertise
- Clear role definition
- Project visibility and profile
- Agreement and distribution of work
- Good learning climate
- Integration of team and project objectives

- Desire to achieve
- Common goals
- Challenge of project
- Rewards and recognitions
- Participation

- Mutual trust and respect

RESTRAINING FORCES

- Poor team organization
- Poor leadership
- Uncertain objectives
- Low visibility of the project

- Team members overloaded
- Unequal talent distribution

- Communication barriers
- Uncertain rewards
- Resistance to project
- Little commitment or ownership in project

- Limited prior team experience
- Lack of encouragement for new ideas

Project managers should try to increase the intensity of driving forces to optimize the level of team motivation, while controlling or reducing the restraining forces in order to keep the project team motivated.

After analyzing the driving and restraining forces, project managers can use following guidelines to motivate their project teams:

- Present the challenges
- Encourage competition
- Encourage and provide professional development
- Provide an open, flexible and supportive environment
- Create an atmosphere of mutual trust and respect
- Emphasize the importance of synergy
- Give regular reviews and feedback. Positive reinforcement and feedback motivates people.
- Use the team reward system.

Inspiring High Team Performance

- Recognize individual differences and capitalize on diversity.
- *Don't ignore money.*

  Project managers should use the VIP approach to motivate team members:

  V = Validation (explain *why* things must be done)

  I = Information (provide access to all relevant information)

  P = Participation (involve team members in developing solutions and making decisions).

Team motivation has a very strong overall influence on project success and is an important factor in all phases of the project. Team motivation has been found to be a very strong driver and, if lacking, can become a strong restraint in team performance. Figure 5.2 shows motivational techniques in a nutshell.

Managing Team Morale

Morale determines attitude—it is a little thing that makes a BIG difference.
— *Anonymous*

To manage projects effectively under time, cost and quality constraints, it is essential that the morale of the project team remain high throughout the project life cycle. A project team with high morale has a strong sense of shared purpose, direction, and a commitment to peak performance. The project manager must do everything possible to combat negative sources that may lower the morale of project team members. Since morale is a complex, dynamic behavioral variable, most project managers want to address the issue of team morale but are uncertain how to do so. Morale can be viewed as the mental attitude of either an individual or the team with regard to the project function or task.

Key factors of team morale. In essence, the level of team morale is a function of four key factors: the job itself (a sense of the job's importance), the project team, project management practices, and economic rewards and recognition. Positive morale results from a positive attitude in all these areas.

Robert Levering, in his book *A Great Place to Work*, points out that high morale, in some projects, is related to the pride in what project participants do (the job itself), enjoying the people you are working with (the project team), and trusting the people you work for (in terms of project leadership, project management practices, economic rewards, and recognition).[7]

Recommendations for managing team morale. There are several ways to improve team morale. Most of these approaches emphasize the importance of understanding and appreciating the needs and objectives of the team members, which influence their behavior. Before project managers can start to improve morale, they should review the four areas of morale mentioned earlier and follow these recommendations for developing the best attitudes among project team members.[8]

206

Figure 5.2 Motivational Techniques in a Nutshell

Manifest confidence when delegating
(helps build mutual trust)

Open communication
(increases mutual understanding and respect)

Tolerance for failure
(develops creativity)

Involve project participants
(increase acceptance and commitment)

Value the efforts and recognize good performance
(what gets rewarded, gets done)

Align project objectives to individual objectives
(people are eager to satisfy their needs)

Trust your team members and be trustworthy
(vital for motivation)

Empower project team members appropriately
(especially for decision making and implementation)

Sense of job importance. Project team members must feel a sense of meaning and importance in their job, challenge in the work and a feeling of accomplishment. This includes:

- *Job Importance.* It has been said that people do not fear extinction; they fear extinction without meaning. An opportunity to do something of value on a project that can be appreciated for years to come, is a powerful motivating factor. Because work is an important source of meaning and personal identity, an appropriate match of the person to the job itself can have a significant impact on morale.[9] Project managers should take every possible step to match job requirements to the attributes of individual team members. They must consider the interests, skills and goals of team members because the success of the project depends mainly upon placing the right people in the right job.

- *Job Challenge.* A challenging project assignment helps maintain the team member's interest, keep job skills current and increase productivity.[10] Management should look for opportunities to provide challenges when doing performance appraisals and planning because tackling new and exciting tasks stimulates an individual's interest, improves skills and creates a more flexible contributor. To provide job challenge, project managers

Inspiring High Team Performance

should encourage team members' involvement in the decision-making process by using task forces, employee committees, and quality improvement teams.

- *Job Accomplishment.* A sense of accomplishment based on competent performance also increases the morale of project team members. Project managers can ensure high productivity by providing good planning (including mission and goals based on shared values), organization, allocation and coordination of resources, and leadership practices. Project leaders should act more as coach and coordinator, rather than as bottleneck and enforcer. Key roles of an effective leader are to *challenge* the process, *inspire* a shared vision, *enable (facilitate)* others to do their best, *encourage* the heart, *encourage* new ideas, and *stimulate* creativity.[11]

- *System for monitoring and control.* Project management and team management require simple but effective reporting and control systems. Emphasis is on keeping the proper records and documentation, maintaining order, making timely and sound decisions, and seeing plans through to completion. Project managers should emphasize team members' involvement in monitoring and designing corrective actions to ensure ongoing quality control, achieve total quality management and achieve key project objectives within constraints.

Teamwork. Teamwork among project participants or stakeholders (external or internal) is a key attitude to improving morale. It includes a sense of team pride, good relations among team members, and a spirit of teamwork among all project stakeholders.

Previous chapters have covered in detail the concepts and techniques of team building, team motivation, team leadership and team decision-making. Here's a brief description of how these three areas relate to the importance of sustaining high morale:

- *Team pride.* The project team determines the standard of job performance and can have a significant impact on the productivity of individual team members. With team pride, team members believe in the capabilities of the project team that results in increased enthusiasm and energy to perform. Help build team/group pride by providing group rewards, setting professional standards of behavior and work ethics, and assigning complete tasks to work groups. For example, AT&T implemented work design changes in core job dimensions on a project, such as variety, autonomy, feedback, challenge, meaning and task, and identity. These changes resulted in cost savings as well as improvements in efficiency, worker attitudes and turnover. [12,13]

- *Good relations among team members.* Social needs (especially on projects with longer durations) are very important. The project manager should not overlook satisfying the social needs of project team members. Some constructive ways to meet social needs are orientation training for new team members, regular progress meetings, quality circles, and a

208

willingness to help employees with job related problems. Other strategies that address social needs are lounge areas, ride-sharing to and from work, picnics, holiday parties, and athletic teams.

Communication needs are closely related to social needs. Communication problems cause frustration, low morale and reduced productivity. Where employees *want* to get information could be very different from where they actually *do* get information (see Figure 5.3). The project manager can increase communication with and among team members through small group meetings and the involvement of top management. They should decrease dependence on the grapevine and spreading of rumors that may have negative impact on team morale.

- *Teamwork.* As mentioned earlier, project managers' success depends upon the performance of the project team. Teamwork ensures an energy output greater than the sum of the efforts put in. Harmony increases human energy, discord decreases energy. Therefore team spirit leads to creation of energy. Project managers can encourage effective teamwork by using examples and reinforcement. Project leaders should themselves behave cooperatively and reward team members who help their co-team members. If project managers are self-centered, protect their own interests and ego, and go after personal rewards and credits rather than caring for the project team, they will discourage teamwork, reduce employee morale, and reduce overall productivity and quality.

Management's concern about employee welfare. To increase project morale, especially where the project manager may have only limited authority over the policies for the whole organization, management must show it cares about all employees, including those working on projects. This can be done through:

- *Management fairness.* Employees expect a just reward for their contributions and fair treatment for their efforts. If employees are treated fairly, they sustain a high level of productivity and commitment to the organization.[14] Project managers who involve team members in making decisions promote democracy and dignity. Participation leads to involvement which in turn leads to ownership and finally to commitment.

- *Organizational goals.* When the individual's and the organization's goals are in conflict, morale and performance fall. Management should try to set goals with input from employees. On a project, the basic project goals are already set by top management or a client but the project manager can still set short-term goals with input from project team members. Genuine goal incongruence, on the other hand, must be addressed. If it persists, the manager must be willing either to incorporate the individual's goals, or begin the process of disassociation of an incompatible contributor.[15]

- *Management concern.* If management fails to show concern for the welfare of people working on a project, dissatisfaction will increase *and*

Figure 5.3 Where Employees Go for Information

Where they want to get information (in rank order)	Where they actually get information (in rank order)
1. Immediate supervisor	1. Immediate supervisor
2. Small-group meetings	2. Grapevine
3. Top executives	3. Employee handbook
4. Employee handbook	4. Bulletin boards
5. Orientation programs	5. Small-group meetings
6. Regular general employee publications	6. Regular general employee publications
7. Annual business report to employees	7. Annual business report to employees
8. Regular local employee publications	8. Regular local employee publications
9. Bulletin boards	9. Mass meetings
10. Upward communications programs	10. Unions
11. Mass meetings	11. Orientation programs
12. Audiovisual programs	12. Top executives
13. Unions	13. Audiovisual programs
14. Mass media	14. Mass media
15. Grapevine	15. Upward communications programs

Source: "Where Employees Go for Information" by Selma Friedman. *Administrative Management.* Sept. 1981.

job performance will decrease. Lack of trust, respect and loyalty characterize this relationship. Managers and employees then fail to listen to each other and everyone protects his/her own interest with little regard for organizational success.

The most effective and least expensive way to promote concern for employee welfare is to cooperate meaningfully in day-to-day contacts related to work problems on and off the job. A willingness to listen, talk and demonstrate sincere responsiveness to each other increases the morale and job performance of management and project teams.

Team rewards and recognition. Project teams thrive on rewards and recognition that act as very effective positive reinforcement. Recognition is one of the most important motivational tools. Professionals look for challenges and expect appropriate rewards and recognition when they

210

meet those challenges successfully. It is important to understand how and why giving proper rewards and recognition motivates team members and how this approach increases performance and contributes to positive reinforcement.

Rewards and recognition—a positive approach. Project managers score high when team goals and project goals are accomplished and team performance is appropriately recognized. There are many forms of recognition, such as praise, opportunities for growth, and economic rewards.

Rewards. In addition to acting only to correct significant deviations, project managers should not ignore the evidence that rewards strengthen desirable behavior.[16] The project manager should not take high performance as guaranteed and assume it will continue indefinitely unless it is positively reinforced with proper rewards in a timely manner. The most obvious reward would be pay, but it is only the tip of the iceberg. Project managers often control and therefore should use a number of other rewards such as praise, desirable work assignment, status symbol, promotion, awards could be in front of peers to inspire others and not turn them off, and special rewards (such as conferences or other training or travel opportunities).

To influence human behavior to achieve high productivity, desirable performance needs to be reinforced in order to strengthen it and reduce the likelihood of it turning into undesirable behavior.

Recognition. One of the most powerful forms of recognition is praise and therefore the importance of praise in a project environment should never be overlooked. Along with praise for good performance, recognition may also encompass giving an opportunity to identify and correct poor performance. It is counterproductive to approach someone on the project team with "Well, you screwed up again!" On the other hand it is constructive to lead the project team members to realize their mistake, to induce them to think harder about their task and to decide for themselves how their performance can be improved.[17]

Some managers use praise effectively, others use it poorly or not at all. Figure 5.4 shows some typical behaviors of project leaders that lead to effective or ineffective use of praise.[18]

Rewards versus reinforcement. Some project managers are often unclear about the difference between these two terms. A reward is an event that a person finds desirable or pleasant. How a reward acts as a reinforcer, is subjective to the individual. For example, a project manager who praises a particular team member, for doing a particular task that no other team member could do, may believe that it would reinforce desired behavior and also inspire other team members to do better. But later, the project manager may learn that the particular team member was not treated in a friendly manner by other team members and therefore that team member

Figure 5.4 Using Praise Effectively—Where will You Be?

Effective	Ineffective
Project leaders who think it's important to help people feel good about themselves.	Those who are insensitive to the needs of others.
Project leaders who give periodic praise to team members for meeting job requirements.	Those who think praise is improper for persons who meet, but do not exceed, job requirements.
Project leaders who understand people respond better if praised for what they do well than if criticized for what they do wrong.	Those who only look for what is being done wrong and consistently give only negative feedback.
Project leaders who give sincere praise for reasons the receiver can understand (i.e., be specific).	Those who are insincere and only use praise (as lip service) to get something they want.
Project leaders who praise teamwork but also recognize individual contributions to final results.	Those who do not go to the trouble to reward teamwork or identify individual contributions.

Praise Given When Earned Rewards The Giver As Well As The Receiver

Source: Paul C. DInsmore and Manual M. Benitez, 1993, "Challenges in Managing International Projects," in *AMA Handbook of PRoject Management*, Paul C. DInsmore, ed., New York, NY: AMACOM, pp 463-464. By permission of the publisher.

may shy away from consistently high performance. To qualify reward as a reinforcer, it must increase the frequency of the behavior it follows.

Enhancing performance through reward system. The main idea of rewarding someone for a job well done is to create positive reinforcement that should further enhance the performance. However, increased performance will only happen if the reward is regarded as fairly important by that person. It should also be noted that relative importance of the needs and rewards may change with time, experience and circumstances of the individual. Like other employees, in addition to promotions and monetary rewards, individuals working on a project team view seminars, conferences, profit sharing, opportunities to engage in challenging assignments and the achievement of challenging goals (positive reinforcement) as rewards.[19]

Another reward often used in a project environment is *banking time off*. Banking time off can be used as an effective reward system to meet a tight project schedule. Some key members of the project team may end up working much harder and should be allowed to bank time off that can be used for extended vacations, etc. However there should be a mutual understanding that very long vacations will not be taken to avoid a significant negative impact on the overall productivity and project schedule. Project managers should provide guidelines about how much time can be taken off consecutively during slack time and for how long can employee retain his/her banked time.

Two other contemporary reward systems include skill-based pay, and flexible fringe benefits.[19] However, these are more applicable in an ongoing operation rather than in a project environment.

People feel motivated if they are valued and their level of motivation depends upon the values placed by their senior management, project managers and other team members. However, many people feel that this value can only be demonstrated by the rewards given to them.

Is money the only motivator? Project managers must not ignore the value of money. Money is by far the most important aspect of any reward system but wide and unfair ranges in the pay structure can actually demotivate team members. It is hard to build effective teams when team members feel that they are paid relatively less than their counterparts in the industry or certain "stars" are overpaid. It is important that all team members are paid fairly based on their skills, talents and contributions to project objectives. It is well to remember the old cliché—"you get what you pay for and if you pay peanuts, you get monkeys."

Money however is not the only effective reward. There are several other subtle "perks" that can be included into a reward package. The list can be endless but significant components of a reward system may include:[19]

- Private office, an office with a carpet and/or a door
- Use of a company car
- Assignment of a secretary
- Reserved parking space
- Flexible work schedule
- Opportunity for telecommuting (if desired)
- After hours educational reimbursement
- In-house training opportunities (to give and get training)
- Stock purchase options
- Holidays and vacation benefits
- Additional health and life insurance at cheaper rates.

Some of above benefits may be a part of an organizational standard benefit plan; others can be implemented for selected projects as requested by the project manager.

Although the use of cash incentives to reward outstanding individual performance is desirable, it can have negative impact if implemented without team consensus. Instead, team incentive rewards are more effective motivators. Unfortunately, few organizations have the procedures or funds to implement financial incentives, but exceptions can be made for high profile and highly profitable projects. In general, project managers should use public recognition and outstanding merit/performance reviews as rewards. A good rule for the project manager is to give the project team all of the glory possible during the life cycle of the project; as there may be little left at the end. Good project managers realize that they can only shine if their team members shine.

There are strengths and weaknesses of any reward system. Project managers, with the help of the human resource department, must evaluate each system before implementation.

Before dramatic improvements in project team performance can be achieved, the project manager should review the morale of team members based on the four key ingredients: the job itself, the project team, management practices and team rewards and recognition (economic and others). Any necessary corrections should be implemented to build a loyal, satisfied and productive project team that is committed to do its best and meet the project objectives throughout its life cycle.

Team Leadership

Real leaders are ordinary people with extraordinary results.

— Anonymous

Teamwork is the by-product of good leadership. Good leadership makes everybody's work more effective and therefore more rewarding. Project leaders must foster an environment where team members are involved, have job satisfaction and mutual trust. They must stimulate the drivers and minimize the barriers in order to develop effective project teams having a high degree of mutual trust and willingness to share information readily and openly among team members.

What leadership is and what it is not

In general terms, leadership is an ability to get things done through others while winning their respect, confidence, loyalty, willing cooperation and commitment. Respect and trust rather than fear and submission are the key elements of effective leadership. It involves focusing the efforts of a group of people towards a common goal and enabling them to work as a team. Leadership is getting people to do things for you even when they don't work for you. A leader should be directive in a democratic way and should enhance and complement efforts of individuals on a project team. The leader is not one person dominating another or a group of people. The project leader is the focal point who acts as required and provides ad-

214

Figure 5.5 Project Life Cycle vs. Leadership and Management Skills

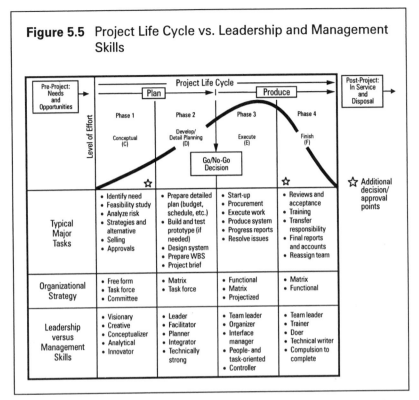

Source: Vijay K. Verma and R. Max Wideman. 1994. Project Manager to Project Leader? and the Rocky Road Between. *Proceedings of the 25th Annual Seminar/Symposium of the Project Management Institute.* Upper Darby, PA: Project Management Institute, pp. 627–633.

vice, encouragement and support, whenever needed to meet project goals, throughout the project life cycle.

In simple terms, project leaders focus on *the right things to do* whereas project managers emphasize *doing the things right*. Leadership and management skills needed for different phases of the project life cycle may change as the project progresses through its life cycle as shown in Figure 5.5. Project leadership is essential during the planning phase of the project to ensure smooth sailing during the producing phase of the project.[20]

The keys to leadership

When you cease to dream you cease to live.

— *Malcolm S. Forbes*

Achieving the goal or final aim is the ultimate test of leadership. The first and the most important responsibility of a leader is to define the objective in order to focus and achieve concerted team work. Also, no one will follow a team leader who does not know where he or she is going, because "A blind man leading a blind man results in both falling into a ditch."

Inspiring High Team Performance

Once the team's tasks are settled and the team is accepted, individuals can go to work and contribute according to their strengths and skills. To be effective, goals and goal setting process should be agreed upon with team members. Project leaders should use SMART approach for setting goals if goals should be Specific, Measurable, Attainable (realistic but challenging), Results-oriented and Rewardable, and Time-bounded.

The leader must ensure that individual team members feel that their tasks/efforts are making an appreciable contribution to the team's overall performance. Three key elements to team leadership are:

The core responsibility of a leader. This combines three elements in a project—the task, the team and the individual.[21] To fulfill the three areas of responsibility, project team leaders must perform certain key functions by themselves or through delegation or sharing. Some of the general functions that the project team leaders must perform are: [21]

Visioning and strategizing. Developing a shared vision and deriving goals and objectives to realize the vision; seeking and analyzing all external and internal information; developing the strategies and goals with the project team; preparing a workable plan and implementing it by using a right decision-making framework.

Communicating and building trust. Creating openness in communication; communicating project plans and giving new information to the team to keep them informed and updated on a regular basis; receiving information from the team, summarizing suggestions and ideas clearly and communicating to appropriate team members for action and follow up; building trust by showing confidence in team members in terms of generating new ideas and problem solving; empowering the project team to an appropriate level.

Team building. Developing effective project teams; briefing the project team on its aims and plan with explanation on *why* these are necessary; setting team standards and performance measurement criteria; getting the tasks done according to the organization's overall policy and various constraints; inspiring high team performance and managing team morale throughout the project life cycle.

Influencing. Influencing top management, client and other stakeholders; communicating effectively and keeping discussion relevant; developing an appropriate power base, balancing total power and skillful and thoughtful application of power; managing project politics effectively.

Supporting. Expressing acceptance of persons, their ideas and their contributions; encouraging teams/individuals, recognizing and rewarding teams and individuals; creating team spirit; relieving tension with humor; reconciling disagreements and resolving conflicts using a win-win strategy.

Evaluating/monitoring. Checking the feasibility of an idea; testing the consequences of a proposed solution; evaluating team performance; help-

216

ing the project team to evaluate its own performance against standards and achieve its best.

The three main areas of responsibility of a team leader include achieving the task, developing individual team members, and building and inspiring the project team. [21]

It must be emphasized that the project team leader is accountable for all three areas of responsibility, even if some of the functions are delegated to team members. The team leader's range of function is normally much wider than that of any team member. It must be remembered that a project team manager can be appointed but a project team leader's appointment has to be ratified in the hearts and minds of team members.

For building and maintaining effective project teams, the project team leaders must take time to understand individual team members as persons both in terms of what they share in common and what differentiates them. If team leaders give to their team members proper respect and trust, real challenges and responsibilities together with a degree of independence and encouragement to be creative and innovative, then the team members will reward their leader with their best. On the other hand if team leaders treat team members as statistics, numbers and things, they will respond with no spark of enthusiasm, or ounce of initiative, and will lack conviction and commitment to the team's goals and objectives. They will not discover through their team leader that "I am larger and better than I thought."

Praise and criticism. Another important factor associated with team leadership is the creative use of praise and criticism. Both are important at the right place and at the right time. For high achievers and those who take pride in their work, judicious praise and recognition for a job well done will result in positive reinforcement leading to even better performance.

However, it should be remembered that praise is not a substitute for money or financial incentive because praise alone does not fill an empty stomach. But it still meets a very basic human need. On the other hand, criticism, given firmly and tactfully in a positive and constructive manner, should not only improve standards and point to weak areas but should also strengthen mutual trust and respect. It will show that the team leader cares about the job quality, team's performance and the importance of individuals' contribution to their maximum potential.

There are some thought-provoking proverbs about praise and blame (see Table 5.3) that can be used by team leaders depending upon the situation and their own personality.[22] They highlight the importance of giving and receiving praise that is like oxygen for the human body.

It is often unfortunate that both team leaders and members have difficulty in giving and receiving praise in an effective manner.

Honesty and integrity. "Basic goodness" in the moral sense is the foundation of leadership. Honesty, integrity, sincerity, moral courage, justice,

Table 5.3 Praise and Blame: Some Proverbs

- An honest man is hurt by praise unjustly bestowed
- Too much praise is a burden
- I praise loudly, I blame softly
- Our praises are our wages
- The most pleasing of all sounds—that of your own praise
- Be sparing in praise and more so in blaming
- Praise a fool and you water his folly
- Praise is always pleasant
- Praise makes good people better and bad people worse.

and fairness all lead to better and more effective teams. If both team members and team leaders have these qualities, then project team energies can be spent on accomplishing the tasks, goals and objectives and not on infighting, politicking, back-stabbing, mutual suspicion, intrigue and destructive criticisms, all of which lead to an unpleasant and unhealthy atmosphere that is not conducive to nurturing any team spirit.

The principles of leadership sound simple, obvious and commonsensical but practicing them is not easy. The three responsibility areas mentioned earlier should serve as a good guide to understanding relationships between the tasks, the individual team members and the team. An appropriate use of praise and criticism leads to positive reinforcement and higher performance level of the team as a whole. An effective team leader must be able to create a true team spirit and an environment that is conducive enough to encourage everyone to work together and help each other win by using the basic values such as mutual trust, respect, honesty and integrity, etc. A team leader must make demands on himself or herself before making demands on team members.

Teamwork is no accident, it is the by product of good leadership. Figure 5.6 shows important factors to inspire a high team performance on an ongoing basis.

Common leadership styles

Leaders are like eagles, they don't flock, you find them one at a time.

— Anonymous

Like team management styles, there are also some team leadership styles that are commonly used in a project environment. Although some of these leadership styles have similar characteristics to those in management styles, yet it should be remembered that leadership focuses on effectiveness (doing the right things) where managership focuses on efficiency (do-

Figure 5.6 Guidelines for Inspiring High Team Performance

I — Identify a shared vision

N — Nurture creativity and innovation through effective leadership

S — Share responsibilities and success

P — Prepare an action plan using participative style

I — Improve communication and trust within the project team

R — Reward and recognize good performance

E — Enable others to do their best and help each other win through facilitation

ing the things right). Successful project managers should also have leadership skills. They should be able to modify their leadership styles according to the situation. Five commonly used team leadership styles are autocratic, consultative/autocratic, consensus, shareholder, and shared/collaborative leadership. [23] These styles are described in Chapter 3.

To be successful in a project environment, the concept of shared leadership is very effective.[23] Shared leadership is more than just participative management. It involves giving as much autonomy to the project team as it can accept. The project managers are willing to forego some of their authority and power to control and share these with the team members. They are willing to let project teams take on as much leadership as possible.

Shared leadership challenges project team members and encourages them to actively participate in problem solving and decision-making; which leads to more and wider acceptance, and hence to stronger commitment in implementing decisions and solutions. In such cases, project teams accept responsibility for the success or failure of the project. Successful project managers tend to use shared leadership approach because it offloads some of their workload and creates a real team spirit. Project team members take the ownership of their tasks that is critical to successful empowerment.

Like general management, the modern view of project management has changed significantly. Modern project managers solve problems collectively and encourage most project stakeholders to contribute to developing solutions and action plans. In this context, a modern project manager is more like a coach, a facilitator, developer and a team builder.[24] Like a coach of a football team, the project manager should develop effective project teams and inspire high performance. They must develop a shared leadership with the project team members, client and other major stakeholders to achieve maximum human synergy to be winners.

As the project team members mature and become more committed, shared leadership becomes more effective because it involves empowering the project team. The concept of empowerment and Self-Motivated Project Teams is discussed in the next chapter in more details.

According to Slevin,[25] the key to effective leadership is to be aware of your dominant leadership style and being able to modify that style depending upon the leadership situations and other associated factors. Slevin also developed a leadership model and a diagnostic tool—the Jerrel/Slevin Management Instrument, which can be used to provide feedback to managers regarding their management styles.[26]

Effective team leadership is vital for high team performance. It is aimed to *create* an environment where all team members are professionally challenged, feel involved, satisfied, and valued. It leads to high degree of mutual trust that leads to effective communication, better working relationships, increased motivation, higher morale, and stronger commitment to achieve high performance.

It is important to recognize that there may be a slight difference between the team manager and team leader, but both are essential to achieve high team performance. The team leader must combine the elements of achieving the task and building and maintaining the team, while at the same time encouraging the creative and innovative potential of project team members. Effective team leaders must be able to change their leadership styles to suit the project participants and project organizational climate.

Roles and responsibilities of leaders

Leadership is making people do what they don't want to do, and like it.
— *Harry S. Truman*

The roles of team leaders are undergoing a radical change. Successful team leaders must be able to pass on to the team the responsibilities traditionally held by team managers or supervisors. They must establish team boundaries and then manage these boundaries effectively by using coaching and facilitating skills.

The traditional manager vs. the team leader. Traditional project managers plan, organize, direct, and control the project activities whereas team leaders set the vision, establish mission, set directions, align people, and motivate and inspire team members. The emphasis has shifted from *control and command* to *freedom and collaboration*.

In addition to the three attributes of successful leaders suggested by Posey and Klein—creating mutual trust and respect among the leader and

220

team members, making sure that the job gets done, and providing leadership in getting problems resolved[27]—leaders in self-managed work teams should have these characteristics:[28]

- Focus less on tasks (the work) and more on relationships (the process)
- Design and develop work process rather than simply monitoring work operations
- Work on developing the whole team rather than individuals.

Regardless of organizational structure—teams or no teams, empowered or not—goals have to be accomplished through planning the activities, assigning responsibilities and allocating resources. The role of team leaders expands beyond the immediate accomplishment of the task.

In Fisher's terminology, traditional managers act more like sheep herders: they focus on the task, activities, procedures, and policies and supervise the team by following behind team members. On the other hand, team leaders act like shepherds, developing the team members at personal and professional level through training, focusing on the process and work environment, leading by staying in front of the team members, creating more leaders, removing bottlenecks and obstacles, solving problems, encouraging independent thinking and creating self-reliance.[28]

Although traditional managers may get the job done, there are two major problems with their role as sheep herders:[28] First, it's inappropriate because self-managed teams are looking for more autonomy and sense of accomplishment. Secondly, it creates (though unintentionally) an organizational culture characterized by low risk-taking, initiative and tolerance for failure and thus discourages creativity and innovation.

Qualities of successful leaders. Leaders must have an ability to communicate the vision clearly and then inspire, motivate and support people to work towards the vision. There are twelve major qualities that make a team leader effective and successful. A leader:[29]

- Has a mission that matters (*The secret of building charisma*)
- Is a big thinker (*The magnet that attracts others*)
- Has high ethics (*Builds trust with your followers*)
- Is a change master (*Creates the future*)
- Is sensitive (*Inspires loyalty*)
- Is a risk taker (*Expands the possible*)
- Is a decision maker (*Releases potential of team members*)
- Uses power wisely (*Needed to master influence*)
- Communicates effectively (*Forges productive relationships*)
- Is a team builder (*Maximizes people potential*)
- Is courageous/energetic (*Strengthens problem solving*)
- Is committed (*The clue to success*).

And, above all, a leader has a sense of humor!

Self-Assessment Exercise E will help you determine if your team is a high-performance team.

Summary

Real teamwork and effective team leadership are vital for inspiring high team performance. Effective project managers must be able to foster an environment where team members are professionally satisfied, involved and have mutual trust and respect. Effective team leadership leads to good morale, higher quality of information exchange, and the maximum potential of everyone involved in the project.

Effective communication is the key to high team performance. Project managers must be able to coordinate and integrate the efforts of team members very effectively. Communication skills of project managers are becoming increasingly important because of overlapping areas of responsibilities, cultural diversity, scarce resources and changing priorities. Open communication among team members creates mutual trust, good working relationships, and better understanding. It clarifies roles, responsibilities and expectations of the project team members and facilitates conflict management.

Project managers must encourage task and relationship openness, set clear priorities, goals and agreements, create a permissive environment, create partnership openness by respecting each other's opinions and ideas, and encourage innovations and creativity. They must give positive feedback and positive reinforcement immediately for good performance. Also, they must confront poor performance without raising defensiveness by being specific, staying with facts and being neutral. Project managers must be very assertive when dealing with poor performers.

Trust and motivation are key factors for high team performance. Trust leads to effective communication, better working relationships, win/win negotiations, and effective conflict resolutions. Project managers must develop trust within the project team by using practical ideas that include walking their talk, creating an environment that encourages interaction and interdependence; and expressing and demonstrating genuine and sincere care, interest and confidence in their team members. They must communicate openly and act as coaches and facilitators to maximize creative potential of all team members. Every effort should be made by the project managers and all project participants to develop and maintain mutual trust with each other.

Project managers must themselves be motivated and motivate their project team and other project stakeholders. They must be aware of driving and restraining forces to team motivation and key factors of team morale that include the job itself, the project teams, the project management practices, and economic rewards and recognition. They must create an environment that nurtures high motivation, morale, and creativity to achieve high team performance. Trust leads to effective communication, motivation leads to higher commitment, and team morale leads to top perfor-

222

Figure 5.7 Important Elements of Power to Motivate

$$P = I^2R$$

where

P = Power to motivate others and feel motivated

I = Involvement in making project plans and participate in making decisions to implement the plans

I = Information access to relevant information to help do the project tasks effectively

R = Reasons/Respect: Explain to people why they should increase their efforts and above all they must be respected for their efforts, initiatives and creativity

---

mance on an ongoing basis; and all of these are vital for inspiring high team performance.

High team performance is a by-product of effective team leadership. Effective project managers must be aware of the difference between project leadership (doing the right things) and project managership (doing the things right). They must be aware of strengths and limitations of various theories, models and various team management and leadership styles and apply them according to the project task, team members and overall situation. They must use different leadership and management skills during different phases of the project life cycle. To inspire high team performance, project team leaders should use a shared leadership style that emphasizes participative style, empowerment, and trust.

In a nutshell the guidelines to INSPIRE a high team performance include—Identify a shared vision, Nurture creativity through effective team leadership, Share responsibilities and success, Prepare action plan using participative style, Improve communication and trust, Recognize good performance, and Enable others to do their best and help each other win.

About Self-Managed Work Teams   **226**
What are self-managed work teams?   226
Why SMWTs?   228
SMWTs vs. the traditional model   230

Empowerment: A Key Element of SMWTs and SMPTs: (The Self-Motivated Project Team)   **232**
What is empowerment?   232
Why empowerment   234
Main variables of empowerment   235

Fostering an SMPT Culture Through Empowerment   **235**
Principles of empowering people   236
Gaining and sharing power   237
Main components of SMPT culture   239
Changing organizational climate to foster SMPT culture   240

Creating and Maintaining SMPTs   **242**
Preparing for SMPTs   243
Building SMPTs   247
Facilitating SMPTs for success   251

Leadership in SMPTs   **256**
Roles and responsibilities of SMPT leaders   256
Problems during transitions   260
The values of SMPT leaders   260
SMPTs and their leaders in a nutshell   262
What's next for SMPTs?   262

Summary   **265**

It is easy to get good players, it is harder to get them to play as a team.

—Casey Stengal

6

From Self-Managed Work Teams to Self-Motivated Project Teams

A S TRADITIONAL MANAGEMENT philosophies prove too slow and too unresponsive to meet global competition, organizations are striving to be more flexible and adaptive. Progressive organizations are questioning not only organizational structures, but the basic paradigm of hierarchical work systems. To meet the challenges of accelerating change, projects are an effective management mode.

The trend to "empower" the workforce has led to increased quality and performance. At the same time, workers have experienced more job satisfaction. In such a work environment, team members not only become multifunctional in the core skills, but also acquire leadership and interpersonal skills, which are the key to sustaining a Self-Managed Work Team (SMWT).[1]

Managing a project is different from managing an ongoing organization. Projects involve short-term, crossfunctional team groupings, intensive learning curves and the need to focus on very specialized progressive objectives within specified constraints. In addition, it is essential to have one person responsible for managing all aspects of the projects and who interfaces with the client and other project stakeholders.[2] Therefore, the SMWT concept in a project environment is not entirely satisfactory. Yet self-management is not only possible on projects, but desirable.

Empowerment increases mutual trust among top management, project manager and team members. The project team becomes self-motivated. They may still need a team leader, but a mature team practically manages itself, within boundaries established by the project manager. Because self-motivation is such an important factor in the goal-oriented project environment, we call the resulting teams Self-Motivated Project Teams (SMPTs). These are similar to SMWTs in ongoing organizations, except that SMPTs must combine the valuable attributes of the SMWT with an attitude that satisfies the project environment in terms of project management process and constraints. ■

About Self-Managed Work Teams

When I started this business of teams, I was anxious to get it done and get back to my real job. Then I realized that, hey, this is my real job.

— *Ralph Stayer, CEO of Johnsonville Foods*

People are basically social creatures; that's why we usually find it more productive and fun to work in a team than alone. A team can communicate with its external customers and suppliers in ways that would not be possible for individuals.

An outgrowth of both the loss of worldwide competitive edge and the institutionalization of change has been the new "lean and mean" look of business. Everywhere there is talk of budget cuts, eliminating the fat, flattening organizational structures, cutting overhead and using temporary help. There is increased pressure to become faster, more flexible, and innovative, which can be achieved by implementing SMWT concepts.

In this environment, team players are critical to success. As the number of people decreases while the volume of work and the standards remain the same, organizations will need people who do quality work the first time, pitch in to help others out, create a cooperative atmosphere, and challenge others to do the best job possible. All this can only be accomplished through an effective teamwork, and this means building empowered teams and eventually creating self-managed work teams (SMWTs).

The concept of SMWTs in a project environment is both questionable and desirable. It is questionable because of the nature of the project environment, where there are continuous deadlines and insufficient time to change organizational culture in order to create SMWTs. At the same time, it is desirable because it increases performance, adaptability, quality, and innovation, all of which are necessary to compete globally. Moreover, people working in a project environment are generally more self-motivated and driven by project goals. A mature self-motivated team in a project environment (SMPT) is similar to an SMWT in an ongoing operation.

What are self-managed work teams?

The best way to get a good idea is to have lots of ideas.

— *Linus Pauling*

Definition: A SMWT is an intact group of employees who define their own goals and formulate plans to achieve those goals. They take day-to-day responsibility for managing themselves and their tasks with a minimum of direct supervision. They are interdependent and in addition to doing their job assignments, they assume traditional management responsibilities such as vacation scheduling, planning and scheduling work, making production and/or service-related decisions and taking actions to solve problems. Depending upon the level of maturity, they may do their own hiring and performance evaluations.[3,4]

226

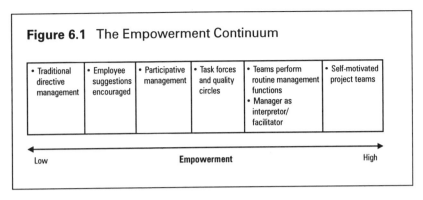

Figure 6.1 The Empowerment Continuum

• Traditional directive management	• Employee suggestions encouraged	• Participative management	• Task forces and quality circles	• Teams perform routine management functions • Manager as interpretor/ facilitator	• Self-motivated project teams

Low   **Empowerment**   High

As you can see from this definition, empowerment is the main characteristic of SMWTs. It gives people greater control over their jobs by giving them opportunities to take on more responsibilities and to make use of their knowledge and learning potential. They experience an increased sense of ownership which leads to increased commitment to produce quality output—and commitment to continuous improvement is essential to remain competitive.

Empowerment can be viewed as a continuum of employee involvement, from seeking employee input in specific and selected areas of the project (lower empowerment) at one end, to task forces and quality circles in the middle, and SMWTs (higher empowerment) at the other end of this continuum.[3,5] Teams operate on this self-management continuum with varying degrees of autonomy, as shown in Figure 6.1. This continuum can also describe the process by which organizations move away from traditional management to teams that eventually become SMWTs.[3,6]

Main characteristics and features of SMWTs. There are many characteristics that differentiate SMWTs from other types of teams. Three of the principal characteristics are:[7]

Intact and stable structure. As defined earlier, an SMWT is an intact group of people working together on a day-to-day basis. This group is dedicated to increase productivity and make continuous improvements by managing themselves and their assignments. This group is more stable than a group brought together for a special purpose, such as a product launch team, a quality action team, project audit team, or a quality circle. However, a long project may provide an intact and stable structure.

Sense of ownership. Work assignments in an SMWT are usually designed to give the team an ownership of a product or a service. It leads to higher commitment from each team member. It requires designing broader job categories and the sharing of work assignments. Rather than specializing in one narrow area or skills, the members of a SMWT are encouraged, at various times, to follow all the jobs of the team. This fits well in a project environment because project teams are usually cross-functional.

From Self-Managed Work Teams to Self-Motivated Project Teams

Whole business focus. SMWTs tend to focus on the whole business rather than on team goals or individual interests only. Consequently, SMWTs are customer-driven and are able to increase customer satisfaction by keeping the big picture in mind. In a project setting, this would mean that the director of a project must focus on all projects that contribute to the organization as a whole, rather than on one specific project only.

SMWTs represent a different way of managing organizations. Some of their operational characteristics are that they:
- Set their own goals and monitor their own work
- Plan, organize, execute, control and improve their own work processes
- Make their own schedule and review their performance as a team
- Prepare their own budgets and coordinate their activities with other departments
- Do their own purchasing
- Are empowered to share various management and leadership functions
- Organize their own training and professional development
- Do their own hiring, firing and disciplining
- Take full responsibility and feel accountable for the quality of their products and services.[1]

SMWTs are notable because they provide significant benefits to both the employers and employees. Employers get a significant competitive advantage because of increased commitment and quality of output from workers where employees get more freedom and control on their jobs and more opportunities to learn different skills and participate in making decisions. Employees feel a sense of accomplishment and a pride of ownership that increases their productivity and quality of output. SMWTs tend to do themselves tasks that are normally done by supervisors in traditional organizational structures.

In some organizations, of course, workers are not ready to take advantage of this freedom and SMWTs may prove too autonomous and costly.

Why SMWTs?

As formal, permanent organizational structures or units that manage their own work, SMWTs can be a strong part of an overall competitive strategy. Empowered teams provide a powerful way of dealing with the pressures of tough global competition, the information revolution and significant change in the expectations of workforce. Organizations must become more efficient, adaptive and sensitive to customer needs. Employees are seeking more job satisfaction and more freedom. SMWTs offer a tool to meet these challenges.

SMWTs provide a way of accomplishing organizational goals and meeting the needs of our changing workforce. They create flexible, self-disciplined, multi-skilled work teams. Team members get an opportunity

228

to participate in decision-making, learn different skills and make valuable contributions to their organizations.

SMWTs also seem to fulfill the need for a cultural shift in today's organization as we face the challenges of increasing effectiveness, quality, service and speed as well as the tasks of flattening hierarchies, taking advantage of technology, and motivating workers by responding to their need for a change in the work environment. If the organizational culture is conducive to SMWTs and the employees are prepared to accept extra responsibility and accountability, SMWTs produce excellent results both for the employer and employees.

Wellins *et al.*, did a survey of 500 organizations that are using SMWT, in conjunction with *Industry Week* magazine and the Association for Quality and Participation. They found a variety of reasons for companies to move toward SMWTs: Quality, productivity, reduced operating costs, increased job satisfaction provided the drivers to change for over 90 percent of the companies surveyed.[1,5]

To expand a little on the results of this survey, some of the major benefits of SMWTs are addressed below.

Improved quality, productivity and service. In the SMWT environment, people feel a sense of job ownership and emphasize continuous improvement. leading to significant leaps in quality, productivity and service. They are trained to perform cross-functional tasks.

Greater flexibility and quick self-correction. SMWTs are faster, effective, adaptive and flexible—all essential team qualities necessary to stay competitive. They communicate better and explore more opportunities and alternatives thanks to a broader knowledge base. The team members in SMWTs are more alert, engaged, proactive and responsive to customer needs than traditionally organized workforces. They are trained to "self-correct:" they are able to identify problems themselves and take corrective actions quickly.

Reduced operating cost. Downsizing, cutthroat competition, and elimination of middle management require work teams to do more and more with less and less. Costs have to be reduced. Empowered work teams provide a means to take on extra responsibility typically reserved for managers or supervisors, thereby reducing overall operating costs.

Faster response to the technology revolution. Advanced manufacturing technologies and information revolution require workers to acquire different and higher-level technical skills and to update these skills continuously. These technologies create closer interdependence and the consequences of failure to work together are serious. SMWTs provide the communication link and responsiveness to take optimum advantage of technological advancements in workplaces.[8]

Fewer and simpler job classifications. With complex technology and growing need for flexibility and fast responsiveness, work teams must have multi-skilled team members who can perform job functions competently. Training is very important. Today, workers are required to perform several job functions, rotate their roles and fill in for one another. SMWTs are designed to facilitate job sharing and cross training.

Psychological benefits to the worker: enhanced enrichment and control. Today's workforce has different values and expectations regarding quality of work life. They want more autonomy, participation in decision-making, responsibility, and empowerment. A Louis Harris poll reported that 77 percent of respondents indicated that they want the freedom to decide how to do their own work. They are willing to accept more challenging work assignments. They value a sense of accomplishment and growth more than pay.[9] These values and wants are more consistent with the concept of self-motivated project teams (SMPTs) as well as SMWTs.

Emphasis on the value of human resources. Projects are done by people. Human resources are one of the most important and biggest assets of any organization. According to an excellent report on the changing workforce by Camevale *et al.*, American employers will no longer be able to select from a field of workers with strong basic skills.[10] Organizations must empower their employees in order to attract and retain the best people.

Organizations are experiencing that, as workers are given more autonomy and ownership, they work harder and feel more committed to producing high-quality results. As workers are given more control of their jobs and more freedom to decide how they will do them, their productivity has increased. Employees who work on projects following the concepts of self-managing teams demonstrate a higher level of motivation, increased self-worth and greater pride in their work making them a self-motivated project team (SMPT). Organizations with such project teams will be able to attract and retain the best people.

SMWTs vs. the traditional model

The classic management structures with stove-pipe functions, rigid bureaucracies, many management levels, and hierarchical chain of command and reporting relationships are becoming obsolete. Now organizations are empowering their employees by giving them more autonomy and opportunity. Work teams set their own goals and select processes to accomplish their goals, i.e., they "manage" themselves. In return, organizations are getting increased quality, customer service, flexibility, and faster responsiveness.

Traditional organizations/management model: The traditional role of management is one of control. Objectives are set by top management alone and are communicated down the chain of command. Figure 6.2 shows a traditional management model.[11]

The major reasons why the traditional management model/philosophy won't work today, are:

230

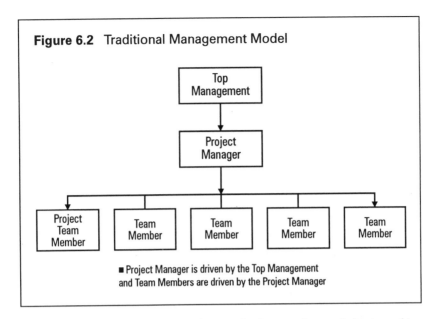

Figure 6.2 Traditional Management Model

■ Project Manager is driven by the Top Management and Team Members are driven by the Project Manager

- Rapidly changing technology has made the creation and sharing of information a critical success factor. In the old model, only top management had access to and control of information.
- Employee expectations and values emphasize challenges, autonomy, participation and sense of ownership. Workers—especially knowledge workers—don't want to be a cog in a machine.
- Tough global competition means organizations need to be faster and more flexible and adaptable.
- Business needs more creativity and innovation, and thus must place more value on self-growth and job satisfaction.

SMWT model. As teams mature, they are able to take more responsibility, make decisions and plan, organize, and manage their own work. The main advantages of SMWTs are improved productivity, quality, and service becuase of higher commitment and ownership, greater flexibility, reduced operating costs, better employee morale and attitude. They provide cross-functional training, faster response to technology revolution, a sense of job enrichment and self-control for the worker, increased collaboration and cooperation, whole-business focus, and continuous improvement. Figure 6.3 shows a model for typical SMWTs.

However, they do have some disadvantages. For example, there is no formal permanent team manager/leader; there may be potential confusion in roles and reporting relationships; it may be difficult to align everyone's interests or to define and enforce the boundaries of freedom. All these challenges can lead to an environment that may at times seem chaotic. It is also important to note that SMWTs don't work very well when the objectives are unrealistic or when the technology is inappropriate for the task.

The origin of SMWTs is attributed to the early work of Eric Trist[12] who challenged the fundamental assumptions of scientific management. Trist introduced the idea of forming work teams having a responsibility for an entire operation and optimizing the interface between people (the social system) and their tools (the technical system) in order to increase productivity, job satisfaction and meet the values of an experienced workforce.[12]

SMWTs are notable because they outperform their traditional counterparts. A survey of the transition to SMWTs in seven countries showed that 93 percent reported improved productivity, 86 percent reported lower operating costs, 86 percent reported improved quality, and 70 percent reported better employee attitudes.[13]

As outlined earlier, in a project environment, SMPTs are conceptually similar to SMWTs in ongoing operations.

Empowerment: A Key Element of SMWTs and SMPTs

Empowerment is not a single change, but a total shift of everything about the way you do business and work together. There are no short cuts.
— Cynthia D. Scott and Dennis T. Jaffe in Empowerment

How can organizations achieve continuous improvement under the pressures to do more and more with less and less? The answer lies in "people power." People want to make a difference in their organizations. They are seeking job satisfaction and opportunities to participate in the decision-making process. They want to have more freedom about their work and work processes.

Organizations feel challenged to cope with changing expectations of the workforce. Yet progressive organizations who are willing to take risks and give more autonomy to their workers can be assured of higher productivity. The progressive organization empowers employees and expects them to use the power in a responsible and accountable manner. Successful leaders believe that empowerment provides more energy and creates a sense of ownership of tasks—prerequisites for continuous improvement.

What is empowerment?

People represent the most valuable resource of any organization. Most people want to make a noticeable contribution to organizational objectives and organizations also want such people. However, there is a lot of frustration in workplaces because neither management nor employees know how to nurture human creativity and initiative. Empowerment is new fuel for the growing workplace because it breaks down these barriers to creativity.

Definition: Empowerment is a combination of three words:

232

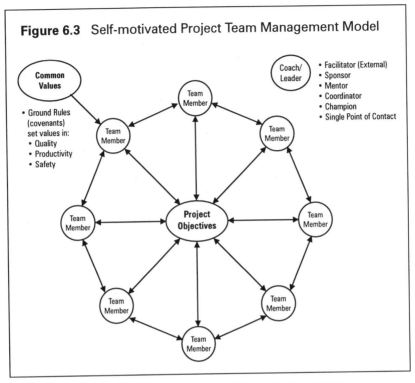

Figure 6.3 Self-motivated Project Team Management Model

Common Values

- Ground Rules (covenants) set values in:
  - Quality
  - Productivity
  - Safety

Team Member

Team Member

Team Member

Team Member

Project Objectives

Team Member

Team Member

Team Member

Team Member

Coach/ Leader

- Facilitator (External)
- Sponsor
- Mentor
- Coordinator
- Champion
- Single Point of Contact

Adapted from *Implementing Self-Directed Work Teams Workbook.* 1993. Boulder. Colo.: Career Track, p. 3

- Prefix *em* means to "put onto" or "to cover with."
- *Power* means control, authority, dominion.
- *We* (at the center of the word) implies sharing responsibilities.[14]

Then, empowering means passing on authority, responsibility and accountability. To this must be added "reliability" on the part of the employee. Empowerment occurs when reliable employees are given power to manage their work and work process. They then experience a sense of ownership, freedom, and control over their jobs.

Empowerment is indeed a *different* way of working together. It means giving employees control and freedom over their tasks in a way that employees experience a sense of ownership. It is facilitated by a combination of factors, which include organizational values and leadership actions; rewards, recognition and training systems; and organizational design and working relationships.[14] Empowerment could be at all levels—individual, team and organizational. Empowerment influences employees, teams and organizations in terms of how they work, feel and achieve results.[15]

Empowered team members share power, responsibility, accountability, communication, expectations, and rewards in ways that are very different

From Self-Managed Work Teams to Self-Motivated Project Teams

from work relationships in traditional hierarchical organizations.[15] The empowered organization is structured in a free format based upon more trust and confidence in its human resources. The work climate encourages people to do what needs to be done to achieve the best results. People do more than just what is required of them and are rewarded and recognized for taking extra initiative. Other actions that characterize an empowered workplace include:[15]

- Enhancing the breadth and depth of each task
- Expanding the skills and opportunities to learn new things
- Encouraging creativity and innovation
- Giving freedom to decide how the task should be done
- Allowing people to make decisions and develop plans to implement them
- Giving responsibility for customer satisfaction and marketing
- Emphasizing the "big picture" (project goals)
- Giving them control over their jobs for evaluations and corrective actions
- Providing a sense of ownership and accountability.

Why empowerment?

Empowerment is not merely a fashionable or trendy concept; it is essential to survive in the 21st century. The typical organization is under attack from outside and from within. Externally, there is tough global competition, rapidly changing technology, pressures for high quality and service, growing need to be faster and flexible, and above all limited resources. Internally, employees feel shortchanged, overworked, underpaid and not properly recognized. They feel lack of opportunities to learn new skills, to grow, and to take greater ownership of their jobs. They are seeking job satisfaction, meaningful work, and a sense of accomplishment. They want to make a contribution to organizational goals. Organizations must adapt to these changes and develop appropriate strategies to get the job done.

Empowerment makes employees aware of their responsibility, authority, the boundaries of freedom, and their commitment to reliability and accountability. For managers who are caught in the middle, who feel pressed by new demands from outside, above, and employees at the same time, empowerment helps build effective teams to achieve human synergy and make the organization work. In a world where information and change are a "click of the mouse" away, the entire work force must be empowered to learn and act quickly. Employees need to be given the information and freedom to think and adapt decisively using their own expertise and experience. Access to information, power to initiate action and the responsibility to take ownership produces a better relationship between employees, management and the customer.

Main variables of empowerment

In a broad sense, empowerment means giving away control and authority. It's success is dependent on four important variables:[3]

234

- *Authority* to make and implement decisions regarding resources
- *Accountability* to achieve higher commitment and sensible use of authority
- *Resources,* that is the budget, equipment, time and training to do the task
- *Information* that is complete and accurate on which to base sound decisions.

To be properly empowered, it is important to have all four variables. In a project environment, if any of these variables is missing, empowerment will fail and project managers will not get the expected increase in performance. For example, authority without proper resources (skills, training, time and budget) and accurate and timely information is only permission. Also, if project team members do not feel accountable, the authority and resources given to them and providing them an access to all business information will lead to poor results. A sense of ownership and a sense of strong commitment is created when people possess all four variables.[3]

Bumps in the road to empowerment are inevitable. People always resist changes. Due to downsizing in most organizations, people are always reacting, fighting crisis. They don't really have the time or energy to be innovative or creative. Here are some major bumps in the road to SMPTs:[15]

- *Inertia* creates difficulty in getting started. People may feel comfortable with the status quo and be reluctant to accept extra freedom and take more responsibility.
- *Lack of self confidence* in the potential of project teams and team members can slow down empowerment.
- *Anger* towards those who are keen at making empowerment work.
- *Confusion* due to the many ways to implement empowerment and no one with real experience.

The road to empowerment is not smooth. Project managers must consider empowerment as a journey with several bridges and bumps along the way which can only be crossed with careful planning, training and sincere commitment from management.

Fostering an SMPT Culture Through Empowerment

No matter what is your business, teams are the wave of the future.
— *Jerry Junkins, late CEO of Texas Instruments*

In the 21st century, organizations will derive their competitive advantages not just from new technology but from dedication, the quality of commitment and the competency of their human resources. Human capital—the results of employee energy and creativity—will be their most valuable asset. Fostering an SMPT culture and building SMPTs will become the key to survival and growth of most business organizations.

However, fostering an SMPT culture is not easy. Like any other cultural changes, it involves changing the basic philosophy of management, teamwork and team building and the way people view their organizational climates and working relationships. It requires a real change at all levels in the organization—whole organization, project teams, and project team members. To create such a change, each of these levels of organization must be prepared and committed to cooperate in this challenging endeavor—a cultural change process. Empowerment is the vital component of SMPT culture. Fostering an SMPT culture involves analysis and understanding of principles of empowering people, gaining and sharing power from several sources, the sources of power, the main components of SMPT culture, and how to change organizational climate to achieve effective empowerment.

Principles of empowering people

Empowerment is an essential element of SMPTs that must be accepted as a concept by the entire organization if it is to be successful. Commitment from all members is essential in order to reap the rewards.

The empowerment referred to so far in this chapter is more individual than team or organizational. While empowerment on an individual basis is good, as a concept to improve results, a project team must be motivated as a whole to qualify as an SMPT and be truly successful. So not only does an organization need to give project teams increased decision-making discretion but team members must give each other the same opportunities. They need to support and promote each other versus competing to finish their own tasks first and better than everyone else.

There are ten major principles of empowering team members in order to foster an SMPT culture:[16]

1. Inform them of their responsibilities.
2. Give them authority equal to their responsibilities.
3. Set standards of excellence.
4. Provide them with training.
5. Give them knowledge and information.
6. Provide them with feedback.
7. Recognize them for good performance.
8. Trust them and support them.
9. Have some tolerance for failure.
10. Treat them with dignity and respect.

These principles must be followed in order for empowerment to be a valuable tool. It is not an easy concept to accept and implement because it is not a one-time process; it is one aspect of continuous improvement.

The purpose of empowerment is to provide the employees greater involvement in making decisions that impact on project goals and on the project management process. The idea is that each team member will have more responsibility and, therefore, a greater personal stake in the project as well as in the organization, ultimately leading to higher quality of work output at greater rates. Empowerment is the cornerstone of the next century's management concept, which is an employee-focused approach to management.

Gaining and sharing power

Empowerment means giving away or sharing power. What are the sources of power that can be given to empower people so that they can manage projects effectively? How can an organization begin to move towards this new paradigm? How can freedom and control be balanced?

Sources of power. Power is central to empowerment. It represents an ability to influence other people, which is instrumental in getting the project done. To a certain extent, project managers must have a balanced combination of various types of power and above all they must know how to use it wisely and give to others carefully. The sources of power in an organization are authority, accountability, commitment, information, influence, network and earned/personal power.[17]

Authority or positional power is based on position on the organizational chart. It refers to the chain of command—a manager's right to control and command subordinates. A manager does not have real authority unless there are boxes coming out of his or her box on the organizational chart.

Accountability power is based on mutual agreement as a contract, not an expectation. It is an essential element of empowerment. Being accountable means being responsible and answerable. It requires one to report, explain or justify. Being able to hold someone accountable, responsible and answerable, gives you the power and increases your ability to get the job done. In a project environment, accountability issues can be enforced by agreeing on and signing contracts that are normally done with the client, contractors, subcontractors, vendors, and suppliers.

Commitment power is based on participation. It means buy-in, ownership and motivation. People support what they create. Genuine involvement/participation leads to acceptance that is essential to obtain commitment. In a project environment, a highly committed team defines its goals and then plans and executes the work. It increases the chances of producing high quality results. High and genuine participative management creates an environment conducive to total quality management.

Information power can be organizational or personal. It may be obtained in three ways: by becoming a focal point for information (has to be given formally); by earning personal power based on knowledge (technical, organizational or special skills); or by acquiring information using organizational politics.

Some managers use "management by walking around" to get better information to build upon their information power.

Influence power represents personal power earned through alliances (professional, social, or others); interpersonal skills (communication, negotiation, conflict resolution and leadership); and charisma. It stays with you even if you change jobs or organizations. It includes network power, which is very effective in managing projects. Influence power is increased by doing favors and then being able to call in owed favors.

From Self-Managed Work Teams to Self-Motivated Project Teams

Network power is based on personal and business contacts. It involves doing and receiving favors.

Earned/personal power is earned based on knowledge, experience, skills and professional reputation.

Once project managers are well aware of these major sources of power, they must try to increase their power by increasing any of these sources of power as much as possible. In a project environment, it can be done by using the following techniques: [17]

- To gain authority, rely on the executive sponsor or project champion in order to maintain high priority and corporate visibility for the project.
- To gain accountability, negotiate agreements/contracts for work and accountability. Negotiate with functional managers for work packages, and hold their personnel accountable for delivering the agreed upon work within budget and on schedule. Team members negotiate agreements with their project managers for their assignments.
- To gain commitment, use a participative management style to get people to buy in and gain wider acceptance about goals and plans to accomplish those goals. People support what they create. It is better to involve upper management and customer in defining goals. Remember, commitment means quality!
- To gain information, sharpen your interpersonal skills. Refine and use listening skills. It is helpful to be formally designated as focal point of project information such as communication, decisions, status report, and rewards. To make it work, it should be backed up with appropriate action when people try to go around you.
- To gain influence, increase interpersonal skills especially communication and alliances. Project managers can increase their influence power by acquiring interpersonal skills, especially communication, facilitation, negotiating, conflict resolution and leadership. They should also establish alliances with a wide variety of people. They should either themselves become technically, organizationally, and politically knowledgeable, or ensure that there is someone with this knowledge on the project team.
- To gain network power, build alliances and keep up the contacts with people you meet.
- To gain earned power, acquire and demonstrate a high level of knowledge, experience and professional excellence. Above all, they should be approachable for help.

It is important that project managers appreciate various sources of power and how different types of power can be acquired or increased. Most important is the ability to balance it and use it wisely. These ideas can also help them in empowering their project team members.

Main components of SMPT culture

Empowerment, essential for building an SMPT culture, is not a single change. It is rather a total shift in the way people work together.[15] It cannot be created unless it is supported by individual attitudes and mindsets, team behaviors, and organizational values. The three main components of empowerment, shown in Figure 6.4, include the following:[15]

Mindsets represent the fundamental component of SMPT culture. Employees become more self-motivated, responsible, accountable and prepared to self-manage their work. Creating SMPT culture involves a series of shifts of mind (as compared to a traditional organization) in terms of how the organization is structured and how managers and employees approach their work. Some of these shifts are shown in Table 6.1.[15]

Drastic shifts are required in mindsets of both the project manager/leader and team members. *Project managers* must act more as *coaches* or *facilitators*. They should challenge assumptions but support creativity and innovation. They should foster a learning environment, promote shared information and collaborative problem solving. They must focus on developing people and their horizons and appreciate diversity of style and behavior. Above all, managers must "walk their talk."

Employees also need to change their mindset to create SMPTs. They should take responsibility for actions and accept accountability for outcomes. They should seek to solve problems rather than pointing fingers. They should find ways of working together and support each other. Above all, they must communicate effectively by sharing information, seeking feedback and supporting other team members' ideas.

Team relationships are important in creating SMPTs. Teams must focus on process as well as content. They communicate effectively, sharing information, giving and receiving feedback. Fostering an SMPT culture requires three major shifts in relationships for everyone in an organization:[15]

- *Attend to process.* In addition to reaching their goals, SMPTs attend to the process regarding how it gets there and how it can be improved.
- *Take responsibility.* In an SMPT, everyone feels responsible for meeting project objectives, not only the project leader/manager. Everyone presents ideas and suggestions which are evaluated objectively and implemented if found suitable.
- *Seek learning.* Traditional organizations typically react to management plans or to the changing environment. SMPT members are willing to accept more responsibility and accountability, take actions, share information, take risks, speak out and solve problems in a collaborative manner. They don't wait for directions and are not afraid of failures.

Organizational structures focus on policies, procedures and incentives that match the value of empowerment. In the 21st century, organizations must produce high quality products and services, make continuous improvements and learn to do more and more with less and less. SMPTs rec-

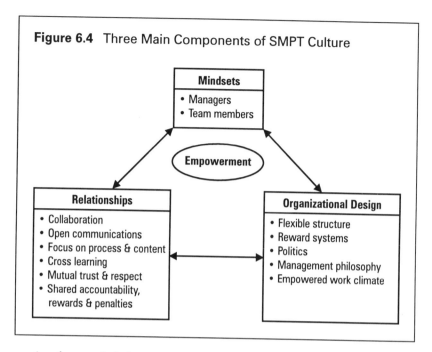

Figure 6.4 Three Main Components of SMPT Culture

Mindsets
- Managers
- Team members

Empowerment

Relationships
- Collaboration
- Open communications
- Focus on process & content
- Cross learning
- Mutual trust & respect
- Shared accountability, rewards & penalties

Organizational Design
- Flexible structure
- Reward systems
- Politics
- Management philosophy
- Empowered work climate

ognize that needed changes won't come in the form of an edict from top management and they must develop innovative approaches themselves.

SMPTs work towards accomplishing organizational objectives and also step back and evaluate how they are reaching these goals. They review their work processes and redesign their way of working. They recognize that this is not a one-time event, but a continuous process.

SMPTs are committed to high quality. Management must recognize that the people who are doing a task are the best people to redesign it for making improvements—not a team of outside consultants. Organizations must provide work autonomy and job flexibility. They must focus on human capital and continuously develop and maintain high team performance. They should create a sense of community in the workplace where people can feel good about working together. Organizations must create a climate where employees can manage their stress effectively by supporting each other and can see career development opportunities.

Changing organizational climate to foster SMPT culture

Creating an SMPT culture involves changing the culture of whole organization and its management philosophy. Empowerment is the key to an SMPT culture. It is often thought to be something managers do *to* their subordinates. In fact, it is more than this, it is a *process,* something that happens in a working relationship between people.

Table 6.1 Shifts from Traditional to SMPT Culture

Traditional	SMPT
• Waiting for directions	• Take action
• Reactive	• Proactive and innovative
• Focus on content	• Focus on process and content
• Emphasis on quantity	• Emphasis on quality and quantity
• Boss responsible	• All responsible
• Finger pointing	• Problem solving
• Focus on individual tasks	• Focus on whole job
• Competitive	• Collaborative
• Driven by manager/supervisor	• Driven by objectives

From the inside to the outside. This refers to the shift in attitude required within the manager, recognizing that empowering employees does not mean disempowering the managers. Some managers in traditional hierarchical organizations perceive empowering as a threat to their status, power and control when in fact the opposite is true. In an empowered workplace, there is more creativity. Project managers can look at everyone on the team for ideas rather than looking only at their boss for directions. Instead of having sole responsibility for the project, the project manager has help from the whole team because everyone feels a sense of ownership and accountability. There is real teamwork in an empowered workplace. Instead of working alone on their tasks, team members work interdependently towards common goals. The work environment emphasizes *collaboration* (to help each other win) rather than on *competition* (race to increase only individual output).

Empowerment is a novel way of achieving real teamwork, increased task ownership and commitment to overall objectives. It must begin from the inside to the outside, i.e., it must be initiated and supported by the management. By empowering, managers gain more power—defined as the ability to influence and achieve—rather than losing power.

Balancing freedom versus control. Traditionally, managers and supervisors are expected to keep tight control over their employees and work processes. Empowerment is quite different from traditional concepts of control. In an empowered workplace, people are encouraged to plan and decide their own work and work processes. They are free to take actions to make any improvements. However, freedom and control must be balanced with project constraints; otherwise, it can lead to chaos.[15]

In a project environment, when project teams are mature and self motivated, team members can be given freedom to plan their own tasks,

From Self-Managed Work Teams to Self-Motivated Project Teams

work procedures, and working hours. Communication is more open and information is shared more openly and widely. However, the project managers must keep control over quality and resources. This is facilitated because project team members feel themselves more responsible and committed to achieve high quality results within specified constraints.

Project managers must define boundaries (such as end dates, important quality issues, etc.) within which some freedom and flexibility can be provided while enhancing individual creativity and developing high commitment to meet project objectives. Empowerment is finding the right *balance* between freedom and control.

Creating and Maintaining SMPTs

On a day-to-day basis, my passion comes from backing people's efforts, getting them what they need to do the job, educating them, and working with them as members of the team.

— Bill Eaton, Levi Strauss executive committee

Management has to be very serious about committing to the goal of creating SMPTs by applying the empowerment concept. By involving and soliciting advice from the employees with the hands-on knowledge of a problem, solutions will be produced quicker and implemented far easier than if the manager simply instructs the employee what to do. A common phase for this concept is bottom-up empowerment, a radical switch from top-down control.

Is empowerment and self-management a fad? Some organizations try to empower their employees and create SMPTs by running all their people through a series of off-site retreats and seminars by inspiring speakers. The experience is powerful, and the participants get excited about potential changes in their work life. But when they return to their workplaces, full of energy, and begin implementing these changes within their teams, they feel they've hit a brick wall. Things don't seem to change easily and they get frustrated. Creating and maintaining SMPTs involves understanding the empowerment concept, the process of empowerment and team dynamics. Managers must follow three basic steps: preparing for SMPTs, implementing SMPTs, and facilitating SMPTs successfully.

Once there is an organizational commitment to SMPTs the journey can begin. The more an SMPT works together and recognizes its strengths and weaknesses, the more responsibility and accountability teams can take. Since motivation is an intrinsic phenomenon, once the team members are matured and happy with the organizational climate, they become self-motivated to achieve project goals.

Preparing for SMPTs

Plan properly. If you fail to plan, you plan to fail.

A careful and sound preparation for SMPTs is the first basic step of creating and maintaining them. It involves evaluating the organization, the management, the team and the team members in terms of their readiness for empowerment and creating SMPTs effectively.

Is the organization ready? This is the first question to be answered. Organizations that have a supportive organizational culture and work environment are more conducive to SMPTs. Their top management welcomes constructive change. Organizational culture is represented by its total environment, social norms and general management philosophy and behavior. Following are major characteristics of the organizational culture that is more likely to support SMPTs. Such organizations:[18]

- Have a clear and positive vision. Remember, "Nothing happens unless first a vision."
- Have formulated a strategy to meet long- and short-term goals
- Believe in their products and services
- Have social conscience and support the community
- Are people oriented, remembering that people are the biggest asset
- Emphasize cooperation more than competition, which encourages team work
- Set higher quality standards for all functions
- Appreciate the time needed to complete the tasks and processes, and so avoid crises rather than having a "crisis culture"
- Provide good hygiene factors, i.e. fair pay, security, good working conditions, social needs and training, etc. Lack of good hygiene factors causes dissatisfaction.
- Promote teams and team work
- Encourage participation in evaluating work process and designing improvements, since the people doing the work know the most about it
- Have tolerance for failure, because willingness to take risks encourages creativity
- Encourage creativity and innovation by taking the attitude that the "status quo" is not satisfactory
- Recognize and reward for individual and team contributions
- Promote managers who "walk their talk," which enhances trust among employees
- Appreciate and capitalize on cultural differences.

Project managers can evaluate organizational culture by using these characteristics as a checklist to determine if the organization is ready for SMPTs. Then they can formulate a plan to eliminate and/or reduce the impact of organizational cultural characteristics that may become obstacles.

Is management ready? This question relates to the attitude of project managers towards empowering their project team members. Since SMPTs help organizations reach their goals, it is important that organizational goals and SMPTs' functions be compatible. Management must be willing to sponsor SMPTs and committed to help them succeed. Here are six major requirements for management support to implement SMPTs:[18]

Set clear goals. This is one of the most important responsibilities and contributions of management, because SMPTs are driven by goals and objectives. Better still, team members should be involved in setting goals. It is effective to have goals expressed in writing because written agreements tend to clarify the issues where agreement is critical for project success.

Show willingness. Management should demonstrate genuine support for SMPTs, not just lip service. They should be willing to give the level of autonomy that the team is ready for. It is useful to have a management champion/sponsor with enough formal/organizational authority to help SMPTs when they face any problems.

Provide political shields. SMPTs may threaten existing power bases as the power is pushed further down in the hierarchy. Such perceived threats may create political obstacles and roadblocks. To create SMPTs, management must provide political shields so that SMPTs can concentrate on project objectives.

Acquire resources. SMPTs represent a new philosophy of working in teams. They may need additional resources (such as training, consulting services, extra support staff, and special equipment) beyond what is normally required for doing their jobs. Sponsor/champions with organizational authority can help provide the additional resources required.

Give feedback. For most organizations, SMPTs may be a new process and philosophy of working together. Continuous objective evaluation should be done to identify problems so that SMPTs can self-correct quickly before proceeding too far in a wrong direction.

Allow process time. Creating SMPTs is a complex process. Management should have patience rather than expecting quick results. Also, SMPTs need to adjust to making their own decisions and accepting the consequences. They need to establish procedures for completing administrative functions and working together effectively. Management should appreciate the learning curve and allow sufficient time for the process to show results.

Are the team and its members ready? What can SMPTs provide for the team and its members? Are team members willing to take more responsibilities and challenges? Is the temporary absence of a team leader suggesting self-management? Among the many reasons for a team and team members to consider SMPTs are to:[18]
- Learn more skills (cross training)
- Learn management skills and participate in decision-making

244

- Have more freedom and control over their tasks
- Work in an atmosphere of trust and respect
- Become self-motivated and increase self-esteem
- Get a sense of accomplishment
- Learn taking more responsibility and accepting accountability
- Gain financial rewards through skill based pay and profit sharing
- Learn human skills
- Learn managing interfaces and integration
- Learn time management
- Learn how organizational/project politics work.

When a team is empowered and self-motivated and has reached a high maturity level, it should be ready to self-manage. To help the team move towards self-management, project managers must have a kick-off meeting to explain the reasons and values of implementing this new work climate. A good kick-off meeting helps start this system and the project on the right foot. At this meeting, project participants are brought together and unity of purpose can be reinforced. Management can communicate the degree of trust and confidence they have in the teams and their commitment to empower the teams to produce high performance. A kick-off meeting can be organized as an informal meeting or a social event where concerns of team members towards self managing can be addressed and true team spirit can be developed by gaining commitment of team members. Since kick-off meetings are crucial to implementing the SMPT concept, project managers must plan and conduct these meetings carefully.

SMPTs are driven by project objectives and can manage themselves within established boundaries. To help prepare the team and its members, the following questions should be asked.[18]

Will you commit to the results? SMPT members must all agree to stand behind the end result whether it is positive or negative. Positive results are easy to live with and promote the good while the negative are excellent opportunities to learn and grow together as a team.

Can the team withstand peer pressure? Within any team, members can experience peer pressure, but SMPTs do not have a leader to take the brunt of the pressure so the team must be able to bind together as a strong team and stand up and respond to any outside pressures.

Does the team have trust? Team members must trust each other and also be trustworthy themselves. A SMPT begins with trust and only positive reinforcement can enhance that trust. To be trustworthy each member must be willing to open up to the team in the spirit of open communication and the well-being of the team.

Are there clear realistic expectations set out? Once there is trust and all the team members commit to the SMPT, then very clearly communicated and realistic objectives and project expectations must be laid out and understood by all members. One can never over-communicate, therefore the more expectations are discussed and clarified on a continual basis, the better it is. For example, resources must be researched and made well known; expectations and objectives must be identified and listed; and all members must agree to them.

What are the rewards for the SMPT and the individual members? This question must be addressed. Now that the team knows what is expected of them and they understand what they need to contribute for the SMPT to succeed, the next question is what is in it for us and for me?

A pay system must be set up for the SMPT so that the individual members are paid fairly for their hard work. A proper reward system must be set up for the SMPT and the individuals. The rewards must be tied directly to team efforts and results. The expectations and objectives must be specific enough to be tied to financial and emotional rewards. The rewards must be meaningful to the team and the individuals so that they are truly seen as rewards.

Who will do what and how will they do it? The SMPT members are now wanting to start their job. The SMPT must outline each of the tasks and how to do it so that all members understand and can participate. Each task must be outlined and documented so that any of the members can clarify and actually follow through any of the tasks. Once all the tasks are outlined then tasks must be done. Because there is no team leader, the team must agree on what tasks each member does so that there is the trust and confidence that it will be done and done right.

Can the SMPT accomplish short- and long-term goals? If the SMPT members are committed then both short- and long-term goals can be identified and proper objectives can be set. Even if the project is short-term, long-term goals still need to be identified for the corporation's needs. The corporation will benefit from long term planning and so will the SMPT if expectations are clear and clarified.

Has the team had management's help in the past? If the team has had good leadershipin the past then the team members have a good foundation to manage themselves. If the team is new or did not have good management support previously then time will answer this question. Good and open communication and clear expectations will help the team manage themselves.

Will the SMPT have a sponsor or outside helper? Peer pressure helps keep the team in check but without a senior management sponsor the team will not be able to overcome all obstacles and problems. Senior management can facilitate needs of the SMPT and help get resources that the SMPT needs.

Do the team members have all the skills that are needed? It is important that each team member have conceptual, human and technical skills so that at any stage of the project or when any task needs to be done that each member can assist. Team members must be able to work dependently, in-

246

dependently and interdependently. If any member does not possess these skills then the project could have problems that the team cannot solve.

You can assess your team's readiness level for the SMPT concept by using Self Assessment Exercise F in the Appendix, which summarizes these questions for discussion among team members.

Sound planning and preparation is crucial to the successful creation of SMPTs. It involves evaluating the level of readiness at all levels: organization, management, and team and its members.

Building SMPTs

The way I looked at it was that the reward was the freedom to manage myself. That in itself was a gift. I had to work a little harder, but I enjoyed it because I got to make my own decisions and face the consequences. I did not have a babysitter.

— *Robert F. Hicks and Diane Bone in* Self-Managing Teams

Building an SMPT involves a clear understanding of empowerment, empowerment process and paths to empowerment. Project managers must be aware of various bumps in the road to empowerment and develop strategies to pass through them successfully.

Building SMPTs can be a difficult process which must be well-thought out and planned thoroughly. Like every management process it must be planned, organized, executed and monitored. The process of building SMPTs can be broken into four steps.

The first step involves setting the overall ambiance within an organization. In this step, strong advocates of SMPTs explore the feasibility of building SMPTs and changing organizational culture accordingly. It involves evaluating the existing organizational culture, identifying resistant forces and developing strategies to minimize this resistance from key team members and project managers.

The design of an organization is instrumental in building SMPTs. Mechanistic organizations have a rigid, more formal structure. They are based around several levels of hierarchy with control centered tightly at the top. An organic organization creates a looser, more flexible environment. The organic environment is more likely to nurture implementation of SMPTs. Everyone is open to change and willing to adapt to the new challenges, policies and procedures.

Step two involves the training process. Training increases self-confidence and motivation. However, training people to take responsibility can be a daunting task. Many people are afraid of failure and are hesitant to take on more work. With proper and extensive education, people become more confident and willing to tackle any challenge. James Huskett describes the training process as "information instead of instruction."[19] Information gives power. Information gives freedom and choice. Instruction is viewed as authoritarian, coming from the top and, therefore, when imposed, can lead to resentment. Information leads to opportunity for employees. They

From Self-Managed Work Teams to Self-Motivated Project Teams

can gain knowledge and absorb a greater range of job obligations. Information can also be interpreted differently by each person, which can lead to greater ideas. In SMPTs, information is shared openly and widely, which results in better decisions and higher quality output.

Part of this training includes feedback. Feedback should always be *constructive*. Feedback is also considered information. The team members can take their feedback and apply it to make themselves better, more productive team members. Feedback should be presented in a manner that is similar to the goal-setting. The employee should evaluate their performance and rate themselves in addition to evaluation from management. Feedback should take place in a more supportive environment where all aspects of a job can be discussed. The work environment should encourage feedback from the individual, the project manager, other team members or other co-workers, and other project stakeholders. This provides a range of opinions, not just one, and all with intention to help each other win.

Feedback is most effective when it is given in a positive light. The project manager should always try to highlight the strengths of an individual when assessing their performance. Recognition is the ultimate motivator for most people. Feedback should take place on a continuous basis as constant feedback alerts team members about when and what they are doing wrong so that they can take appropriate corrective action immediately. Project managers must be willing to help when the team needs it.

The third step involves gaining commitment of all the team members. It involves building communication links and setting up an effective team communication system that fosters openness. Team members establish roles to improve on a continuous basis the quality of products and services to the client. Team members trust each other, collaborate and work interdependently to maximize overall team performance.

During this step, project leaders should recognize the challenges and problems during transition. They should pass on more control and freedom to team members as teams become more matured and self motivated. Some project leaders may not be successful in building SMPTs because of the lack of coaching skills.

The final step in building SMPTs is evaluating to optimize the impact on the organization. This can be a difficult time because the manager has given up his or her traditional power and authority role but still has the ultimate responsibility to deliver the project deliverables. The project manager wants to be informed, but not overbearing. Among many elements of monitoring, two main elements are *trust* and *fair distribution of workload*. Empowerment is based on trust which many traditional managers have a difficult time dealing with. Knowing that the final responsibility lies with them, the manager must have effective communication with his or her SMPT. The monitoring may involve a casual meeting once a week or a simple report on the progress, but it is essential to keep all parties informed. The more power an employee has, the more responsibility they are willing to accept, and more committed they will be to accomplish project objectives.

Part of the monitoring process also involves ensuring that any team member is not overloaded. By keeping track of their team's workload, the manager must maintain an appropriate balance. An SMPT can be a liberating experience, but it can also grow quite frustrating if the team members bite off more than they can chew.

Stages of maturity for SMPTs. SMPTs evolve through five stages of maturity. The roles and skills requirements of the team leaders change with the maturity level of the team. Also, each stage of maturity presents its own challenges. These stages are:[20]

- Stage 1—Investigation
- Stage 2—Preparation
- Stage 3—Implementation
- Stage 4—Transition
- Stage 5—Maturation.

The time taken to move from investigation stage to maturation stage varies from team to team. As major empowerment changes are made, the team may cycle back and forth through the five stages. Some teams may get stuck in intermediate stages and never reach the maturation level. Critical events may also move teams backwards in the maturity cycle. For example, in the case of even a matured team, changing team membership as the project progresses through its life cycle may move the team back to transition stage in order to define and negotiate new roles and responsibilities. The degree of setback depends upon *who* moves in and out and the *timing* in the project life cycle when the team membership changes.

Figure 6.5 shows how these five stages of an SMPT maturity cycle relate to the four steps of building an SMPT discussed earlier. The four steps of building an SMPT outline major actions and outcomes as the team starts producing an optimum output and the SMPT concept is recognized as an appropriate strategy to manage projects and even the whole organization.

Challenges in building SMPTs. Many project directors, project managers and clients raise the concern of the risk involved in SMPTs. Of course, there is risk involved, because the project environment is very dynamic and project teams are expected to be very flexible, fast, and responsive to client needs. Like any system, it will be successful only if implemented properly. Some the challenges and difficulties that may arise include:

Geographic separation can make the implementation of SMPTs difficult because team members may not be able to see each other every day. This becomes even more important when the project team is working on a global project and the team members are dispersed throughout different

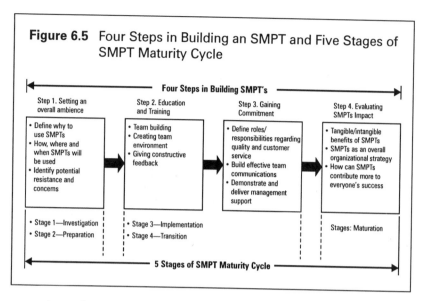

Figure 6.5 Four Steps in Building an SMPT and Five Stages of SMPT Maturity Cycle

|◄─────── **Four Steps in Building SMPT's** ───────►|

Step 1. Setting an overall ambience	Step 2. Education and Training	Step 3. Gaining Commitment	Step 4. Evaluating SMPTs Impact
• Define why to use SMPTs • How, where and when SMPTs will be used • Identify potential resistance and concerns	• Team building • Creating team environment • Giving constructive feedback	• Define roles/ responsibilities regarding quality and customer service • Build effective team communications • Demonstrate and deliver management support	• Tangible/intangible benefits of SMPTs • SMPTs as an overall organizational strategy • How can SMPTs contribute more to everyone's success
• Stage 1—Investigation • Stage 2—Preparation	• Stage 3—Implementation • Stage 4—Transition		Stages: Maturation

|◄─────── **5 Stages of SMPT Maturity Cycle** ───────►|

countries and regions. Modern technology can help solve some communication problems due to different time zones but personal interactions are important. A good kick-off meeting (as an informal meeting or a social event) is crucial to implementing SMPT. Also, periodic status meetings should be organized to encourage open communications and maintain unity of purpose.

Low interdependence can pose problems, especially when team members become too independent and the tasks they are working on are highly specialized.

Task limitations may sometimes inhibit the use of SMPTs. For example, for emergency tasks (such as fire fighting, rescue operation, etc.), it is essential to have a captain or a leader rather than team members managing themselves.

Organizational limitations generally represent the most common reasons of SMPTs failure. Incompatible organizational culture and lack of management commitment to the whole change process are the single biggest reasons. Other reasons include:[3]

- Impatience (expecting immediate results)
- Unwillingness to change personal management styles (from control to collaboration)
- Unwillingness to change organizational structure (from pyramid to circle)
- Insufficient budget and time (for training and acquiring new skills).

Sometimes, even when SMPTs are implemented properly, failures can happen. SMPTs are not a substitute for sound business basics. If no one wants to buy your product or service, SMPTs won't help. Nor will they

250 ─────────────────────────

help if you are in the wrong business or not using the right technology. However, SMPTs can increase your chances of success because they increase the human potential across the whole organization leading to high performance.[3] Project managers must try to overcome the obstacles and roadblocks normally encountered during implementation of SMPTs.

AFTER PREPARING FOR SMPTs the next step is to build SMPTs. Project managers must be aware of the empowerment process, which is crucial in building SMPTs. They must go through the four steps in building SMPTs patiently and systematically. They must understand stages in maturity cycle of SMPTs and evaluate what is expected of them during each stage. They must be aware of various challenges and difficulties in implementing SMPTs and develop strategies to overcome them.

Facilitating SMPTs for success

If there has been one failing within our organization over the years, it's that we haven't tried to dispel the notion that our success comes out of a computer. It doesn't. It comes out of the sweat glands of our coaches and players.
— Tom Landry, former head coach, Dallas Cowboys

The success of SMPTs can be achieved by changing organizational culture, gaining management support and commitment to this change process and using facilitative skills.

Guidelines for management. The process of creating SMPTs is very delicate. Its success depends upon genuine support from the management through the life cycle of its maturity, from investigation to maturation. Managers should use the following guidelines to help them manage decisions on who should be involved, how to proceed and what to expect.[18]

Select for success. In an organization, some teams are more self-motivated and mature than others. The probability of success in creating SMPTs can be increased by selecting such teams as candidates for SMPTs because they already have many of the following desirable characteristics as:[18]

- Work well together
- Require low management maintenance; interested in self-management
- Have positive, forward-looking attitudes
- Willing to be a "test case" for creating SMPTs as a pilot project
- Interested in sharing responsibility and accountability
- High level of mutual trust, respect and urge to help each other
- High level of commitment to accomplish project objectives.

Create successful experiences. Management should document, communicate and publicize the early successes of SMPTs in order to gain more support and confidence from the whole organization. News of success will help gain acceptance for creating more SMPTs.

From Self-Managed Work Teams to Self-Motivated Project Teams

Go slow to go fast. As an innovative style of management, the SMPT needs resources, commitment and time. Management should have patience rather than expecting great results immediately.

Practice written agreements. A written agreement between the management and SMPT will clarify team ground rules and expectations of both parties. It may address the reasons why the team wants to be self-managing and how it plans to accomplish this. This is necessary as an SMPT may follow different procedures and policies with respect to work schedules, salary administration, performance appraisal systems and incentives, etc.

Emphasize both short- and long-term goals. Short-term productivity of SMPTs may increase due to energy and enthusiasm of team members in the early stages of creating SMPTs. However, without long-term goals of continuously improving work environment, sharing more responsibility and accountability and exploring opportunities for professional development and growth, SMPTs will fail as the "honeymoon period" ends.

Facilitative skills. Project managers can play a key role in increasing the success of SMPTs. They must learn to act more like a "coach" than a manager or supervisor. Facilitative skills must be used in problem solving, consensus building, self-correction (by the team), and management of the team's process with respect to tasks and relationships.[21]

Problem solving. SMPTs do not have supervisors to handle disputes or provide solutions to problems. Therefore, it is important that SMPTs be prepared to solve both technical and non-technical problems, which means dealing with both open-ended problems (those having many possible solutions) and close-ended problems (those have single solutions or sets of solutions), as they arise.

When an SMPT is faced with a problem, the group must collectively determine a list of possible outcomes. To ensure that the SMPT comes up with the best possible solution, the following process should be followed:
- Keep the group small (five to nine members).
- Announce the meeting in advance.
- Use a round robin approach for collecting ideas.
- Encourage people to discuss the idea with the group, not only with the originator.
- Rephrase criticism in a positive way.
- Ask for positive remarks from negative people.
- Set an example by clarifying ideas, not defending them.[21]

Consensus building. Consensus creates a deeper commitment among team members for carrying out team decisions because the members have been heard and their contributions considered. Team consensus is an important part of SMPTs. It is a process, not an outcome. It involves discussing openly and honestly the ideas and concerns of team members and then persuading team members to buy into a specific idea or solution.

252

The three power bases used to influence members in SMPTs and gain consensus are:[21]

- Expertise (based on knowledge and experience)
- Personal credibility (based on commitment to the team's interest and interpersonal skills)
- Political power (based upon formal/informal contacts).

Perceived power stems from how others view one's level of expertise on a specific topic and/or one's political power (connections to people outside the group).

Four steps which can be taken to contribute towards building team consensus are:

Encourage all participants to have a full say. It is important to create an open environment where people can feel comfortable putting forward ideas for group discussion.

Emphasize positives. Negative feedback isn't good for group morale and discourages open communication. Counter negative feedback by asking members to comment on what is good about a specific suggestion.

Find out how serious the negatives are. If there are negative consequences to an idea, present your opinions to the group in the form of a solution. This way you are able to point out the problem but in a positive light, which is less offensive to the originator of the idea.

Keep summing up the areas of agreement. Summarize the areas that everyone agrees upon. This should eventually bring forward the best solution to the problem. Gradually the group members should be able to see that one solution is more viable than the rest and consensus will be gained.[21]

Reaching consensus does not imply there is no conflict within a team. A critical exchange of ideas is healthy for building consensus and conflict and tension caused by controversial ideas are natural. SMPTs can view consensus as "controlled conflict" that leads to high commitment and productivity.[21] Consensus is not 100 percent agreement; in fact, 100 percent agreement is a myth. After consensus is reached, team members should feel "It may not be exactly what I wanted but it is certainly something I can live with."

Self-correction. The ability of SMPTs to self-correct is crucial. Without a supervisor to lead the way, a SMPT is forced to come up with its own solutions. Even decisions made through group consensus can lead to problems. Thus, it is important to detect potential problems in early stages and correct them right away. When correcting a problem, a SMPT should use the following guidelines:

Practice leveling. Open communication is the key to detecting and solving a problem. Team members should be encouraged to discuss their concerns with each other. If there is a lack of mutual trust and genuine support, team members may be wary of voicing their opinions and a problem can go undetected and grow out of control.

From Self-Managed Work Teams to Self-Motivated Project Teams

Find problems—don't point fingers. Rational problem solving requires rational people. Ownership of successes and failures must be shared by all members of the team. Pointing fingers can lead to lack of trust, defensive behavior, low morale and poor communication among team members.

Look carefully at what you are doing. Evaluate your process; then process your evaluation. Determine what needs to be changed to prevent the same problem from occurring again. Learn from your mistakes. [21]

Process management. Process management refers to how a SMPT goes about doing specific tasks. SMPTs must manage both task-process issues and people-process issues. Task-process issues refer to the relationship between team members and their work. People-process issues refers to how the team members relate to one another. The majority of problems are caused by poor management of team's process, which affects cohesiveness, commitment and productivity. SMPTs can use these guidelines to manage task processes:

- Clarify your purpose and specify your outcomes.
- Seek alternative methods and procedures for achieving your outcomes.
- Make your task structure explicit.
- Stick to the subject.
- Summarize.
- Monitor your time.
- Identify task assignments and/or "next step" at the end of your session.[21]

Project managers can also use the following set of guidelines to help manage people-processes:

Provide opportunities for everyone to contribute. Everyone should be contributing in open discussion. If some members are not, be sure to solicit their input on a regular basis.

Separate content from personalities. Fostering a professional attitude amongst team members will help ensure that no one gets hurt feelings when ideas are criticized. People should be able to distinguish negative feedback on an idea from a personal attack.

Reduce and reconcile misunderstandings and disagreements. Make sure that disagreements are dealt with and that team members come to an understanding. Personal differences should be dealt with promptly. Personal attacks should be avoided.

Provide recognition for team process. Create a way of tracking team progress and make everyone aware when you have all met a deadline, quota or small milestone towards reaching a goal. It is important to know that you are moving towards achieving your team's objectives. This creates a positive climate and a sense of accomplishment.

Provide a fair hearing for all ideas and comments. Give everyone's ideas and comments equal attention. Team members need to feel that they are being taken seriously by everyone and that their individual contributions are valued by the group.

Help the group focus on "win-win" solutions. It is important for team members to not only feel that they are helping meet the needs of the group, but also that they get what they need out of the process (more experience, a new skill). What is best for the team should also benefit everyone individually. [21]

A continuing theme throughout the SMPT facilitation process is open communication. Problem solving, consensus building, self-correction and process management each rely heavily on consistent open communication amongst team members. Good communication creates trust and heightens team moral. Without open communication, people will be less likely to express their opinions which may result in tension and/or conflict within the team unit. Ultimately it is important that each SMPT member feel that they are contributing towards the team's performance. It is hard to establish hard and fast rules for how team members should treat each other. However, effective management of task processes establishes the definition, structure and process of achieving the task and effective management of people processes establishes good working relationships and true teamwork, leading to human synergy.

Developing people skills. SMPTs require a high degree of interdependence. They seldom fail due to lack of technical knowledge and skills; the majority of team failures are caused by poor people-process skills, which can be developed through training. However, technical specialists in teams often do not appreciate this problem and therefore normally resist the need to acquire training in developing their people skills. The major human skills necessary to facilitate the success of SMPTs are:[21]

- Problem solving
- Decision-making
- Confrontation and conflict resolution
- Managing time (and meetings)
- Communication skills (listening and feedback)
- Participative management
- Influencing
- Boundary management
- Managing project politics positively.

Like individuals, teams mature with time. Members in SMPTs should assess themselves regarding their people-process skills in the beginning stages, set a goal and develop a plan of action to enhance these skills and then evaluate them again as the team reaches maturity. Continuous improvement is one of the main goals of a team and it must be followed by developing the people skills of team members through training. Training can be provided in-house and/or obtained by attending off-site seminars and workshops. Management must commit to providing sufficient resources and training in order to help develop and grow team members in order to enhance the success of SMPTs.

From Self-Managed Work Teams to Self-Motivated Project Teams

Leadership in SMPTs

A leader is best when people barely know he exists, not so good when people obey and acclaim him, worse when they despise him. But of a good leader, who talks little, when his work is done, his aim fulfilled, they will say "We did this ourselves."

— *Lao Tzu (about 550 BC)*

The leadership in SMPTs is quite complex because of the changing roles of leader for SMPTs and the problems they encounter during transition. To understand it, it is important to look at more than just actions and activities. It involves analyzing how these leaders think and what they value.

Roles and responsibilities of SMPT leaders

As teams are empowered and self-motivated, they assume many of the responsibilities that were traditionally reserved by managers and supervisors in hierarchical organizations. This raises the question: If teams start managing themselves, do we need the team leaders, and if so what are their roles? Self-management concept changes the roles of managers radically. They fear loss of power and status which raises anger, stress, ambiguity and resistance. For some managers, this transition is easy but for many it is not.

Yet SMPTs are not *leaderless*. They have leaders but their role has changed.

Team leaders work *on* the system, whereas the managers work *in* the system; that is, team leaders develop the system and guidelines and the managers use those systems to manage the tasks. Team leaders act mainly as boundary managers to manage the impact of the project environment on the project team. They alert the team to such issues as market conditions, technology changes, socioeconomic issues, and government/regulatory issues.[22]

Rethinking leadership responsibilities. As teams are empowered and move along in their journey to self-management, the role of leaders has to be redefined. Some important factors needed to rethink leadership responsibilities are:[23]

Transition of leadership responsibilities normally spans from two to five years to develop fully SMPT. It is like a journey with bumps along the way. More complex leadership responsibilities such as budgeting may take longer to move down to the team member level. Some traditional responsibilities that organizations have shifted to their teams include:[23]

- Work scheduling, work assignments, holidays and vacation scheduling
- Monitoring progress, identifying problems and taking corrective actions
- Designing and preparing training manuals
- Deciding on moderate capital investments to improve efficiency, quality and reduce downtime
- Responsibility for cross-training, product quality and continual improvement

256

- Schedule the work, set quality standards and explore alternatives to handle large volumes of work successfully.

Shifting proportions of responsibility. This depends upon the culture of organization and maturity level of team members. The Wellins/*Industry Week*/Association for Quality and Participation survey data regarding the distribution of leadership responsibilities for major production tasks and management tasks indicated that the leadership of these tasks was either dominated by a formal leader (outside the team), or the team, or shared by both. The concept of shared leadership reflects more reality in SMPTs than in self-managing work teams.[23]

Fewer managers mean fewer project human resources is a myth about SMPTs. The number of managers and supervisors is reduced because the team members assume many of the responsibilities traditionally held by managers. However, the total number of team members may increase significantly due to their increased workload.

Changing roles. Roles of leaders of SMPTs are changing drastically. Often SMPTs leaders wear three main hats. They are:[24]

- *Administrators*. They help the team meet its objectives through goal-setting, planning, problem solving, and other group processes.
- *Technical advisors*. They provide the team with technical guidance and support and convey skills and knowledge to help the team make its own decisions.
- *Coaches*. They help the team develop as it matures with a final aim of making it a self-managing team.

Leadership dimensions include skills, knowledge and motivations. Wellins *et al.*, conducted in-depth job analyses for positions of both team leaders and group leaders in a few organizations that were building SMPTs. The team leader's position is inside the team. It is held by a team member and is rotated based upon expertise required and project life cycle phases. A group leader assumes responsibilities outside the team and operates in a broader organizational environment assuming many functions as needed.[25] For example, as teams are empowered more, strategic planning becomes more important than operational planning.

Clarifying responsibilities is very important to avoid any confusion. Controllers, planners and inspectors are now replaced with coaches, facilitators and supporters. Leaders should make a role contract with team members. It does not have to be too rigid and changes can be made through mutual consent. A role contract will avoid any surprises when the team assumes responsibility for roles that previously belong to the leaders.

Also, as teams move along the empowerment continuum, leaders roles shift from direct to indirect involvement and therefore leaders can be given new responsibilities:[25] they can coach more teams in the organization, for example. Responsibility charts are very practical to clarify roles and responsibilities.

From Self-Managed Work Teams to Self-Motivated Project Teams

Rethinking leadership responsibilities in SMPTs does not mean that there is no need for leaders. Rather it means that there is a major shift in power, and such a shift is difficult for both those who lose power and those who gain it. In reality the role of leaders in SMPTs is expanding.

Team tips for changing leadership roles. Here are some tips used for changing leadership roles when implementing SMPTs:[26]

- *Involve managers and supervisors in change process.* Do "with" them rather than doing "to" them. They should be part of the vision, not just the part of the change.
- *Provide leadership support and training.* The egos and security of managers are on line. They need a new role in the organization. Training should focus on the nature of teamwork, workplace redesign and the ins and outs of SMPTs.
- *Recognize and reward leadership that encourages team work and empowerment.* Reward team performance rather than individual performance and reward behaviors that involve "letting go" and "handing over."
- *Have realistic expectations about the pace of change.* Teams change the way work is done, and leadership skills and behaviors are not developed overnight. It takes time, so have patience.
- *Delegate responsibility when teams are ready.* Let go (delegate) when teams are ready. But delegate, don't abdicate.

Boundary management role. SMPTs manage by themselves but within a boundary that differentiates the team from its surrounding environment. The team leader manages this boundary to optimize the performance of the team and of the organization as a whole. Some points regarding the boundary management role of team leaders are:[27]

Focus areas of boundary managers go beyond the normal team environment. The team leaders spend their energy and efforts on boundary issues which include:[27]

- Interface problems with other project teams
- Interactions with clients, vendors, suppliers and competitors
- Important legal or social issues related to communities
- Forecasting new technologies and economic changes to act proactively rather than reactively
- Building communication links with headquarters and other groups to stay on track
- Communicating with regulatory agencies (regards laws and regulations)
- Training and development opportunities for the team
- Exploring new opportunities and strategic alliances.

As a boundary manager, the team leader manages these issues to help the team adapt successfully to the environment.

Boundary management is a non-traditional role because it encourages teams to assume the full responsibility of throughput, work process, and product quality. For example, Ralph Stayer, CEO of Johnsonville Foods, encouraged work teams to monitor their own progress, compile necessary reports, identify problems and take actions.[28] Effective team leaders do not demand status reports which cost significantly more in lost time and salaries than their benefits. They should develop team potential rather than hinder them in their progress.

Boundary managers work "on" the system as opposed to supervisors who work "in" the system. Boundary managers focus on improving the systems and work processes and redesigning the organizational structures to facilitate collaboration. They provide the big picture view to expand the team's horizon.

Boundary management involves building effective infrastructure to help teams optimize their output, relationship and development. Boundary managers ensure that the organizational system measures the right things, provides regular feedback and timely information regarding the project's results and contributions to the overall organization. They ensure that teams have such working systems in place to reduce hierarchies. They focus on optimizing the whole operation rather than their own departments. They act as cross-organizational collaborators rather than empire builders.

Seven competencies of boundary managers. Successful boundary managers modify organizational structures, build effective infrastructure, and create a climate of cooperation and collaboration. They shield team members from unproductive organization politics. The specific behaviors of successful SMPT leaders can be described by a set of seven competencies:[27,29]

- *Leader.* Increases energy of team members by creating and communicating visions that inspire and motivate team members.
- *Role model.* Demonstrates desired behavior by "walking the talk."
- *Coach.* Teaches and develops team members to their full potential, maintains a balance between authority and responsibility, and accountability.
- *Business analyst.* Understands the "big picture" and is able to transform changes and business threats into opportunities.
- *Barrier buster.* Eliminates barriers to effective team work and challenges the status quo.
- *Facilitator.* Creates a true team climate and bring together resources (necessary tools, information and people) to accomplish goals.
- *Customer advocate.* Flushes out customer needs, develops and maintains close liaison with the customer and focuses on customer satisfaction as the top priority.

Problems during transitions

Leading an SMPT is not easy. Changing from a traditional manager/supervisor to a leader is challenging for both the managers and team members regardless of the management level. Some managers survive this transition while others cannot. Many managers/supervisors face many problems which include the following:[30]

Perceived loss of power or status. This includes organizational power and status symbols. Some managers feel that empowering team members means disempowering them. This is not true. In fact empowering people leads to increased performance and high quality which actually increases the effectiveness and power of managers.

Unclear new role. Often managers and supervisors are not clear of their role as leaders. They are urged not to control or direct any one but are not sure what to do instead, i.e., coach and facilitate. Consequently they follow the wing walker rule, i.e. never let go with one hand before you grab hold with the other one and therefore fail to make a smooth transition. Management should clarify that their new role is expanded to leadership than managership.

Fear of losing their jobs. Sometimes team managers feel that they will not be needed if teams start managing themselves which is not true. Instead, in SMPTs they are needed more to coach, support and teach rather than to command and control.

Double standard syndrome. This refers to the difference in the new way of managing in SMPTs environment compared to the way the managers were managed themselves. Concept of empowerment should be applied throughout the whole organization and this leadership role should be reflected by the top management as well.

Many organizations have tried to introduce SMPT practices without proper planning and evaluation of individual's and manager's skills and organizational culture. Consequently it has threatened managers and supervisors who are critical to success of SMPTs. Above shortfalls and problems have created frustration and resistance as managers make the transition from traditional management roles to roles of leaders.

The values of SMPT leaders

Values provide inner strength to overcome obstacles.

— Anonymous

The three main attributes of successful leaders in both traditional and empowered organizations include creating trust and respect between the project leader and the project team members, making sure that project goals are accomplished, and providing leadership in resolving problems.[23]

Creating SMPTs involves shifting the management paradigm from control to commitment. There are several visible and invisible elements of a leader's role in SMPTs. The visible elements include work ethics, atti-

260 ──────────

tudes, behavior, styles, communication (oral and written), product, etc., communication. The invisible elements include vision, values, assumptions, ideas, commitment, motivation and paradigms, etc. Making Theory X assumptions (that people are lazy, want to be controlled, are not self-motivated, etc.) limits the ability to lead SMPTs. Also, the values and concerns of leaders of SMPTs determine their degree of effectiveness. Successful leaders of SMPTs have three main concerns:[22]

- Importance of managing by vision, which gives the team a sense of purpose and direction
- Need to focus on clients, which emphasizes customer service and quality products
- Emphasis on continuous improvement, which increases values of learning.

In addition, successful leaders of SMPTs have five main values. These are strong beliefs in:[22]

Teamwork. Successful team leaders tend to minimize status differences and salary differentials and discourage the "us against them" attitude. Instead, they emphasize working together to achieve human synergy. These attitudes increase collaboration and shared responsibility.

Work as a part of life. Successful team leaders are genuine and natural in their work relationships; they believe in a healthy balance between the personal and the professional aspects of life.

Promoting diversity. Most project teams have a diverse mix of people with different backgrounds, experience and culture. Successful team leaders capitalize on this diversity by completing the skill mix required and creating an environment where everyone shares accountability and works interdependently to help each other.

Lifelong development of team members, personally and professionally. Successful leaders strongly believe that people appreciate rather than depreciate with time if suitable opportunities are provided to the team members to learn new skills and develop at both personal and professional level.

Elimination of barriers to team performance. Successful team leaders have a strong conviction that main role of management is to create an environment to nurture high team performance. They should have tolerance for failure to expand the possible and maximize human potential. Team leaders should view themselves as servants of the team, providing what the team members need to maximize team performance.

Values held by team leaders of SMPTs are very important because they provide them with inner strength and motivation. When team leaders live their values, they build trust and respect among team members which strengthens working relationships and the commitment to help each other win. For example, a team leader's assumption (invisible) that team members have good ideas is reflected in his or her behavior (invisible), and good team ideas surface.

From Self-Managed Work Teams to Self-Motivated Project Teams

SMPTs and their leaders in a nutshell

Empowerment and SMPTs are not merely trendy concepts, they are essential in order to satisfy the changing expectations of today's work force. Creating SMPTs involves changing the fundamental organizational culture and not just organizational structure. Various values, roles and responsibilities of team leaders have been described in the previous sections. However, here are thoughts that a team leaders must remember to implement SMPTs effectively and successfully:[31]

In SMPTs, people perform multiple tasks, manage themselves with minimum of supervision, and share responsibility and accountability. SMPTs outperform their traditional counterparts. They constitute a journey, rather than the destination: not so much what you do as how it is done.

Because SMPTs are based upon empowerment, all four elements—authority, resources, information, and accountability—must be present. Anything less is a sham.

SMPTs are not "undirected" or "leaderless"; they are directed differently. SMPTs are driven by goals rather than by the managers/supervisors. Thus, the SMPT develops leaders rather than managers. What's the difference? Team leaders work *on* the system, whereas supervisors work *in* the system. They act as boundary managers to manage the impact of the project environment on the project team. They alert the team to rapidly changing business environment, technology, and nature of work force.

The team leader's role changes with the maturity level of the team. Team responsibility expands as the team matures, and this process requires role clarification, a personal need to change, organizational support and self awareness.

Table 6.2 shows ten perspectives for enhanced leadership, teamwork and success.

What's next for SMPTs?

When you have a desire and a commitment to play as a team, excelling is no longer work.

— Anonymous

This novel way of helping people work together will surely impact the future of work. And, as with any radical change, there will be resistance and backlash in response. Here are a few observations regarding the future of self-management:[26]

The general shift towards self-management. Alvin Toffler discussed radical changes in the work environment, noting that workers need to learn new technologies, adapt to flat organizational structures and generate new ideas. Employee empowerment is moving from an experimental stage to business necessity to meet global competition.[32] Jerry Junkins, late CEO of Texas Instruments, stated in *Fortune* magazine, "No matter

Table 6.2 Ten Perspectives for Enhanced Leadership, Teamwork and Success

1. S: (1 letter representing success and satisfaction)
2. WE/US: (2 letters essential to retain relationships)
3. TRY: (3 letters representing perseverance, persistence, courage)
4. TIME: (4 letters representing most valuable thing)
5. TEAMS/TRUST: (5 letters to get human synergy)
6. LISTEN: (6 letters representing most important skill)
7. RESPECT: (7 letters regarding interpersonal skills)
8. INVERTED: (8 letters regarding practical organizational structures)
9. OBJECTIVE/CHALLENGE: (9 letters which keep you focused)
10. EMPOWERING: (10 letters that increase ownership)

what's in your business, teams are the wave of the future." To achieve high quality, it is essential to empower people and create teamwork.[33] Robert Hass, CEO of Levi Strauss, has indicated a trend towards a team-oriented, multi-skilled environment in which the team takes on many of the tasks traditionally done by supervisors and trainers. With some sort of gain-sharing, this leads to higher commitment and employee satisfaction.[34] General Motors' Saturn team approach is an example of a strategy to help the U.S. meet global competition in the global economy.[35]

Expect rapid growth. According to one study, fewer than 10 percent of work areas are currently organized into teams. Most team members, leaders, and practitioners believe that SMPTs will expand rapidly over the next decade.[36]

White collar applications. Productivity and quality has been increased dramatically in the manufacturing sector by focusing on process, technologies, and people. SMPTs have not been widely used for white-collar workers because the productivity of service organizations is difficult to measure and cross-training is difficult and inefficient. However, these difficulties are being resolved and this concept is becoming popular.

Self-directed organizations. We will still need leaders but self-directed teams are making more and more key business decisions. As management recognizes the benefits of teams and empowerment and trust is developed, the teams will start making decisions not just for the team but for the benefit of entire organization.

Global effect. Due to global competitions, many large organizations are involved in international projects and joint ventures. Even autocratic and traditional work cultures are recognizing the value of empowerment and self-management and becoming willing to work together with work cultures who are already more comfortable with this concept.

The need for national support. National support has contributed to teams and employee involvement in countries like Sweden and Japan. Unfortunately, the U.S. lacks a powerful centralized effort to increase participation in the work place. A report published by National Center of Education and the Economy calls for national support to encourage employers to invest more in both the education of their employees and creation of higher involvement work organizations.[36]

The role of organized labor. The unions, like management, must deal with the changing values of today's work force—values that include greater autonomy, participation, freedom, and flexibility. Collaboratively developed and implemented teams provide wins for both management and union. On the whole, the leadership of various national unions, including United Auto Workers, the United Steel Workers of America, and the Communications Workers of America, have supported various forms of teams across the United States.[26] According to Lawrence Bankowski, a national union president, "Deep down manufacturers have to change their culture and their thinking and tap into workers' brains."[37]

Backlash against the team concept. In spite of the fact that empowered teams are essential to survive the tough competition in the future, SMWTs encounter some resistance. Following are some typical negative reactions for work teams:[26]

- Work teams are a foreign concept; they won't work in our organization.
- The concept is great, but difficult to implement.
- It would have worked, but the managers and supervisors ruined everything.
- We tried teams, but employees wouldn't accept the change.

Avoiding backlash. The management and team leaders can take following actions to minimize the negative impact of backlash:[26, 38]

- Plan the creation and implementation of SMWTs. If you fail to plan, you plan to fail.
- Set realistic goals.
- Provide appropriate training at all levels.
- Team building made part of overall strategy.
- Focus on continuous improvement.
- Have patience; "go slow to go fast."
- Manage this change of introducing empowerment effectively; explain its importance, sell the case and provide organizational support.
- Make employment assurances to relieve the perceived fear of loss of job, power, and status.
- Align organizational structures with SMPTs.
- Ensure that financial reports, training, and other tools are consistent to values of high involvement.

264

Summary

The concept of SMWTs in a project environment is both desirable and debatable. It is debatable because of the nature of project environment where there are continuous deadlines and insufficient time to change organizational culture for creating SMWTs and a need to have a project manager who acts a single point of contact for the owner. At the same time, it is revolutionary and desirable because it increases performance, adaptability, quality and innovations which are necessary to compete globally.

In a project environment, the concept of SMWT is not entirely satisfactory. However, a mature self-motivated team in a project environment is practically similar to Self-Managed Work Teams in an ongoing operation. What is required is a combination of the valuable attributes of the SMWT and an attitude that satisfies the project environment. Because self-motivation is such an important factor in the goal-oriented project environment, we call the resulting team a Self-Motivated Project Team (SMPT).

Empowerment and SMPTs represent the wave of the future work environment. SMPTs provide a challenging and dynamic structure, a sense of ownership to their members and whole business focus. They are notable because they provide significant benefits to both the employers and employees. Major benefits of SMPTs include improved quality, productivity and service; greater flexibility and quick self correction; reduced operating cost; faster response to technology revolution; fewer and simpler job classifications; psychological enrichment and control; and emphasize the value of human resources.

Continuous improvement is essential to remain competitive. It can be achieved by building SMPTs to help build commitment and pride of ownership. Empowerment is essential for fostering an SMPT culture and for building SMPTs. It is a different way of working together. It means giving employees control and freedom over their jobs in a way that employees experience a sense of ownership. It is facilitated by a combination of factors, which include organizational values and leadership actions; rewards, recognition and training systems; and job design and working relationships.

There are four main variables of empowerment: authority, accountability, resources and information. A sense of ownership and of strong commitment is created when people have *all* four variables. As teams mature they move along the empowerment continuum by taking more and more responsibility and eventually becoming self-motivated teams.

Empowering means passing on authority, responsibility and accountability. Empowerment occurs when employees are given power to manage their work and work process. Power is central to em*power*ment. It represents an ability to influence project participants to meet project objectives successfully. Project managers must acquire a balanced combination of seven types of power which include authority, accountability, commitment, information, influence, network and earned power. More importantly, they must know how to use these powers wisely and when to share these with team members and how much.

To build an SMPT, it is essential that changes are created in all directions. It requires fostering an SMPT culture by changing its three main components: mindsets of managers and team members, team relationships, and organizational structure. Empowerment is the most vital factor for fostering SMPT culture. Project managers and project leaders must understand the basic principles of empowering people and identify different sources of power to share and gain overall power. They must recognize that SMPT culture requires a change in mindsets, working relationships and organizational design, and organizational climate.

Creating and maintaining SMPTs involves preparing for SMPTs, building SMPTs through empowerment and facilitating SMPTs for success. The success of creating SMPTs depends upon organizational culture, work environment, management philosophy and behavior, and above all readiness level of team members. A sponsor or a champion is critical to success.

Empowerment is the key to building SMPTs. In order to build an SMPT, project leaders should follow four steps which include: setting an overall ambience; education and training; gaining commitment; and evaluating SMPTs on a regular basis. SMPT is an evolutionary process. It goes through five stages of maturity which include investigation, preparation, implementation, transition and maturation. Project leaders must be aware of some challenges and difficulties in implementing SMPTs due to geographic separation, task limitations (e.g., in emergency or crisis situations), and organizational limitations. The circumstances should be evaluated and then SMPTs implemented carefully. SMPTs can be implemented successfully provided there is strong support and commitment from management and team members. The leaders must use facilitative skills: problem solving, consensus building, self correction and managing the process (in terms of task and people).

LEADING AN SMPT is not easy. Changing from a traditional manager/supervisor to a leader is challenging for both the managers and team members. Some traditional managers survive this transition while others cannot. Some of the problems facing traditional managers include a perceived loss of power and status, unclear new role, fear of losing their jobs, adjustment to a different way of managing.

Project managers must act as boundary managers with a focus on emphasizing integration and interfacing; working "on" the system rather than 'in' the system; and building effective infrastructure to help meet project goals. Seven competencies of leaders and boundary managers in SMPTs include leader, role model, coach, business analyst, barrier buster, facilitator, and customer advocate.

Because of severe economic and manpower constraints and consequent "flatter" organizations, management by projects is being recognized as one of the most effective ways of managing organizations. Because self-motivation is such an important factor in the goal-oriented project environment, the Self-Motivated Project Team is central to project success. More research and practical ideas need developing to foster a conducive organizational culture and work climate to build SMPTs. The importance of SMPTs should be reinforced by documenting financial and psychological benefits to both the organization and its people.

References

Chapter 1

1. F.P. Doyle. 1990. People-Power: The Global Human Resource Challenge for the '90s. *Columbia Journal and World Business* (Spring/Summer): pp. 36–45.
2. L.R. Offermann and M.K. Gowing. 1990. Organizations of the Future. *American Psychologist 45*, pp. 95–108.
3. Based on R.M. Kanter, 1991, Transcending Business Boundaries: 12,000 World Managers View Change, *Harvard Business Review* (May–June): pp. 151–164.
4. Based upon Don Hellreigel, John W. Slocum, Jr., and Richard W. Woodman, *Organizational Behavior, Sixth Edition*, St. Paul, MN: West Publishing Company, pp. 719–742.
5. W.B. Johnston. 1991. Global Work Force 2000: The New World Labor Market. *Harvard Business Review* (March–April): p. 115–127. Also A. Redwood, 1990, Human Resources Management in the 1990s, *Business Horizons* (January–February): p. 74.
6. R.W. Woodman. 1990. Issues and Concerns in Organizational Diagnosis. In C.N. Jackson and M.R. Manning (eds.), *Organization Development Annual Volume III: Diagnosing Client Organizations*, Alexandria, VA: American Society for Training and Development, pp. 5–10.
7. Based upon Samuel C. Certo, Steven H. Appelbaum, and Irene Divine, 1989, *Principles of Modern Management: A Canadian Perspective, Third Edition*, Allan and Bacon, Inc., pp. 285–303.
8. Warren C. Bennis, K.D. Benne, and R. Chin (eds.). 1961. *The Planning of Change: Readings in the Applied Behavioral Sciences*. New York: Holt, Rinehard & Winston.
9. William C. Giegold and R.J. Craig. 1976. Whatever Happened to OD? *Industrial Management* (January/February): p. 9–12.
10. John C. Alpin and Duane E. Thompson. 1974. Successful Organizational Change. *Business Horizons* (August): p. 61–66.
11. Richard J. Selfridge and Stanley I. Sokolik. 1975. A Comprehensive View of Organization Development. *MSU Business Topics* (Winter): p. 47.
12. Martin G. Evans. 1974. Failures in OD Programs: What Went Wrong. *Business Horizons* (April): pp. 18–22.
13. W.F. Glueck. 1969. Organization Change in Business and Government. *Academy of Management Journal 12*: pp. 440–441.
14. C.J. Middleton. 1967. How to Set Up a Project Organization. *Harvard Business Review* (March/April): pp. 73–74.
15. Harvey F. Kolodny. 1981. Managing in a Matrix. *Business Horizons 24*: pp. 17–24.
16. J.E. Neumann. 1989. Why People Don't Participate in Organizational Change. In R.W. Woodman and W.A. Pasmore, eds., *Research in Organizational Change and Development 3*, Greenwich, CT: JAI Press, pp. 181–212.
17. For additional perspectives on resistance to change, see C. Argyris, 1990, *Overcoming Organizational Defense*, Boston: Allyn and Bacon; C. Argyris. Reasoning, Action Strategies, and Defensive Routines: The Case of OD Practitioners, in R.W. Woodman and W.A. Pasmore, eds., *Research in Organizational Change and Development 1*. Greenwich, CT: JAI Press, 1987, pp. 89–128; B.A. Spector, 1989, From Bogged Down to Fired Up: Inspiring Organizational Change, *Sloan Management Review* (Summer): pp. 29–34; B.M. Staw, Counterforces to Change, in P.S. Goodman and Associates, eds., *Change in Organizations*, San Francisco: Jossey-Bass, 1982, pp. 87–121.
18. K. Lewin. 1951. *Field Theory in Social Science*. New York: Harper & Row. Also K. Lewin, 1947, Frontiers in Group Dynamics. *Human Relations 1*: pp. 5–41.
19. This strategy for minimizing the resistance to change is based on How Companies Overcome Resistance to Change, *Management Review* (November 1972): pp. 17–25.
20. John P. Kotter and Leonard A. Schlesinger. 1979. Choosing Strategies for Change. *Harvard Business Review* (March/April): pp. 106–113.
21. Arnold S. Judson. 1966. *A Manager's Guide to Making Changes*. New York: Wiley, p. 118.
22. Kurt Lewin. 1947. Frontiers in Group Dynamics: Concept, Method and Reality of Social Sciences: Social Equilibria and Social Change. *Human Relations 1* (June): pp. 5–14.

23. Edgar H. Schein. 1961. Management Development as a Process of Influence. *Industrial Management Review* (May): pp. 59–76.

24. T.G. Cummings and E.F. Huse. 1989. *Organization Development and Change, Fourth Edition.* St. Paul: West, pp. 46–63.

25. Thomas E. Miller. 1988. Teamwork: The Key to Managing Change. *Project Management Handbook, Second Edition.* Eds. David I. Cleland and William R. King. New York: Van Nostrand Reinhold, pp. 802–822.

26. Fritz J. Roethlisberger. 1977. *The Elusive Phenomena.* Boston, MA: Division of Research, Harvard Graduate School of Business Administration, pp. 169–170.

27. Larry E. Greiner. 1967. Patterns of Organizational Change. *Harvard Business Review 45:* pp. 119–130.

28. Vijay K. Verma. 1995. *Organizing Projects for Success.* Upper Darby, PA: Project Management Institute, pp. 32–42. Also, Verma and Wideman, R. Max, 1996, Project Manager to Project Leader? and the Rocky Road Between. *Proceedings of the 25th Annual Seminar/Symposium.* Upper Darby, PA: Project Management Institute, pp. 627–633.

29. *Webster's New Collegiate Dictionary.* 1977. Springfield, MA: G&C Merriam, p. 228.

30. Richard W. Sievert, Jr. 1986. Communication: An Important Construction Tool. *Project Management Journal* (December): p. 77.

31. Gary Robinson and Sandra Robinson. 1994. Notes and handouts for project management course sponsored by the School of Engineering Science and presented by the Department of Continuing Studies, Simon Fraser University, (September): pp. 6–14.

32. Hans J. Thamhain. 1988. Team Building in Project Management. *Project Management Handbook, Second Edition.* Eds. David I. Cleland and William R. King. New York: Van Nostrand Reinhold, pp. 823–831.

33. Skillpath, Inc. 1994. *Coaching and Team Building Skills for Managers and Supervisors.* Mission, KS.: pp. 8–15.

34. Sunny Baker and Kim Baker. 1992. On Time/On Budget: A Step by Step Guide for Managing Any Project. Englewood Cliffs, NJ: Prentice Hall, pp. 211–220. Also Warren C. Bennis, K.D. Benne, and R. Chin, eds., 1961, *The Planning of Change: Readings in the Applied Behavioral Sciences,* New York: Holt, Rinehart & Winston, p. 69.

35. Joan Knutson and Ira Bitz. 1991. *Project Management: How to Plan and Manage Successful Projects.* New York: AMACOM, pp. 96–108.

36. Newton Margulies and John Wallace. 1973. *Organizational Change: Techniques and Applications.* Chicago: Scott, Foresman, p. 14.

Chapter 2

1. David I. Cleland. 1990. *Project Management: Strategic Design and Implementation.* Blue Ridge Summit, PA: TAB Books Inc., pp. 299–322.

2. G.C. Homans. 1959. *The Human Group.* New York: Harcourt, Brace and World 2. Also see J. Miller, 1971, Behavioral Science, *Living Systems: The Group 16:* pp. 302–398.

3. Based upon D. Hellreigel, J.W. Slocum, Jr., and R.W. Woodman, 1992, *Organizational Behavior, Sixth Edition,* St. Paul, MN: West Publishing Company, pp. 311–318, 332–342.

4. G. Hofstede, B. Neuijen, D.D. Ohayv, and G. Sanders. 1990. Measuring Organizational Cultures: A Qualitative and Quantitative Study Across Twenty Cases. *Administrative Science Quarterly 35:* pp. 286–316.

5. T.R. Mitchell and W.G. Scott. 1990. America's Problems and Needed Reforms: Confronting the Ethic of Personal Advantage. *Academy of Management Executive 4:* pp. 23–35.

6. R. Albanese and D.D. van Fleet. 1985. Rational Behavior in Groups: The Free-Riding Tendency. *Academy of Management Review 10:* pp. 244–255.

7. M.E. Schnake. 1991. Equity in Effort: The "Sucker Effect" in Co-Acting Groups, *Journal of Management 17:* pp. 41–55.

8. F.E. Fiedler. 1967. *A Theory of Leadership Effectiveness.* New York: McGraw-Hill.

9. L. Hirchhorn. 1991. *Managing in the New Team Environment.* Reading, MA: Addison-Wesley Press.

10. John Adair. 1986. *Effective Team Building*. Hants, England: Gower Publishing Company Ltd., pp. 6–8, 95–96.

11. *Training in small groups*. 1979. Ed. B. Babington Smith and B.A. Farrel. Pergamon Press, pp. 117–118.

12. D. Francis and D. Young. 1979. *Improving Work Groups: A Practical Manual for Team Building*. University Associates.

13. Harold Kerzner. 1989. *Project Management: A Systems Approach to Planning, Scheduling and Controlling, Third Edition*. New York: Van Nostrand Reinhold, pp. 260–261.

14. T. Mack. 1990. Energizing a Bureaucracy. *Forbes* (September): pp. 16–80.

15. John Cotter. 1983. *Designing Organizations that Work: An Open Sociotechnical Systems Perspective*. John J. Cotter and Associates, Inc.

16. E. Sundstrom, K.P. De Meuse, and D. Futrell. 1990. Work Teams: Applications and Effectiveness. *American Psychologist 45*: pp. 120–133.

17. Tom Peters. 1990. Don't Let Project Teams Become Committees. Inside *Guide Fall 4*, inside *Guide Magazine Limited for Canadian Airlines*, Toronto, ON, Canada, pp. 11, 20.

18. Based upon D. Hellriegel, J.W. Slocum, Jr., and R.W. Woodman, 1992, *Organizational Behavior, Sixth Edition*, St. Paul, MN: West Publishing Company, pp. 318–332.

19. Based upon Steven L. McShane, 1995, *Canadian Organizational Behavior, Second Edition*. Chicago, IL: Richard D. Irwin, Inc., pp. 300–318.

20. For a summary of recent models, see P.S. Goodman, E. Ravlin, and M. Schminke, Understanding Groups in Organizations, *Research in Organizational Behavior 9* (1987): pp. 121–73.

21. J.E. McGrath. 1990. Time Matters in Groups. In *Intellectual Teamwork: Social and Technological Foundations of Cooperative Work*, eds. J. Galegher, R.E. Kraut, and C. Egido, Hillsdale, NJ: Erlbaum, pp. 23–61. Also G.P. Shea and R.A. Guzzo, 1987, Group Effectiveness: What Really Matters? *Sloan Management Review 27*: pp. 33–46.

22. Stephen R. Covey. 1990. *The Seven Habits of Highly Effective People, First Fireside Edition*. New York: Simon and Schuster, Inc., pp. 48–52.

23. R.B. Lacoursiere. 1980. *The Life Cycle of Group Developmental Stage Theory*. New York: Human Services Press.

24. Gary Robinson. 1992. Discussion at PMI West Coast BC Chapter meeting at Vancouver, BC, Canada (October 21).

25. Erika Jones. 1994. *Facilitating Groups to Get Results*. Workshop presented at the 1994 Annual Seminar/Symposium of the Project Management Institute, Vancouver, BC, Canada (October).

26. B.W. Tuckman. 1965. Development Sequence in Small Groups. *Psychological Bulletin 63*: pp. 384–399. Also B.W. Tuckman and M.A.C. Jensen, 1977, Stages of Small Group Development Revisited, *Group and Organization Studies 2*: pp. 419–442, and S.L. Obert, 1983, Developmental Patterns of Organizational Task Groups: A Preliminary Study, *Human Relations 36*: pp. 37–52.

27. B.M. Staw. 1991. *Psychological Dimensions of Organizational Behavior*. New York: Macmillan.

28. C. Steinburg. 1993. The Downfall of Teams. *Training and Development* (February): pp. 9–10. Also see R. Sisco, 1992, Put Your Money Where Your Teams Are, *Training 29* (July): pp. 41–45.

29. S. Worchel and S.I. Shackelford. 1991. Groups Under Stress: The Influence of Group Structure and Environment on Process and Performance. *Personality & Social Psychology Bulletin 17*: pp. 640–647. Also J. Kelly and J. McGrath, 1985, Effects of Time Limits and Task Types on Task Performance and Interaction of Four Person Groups, *Journal of Personality and Social Psychology 49*: pp. 395–407.

30. B. Berelson and G.A. Steiner. 1964. *Human Behavior: An Inventory of Scientific Findings*. New York: Harcourt, Brace and World, pp. 356–360.

31. J. Southerst. 1992. The Next Industrial Revolution. *Canadian Business* (June): pp. 92–101. Also 1986, Quick Moves Keep Bata Competitive, *Industrial Management 10* (November): p. 6.

32. K.G. Stoneman and A.M. Dickinson. 1989. Individual Performance as a Function of Group Contingencies and Group Size. *Journal of Organizational Behavior Management 10*: pp. 131–150. Also A.P. Hare, 1981, Group Size. *American Behavioral Scientist 14*: pp. 695–708.

33. S.M. Colarelli and A.I. Boos. 1992. Sociometric and Ability-Based Assignment to Work Groups: Some Implications for Personnel Selection. *Journal of Organizational Behavior 13*: pp. 187–196. Also D.G. Ancona and D.F. Caldwell, 1992, Demography and Design: Predictors of New Product Team Performance, *Organization Science 3*: pp. 321–341; and J.K. Murnighan and D. Conlon, 1991, The Dynamics of Intense Work Groups: A Study of British String Quartets, *Administrative Science Quarterly 36*: pp. 165–186.

34. W.E. Watson, K. Kumar, and I.K. Michaelson. 1993. Cultural Diversity's Impact on Interaction Process and Performance: Comparing Homogeneous and Diverse Task Groups. *Academy of Management Journal 36*: pp. 590–602. Also C. Kirchmeyer and J. McLellan, 1990, Managing Ethnic Diversity: Utilizing the Creative Potential of a Diverse Workforce to Meet the Challenges of the Future. *Proceedings of the 1990 ASAC Conference, Organizational Behavior Division 11*: pp. 120–129; R.J. Magjuka and T.T. Baldwin, 1991, Team-Based Employee Involvement Programs: Effects of Design and Administration, *Personnel Psychology 44*: pp. 793–812; and Shaw, *Group Dynamics*, pp. 238–261.

35. Based upon D. Hellreigel, J.W. Slocum, Jr., and R.W. Woodman, 1992, *Organizational Behavior, Sixth Edition*, St. Paul, MN: West Publishing Company, pp. 150–162. Also D. Hellreigel and J.W. Slocum, Jr., 1995, Managerial Problem-Solving Styles, *Business Horizons* (December): pp. 29–37.

36. J.E. Driskill, R. Hogan, and E. Salas. 1987. Personality and Group Performance. In C. Hendrick (ed.), *Group Processes and Intergroup Relations*, Newbury Park. CA: Sage, pp. 91–112.

37. L.R. Hoffman. 1979. Applying Experimental Research on Group Problem Solving to Organizations. *Journal of Applied Behavioral Science 15*: pp. 375–391.

38. R.F. Bales. 1970. *Personality and Interpersonal Behavior*. New York: Holt, Rinehard, and Winston. Also M.W. Lustig, 1987, Bales' Interpersonal Rating Forms: Reliability and Dimensionality, *Small Group Behavior 18*: pp. 99–107.

39. K.L. Bettenhausen and J.K. Murnighan. 1991. The Development of an Intragroup Norm and the Effects of Interpersonal and Structural Changes. *Administrative Science Quarterly 36*: pp. 20–35.

40. L.W. Porter, E.E. Lawler, and J.R. Hackman. 1975. *Behavior in Organizations*. New York: McGraw-Hill, pp. 391–394. Also D.C. Feldman, 1984, The Development and Enforcement of Group Norms, *Academy of Management Review 9*: pp. 47–53.

41. J.B. Harvey. 1988. *The Abilene Paradox and Other Mediations on Management*. Lexington, MA: D.C. Heath. Also J.L. Pearce and R.H. Peters, 1985, A Contradictory Norms View of Employer-Employee Exchange, *Journal of Management 11*: pp. 19–30.

42. F.J. Roethlisberger and W.J. Dickson. 1939. *Management and the Worker: Technical versus Social Organization in an Industrial Plant*. Cambridge: Harvard University Press.

43. D.C. Feldman. 1984. The Development and Enforcement of Group Norms. *Academy of Management Review 9*: pp. 47–53. Also see R.S. Spich and R.S. Keleman, 1985, Explicit Norm Structuring Process: A Strategy for Increasing Task-Group Effectiveness, *Group and Organization Studies 10*: pp. 37–59.

44. Jon R. Katzenbach and Douglas K. Smith. 1993. *The Wisdom of Teams*. Boston, MA: Harvard Business School Press, McKensey and Company, pp. 121–123.

45. B. Latané. 1981. The Psychology of Social Impact. *American Psychologist 36*: pp. 343–356. Also C.A. Kiesler and S.B. Kiesler, 1970, *Conformity*, Reading, MA: Addison-Wesley.

46. Porter, Lawler, and Hackman, *Behavior in Organizations*, pp. 399–401; and W.A. Kahn, 1990, Psychological Conditions of Personal Engagement and Disengagement at Work, *Academy of Management Journal 33*: pp. 692-724.

47. L. Coch and J.R.P. French, Jr. 1948. Overcoming Resistance to Change. *Human Relations 1*: pp. 512–532.

48. A. Sinclair. 1992. The Tyranny of a Team Ideology. *Organization Studies 13*, 611–626.

49. S. Simpson. 1991. Dunkley Lumber Sets Itself a New Safety Standard. *Your Workplace Health and Safety*, (fall) 1.

50. Based on D. Bochove. 1993. Culture Shock Proves a Major Component of Work-Study Tour. *Toronto Globe & Mail* (July 6): p. B16. Also D. Robertson, J. Rinehart, C. Huxley and the CAW Research Group at CAMI, 1992, Team Concept and Kaizen: Japanese Production Management in a Unionized Canadian Auto Plant, *Studies in Political Economy 39*: pp. 77–107; R.R. Rehder, 1992, Building Cars as if People Mattered, *Columbia Journal of World Business* 27 (summer): pp. 56–70; and W. List, 1989, CAW Rejects Concept of Work Teams as Not in Workers' Interest, *Toronto Globe & Mail* (October 23): p. B3.

51. R.S. Spich and K. Keleman. 1985. Explicit Norm Structuring Process: A Strategy for Increasing Task-Group Effectiveness. *Group & Organization Studies 19* (March): pp. 37–59.

52 D.I. Levine. 1992. Piece Rates, Output Restriction, and Conformism. *Journal of Economic Psychology 13*: pp. 473–489.

53. Shaw, *Group Dynamics*, pp. 213–216; and Goodman *et al.*, *Understanding Groups in Organizations*, pp. 144–146.

54. P.R. Bernthal and C.A. Insko. 1993. Cohesiveness Without Groupthink: The Interactive Effects of Social and Task Cohesiveness. *Group and Organization Management 18*: pp. 66–87. Also A. Tziner, 1982, Differential Effects of Group Cohesiveness Types: A Clarifying Overview, *Social Behavior and Personality 10*: pp. 227–239.

55. A. Lott and B. Lott. 1965. Group Cohesiveness as Interpersonal Attraction: A Review of Relationships with Antecedent and Consequent Variables. *Psychological Bulletin 64*, 259–309.

56. S.E. Jackson. Team Composition in Organizational Settings: Issues in Managing an Increasingly Diverse Work Force, in *Group Process and Productivity*, eds. Worchel *et al.*, pp. 138–173. And J. Virk, P. Aggarwal, and R.N. Bhan, 1983, Similarity versus Complementarity in Clique Formation, *Journal of Social Psychology 120*: pp. 27–34.

57. W. Piper, M. Marrache, R. Lacroix, A. Richardson, and B. Jones. 1983. Cohesion as a Basic Bond in Groups. *Human Relations 36*: pp. 93–108. Also A. Mikalachki, 1969, *Group Cohesion Reconsidered*, London, ON: School of Business Administration, University of Western Ontario.

58. M.B. Pinto, J.K. Pinto, and J.E. Prescott. 1993. Antecedents and Consequences of Project Team Cross-Functional Cooperation. *Management Science 39*: pp. 1281–1296.

59. J. Zeidenberg. 1990. For Fun and Profit. *Profit* (November): pp. 37–40.

60. J.E. Hautaluoma and R.S. Enge. 1991. Early Socialization into a Work Group: Severity of Initiations Revisited. *Journal of Social Behavior & Personality 6*: pp. 725–748. Also E. Aronson and J. Mills, 1959, The Effects of Severity of Initiation on Liking for a Group, *Journal of Abnormal and Social Psychology 59*: pp. 177–181.

61. Shaw. *Group Dynamics*, p. 215.

62. J.M. McPherson and P.A. Popielarz. 1992. Social Networks and Organizational Dynamics. *American Sociological Review 57*: pp. 153–170. Also Piper *et al.*, *Cohesion as a Basic Bond in Groups*, pp. 93–108.

63. C.A. O'Reilly III, D.F. Caldwell, and W.P. Barnett. 1989. *Work Group Demography, Social Integration and Turnover. Administrative Science Quarterly 34*: pp. 21–37.

64. C.R. Evans and K.L. Dion. 1991. Group Cohesion and Performance: A Meta-Analysis. *Small Group Research 22*: pp. 175–186. Also Goodman *et al.*, *Understanding Groups in Organization*, p. 146; and C.N. Greene, 1989, Cohesion and Productivity in Work Groups. *Small Group Behavior 20* (February): pp. 70–86.

65. R.F. Bales. 1950. *Interaction Process Analysis*. Reading, MA: Addison-Wesley. Also R. Stayer, 1990, How I learned to Let My Workers Lead, *Harvard Business Review* (November–December): pp. 66–69, 72–74, 76, 80, 82, 83.

66. C.E. Larson and F.M.J. Lafasto. 1989. *Teamwork: What Must Go Wrong/What Can Go Wrong*. Newbury Park, CA: Sage.

67. Stephen D. Owens and James Reagan McLaurin. 1993. Cultural Diversity and Projects: What the Project Manager Needs to Know. *Proceedings of PMI'93 Annual Seminar/Symposium*, pp. 229–236.

68. V. Terpstra. 1972. *International Marketing*. Hinsdale, IL: Dryden, p. 83.

272

69. M. Dean Martin. 1981. The Negotiation Differential for International Project Management. *Proceedings of Project Management Institute*; also published as Chapter 38 in Paul C. Dinsmore, ed. *The AMA Handbook of Project Management*, AMACOM, New York.

70. Geert Hofstede. 1993. *Cultures and Organizations: Software of the Mind*. New York: McGraw Hill Book Co., p. 5.

71. Fred Luthan and Richard Hodgetts. 1991. *International Management*. New York: McGraw-Hill Book Co., p. 35.

72. V. Terpstra. 1978. *The Cultural Environment of International Business*. Dallas, TX: South Western Publishing, p. 176.

73. Terpstra, *The Cultural Environment of International Business*, p. 2.

74. G.E. Miracle and G.S. Albaum. 1970. *International Marketing Management*. Homewood, IL: Richard D. Irwin, pp. 8–9.

75. E.T. Hall. 1959. *The Silent Language*, Greenwich, CT: Fawcet, pp. 128–145.

76. L.T. Wells, Jr. 1977. Negotiating With Third World Governments, *Harvard Business Review* 55 (January–February): pp. 72–80.

77. Geert Hofstede. 1993. p. 14; and and Geert Hofstede. 1993. Cultures and Organizations: Software of the Mind, New York, NY: McGraw Hill Book Co., p. 14; and Geert Hofstede. 1993. Cultural Dimensions in People Management: The Socialization Perspective, in Globalizing Management, Creating and Leading the Competitive Organization, New York: John Wiley; and Hampden-Turner, Charles, and Alfons Trompenaars. 1993. The Seven Cultures of Capitalism, New York: Doubleday.

78. Hofstede, 1993. pp. 25-28.

79. Hofstede, 1993. pp. 51, 67.

80. Hofstede, 1993. pp. 82-83.

81. Hofstede, 1993. pp. 261-262.

82. Richard A. Punzo. 1996. Managing Cross Cultural Values in Project Teams. Proceedings of Annual Seminar/Symposium, Upper Darby, PA: Project Management Institute, pp. 863-868; and Training Management Corporation. 1996. Effective Global Manager, Seminar and Workbook, Princeton, NJ.

83. F. Kluckhohn and F.L. Strodtbeck. 1961. Variations in Value Orientations, Evanston, IL: Row, Peterson.

84. Edward T. Hall. 1990. The Silent Language, New York: Doubleday Books, 1990.

85. Stephen Rhinesmith. 1993. A Manager's Guide to Globalization: Six Keys to Success in a Changing World, Homewood, IL: Business One Irwin Press.

86. Edward C. Stewart and Milton J. Bennett. 1991. American Cultural Patterns: A Cross-Cultural Perspective, ref. ed. Yarmouth, ME: Intercultural Press: 1991.

87. Geert Hofstede. 1993. p. 143.

88. P.R. Harris and R.T. Moran. 1991. Managing Cultural Differences, Third Edition, Houston, TX: Gulf Publishing Co., pp. 104-106.

89. This section is based upon a paper by Larry Smith and Jerry Haar, 1993, *Managing International Projects, The AMA Handbook of Project Management*, Ch. 37, ed. Paul C. Dinsmore, pp. 441–448.

90. Lennie Copeland and Lewis Griggs. 1986. *Going International: How to Make Friends and Deal Effectively in the Global Marketplace*. New York: Plume-New American Library.

91. Arvind V. Phatak. 1989. *International Dimensions of Management*. Boston, MA: Kent Publishing.

92. David Clutterbuck. 1980. Breaking Through the Cultural Barrier, *International Management* (December): pp. 41–42. Also Arvind V. Phatak, 1974, *Managing Multinational Corporations*, New York: Praeger.

93. B.M. Bass *et al.* 1979. *Assessment of Managers: An International Comparison*. New York: MacMillan. Also Ronald E. Berenbeim, 1986, *Operating Foreign Subsidiaries: How Independent Can They Be?* New York: Conference Board.

94. Joseph A. Bello. 1986. *Behavioral Problems of Operational Research Implementations in Developing Countries*. Eds. Ukandi G. Damachi and Hans Dieter Seibel, *Management Problems in Africa*. New York: St. Martin's, pp. 232–269.

95. Parviz Asheghian and Bahman Ebrahimi. 1987. *International Business*. New York: Harper & Row.
96. Pierre Casse. 1979. *Training for the Cross-Cultural Milieu*. Washington, DC: SIETAR.
97. Paul C. Dinsmore and Manuel M. Benitez Codas. 1993. Challenges in Managing International Projects. *The AMA Handbook of Project Management*. Ed. by Paul C. Dinsmore, pp. 457–464.

Chapter 3

1. David I. Cleland. 1990. *Project Management: Strategic Design and Implementation*. Blue Ridge Summit, PA: TAB Books, pp. 299–322.
2. Linn C. Stuckenbruck and David Marshall. 1985. *Team Building for Project Managers*. Drexel Hill, PA: Project Management Institute, pp. 3–9, 28, 48–49.
3. J.J. Aquilino. 1977. Multi-skilled Work Teams: Productivity Benefits. CA: *California Management Review* (Summer): pp. 19, 17–22. Also J.D. Aram and C.P. Morgan, 1976, Role of Project Team Collaboration in R&D Performance, *Management Science 22* (June): p. 27; S. Atkins and A. Katcher, 1975, Getting Your Team in Tune, *Nation's Business* (March): pp. 91–93.
4. J.L. Hayes, 1975. Teamwork. *Management Review* (September): pp. 2–3. Also D.S. Hopkins, 1975, Roles of Project Teams and Venture Groups in New Product Development, *Research Management 18* (January): pp. 7–12; L. Bennington, 1972, The Team Approach to Project Management, *Management Review* (January), p. 61.
5. F.E. Katz. 1965. Explaining Informal Work Groups in Complex Organizations. *Administrative Science Quarterly 10*: pp. 204–223.
6. R. Likert. 1976. Improving Cost Performance with Cross-Functional Teams, *Conference Board Record 12* (1975): pp. 51–59. Also *Management Review 65*: pp. 36–42.
7. D.L. Wilemon and H.J. Thamhain. 1983. Team Building in Project Management. *Project Management Quarterly* (June): pp. 73–81.
8. H.J. Thamhain and D.L. Wilemon. 1974. Conflict Management in Project-Oriented Work Environments. *Proceedings of the Sixth Annual Seminar/Symposium*. Drexel Hill, PA: Project Management Institute, p. 87.
9. J.H. Zenger and D.E. Miller. 1974. Building Effective Teams, *Personnel 51*: pp. 20–29.
10. R.B. Maddux. *Team Building: An Exercise in Leadership*. Los Altos, CA: Crisp Publications, Inc., p. 9.
11. Peggy J. Day. 1989. *Team Building: Coaching a Winning Project Team*. Portland, OR: Workshop presented at the Northwest Regional Symposium of the Project Management Institute.
12. D.L. Wilemon and H.J. Thamhain. 1983. *A Model for Developing High Performance Project Teams*, Houston, TX: PMI Seminar/Symposium, pp. III–H11 to III–H12.
13. Harold Kerzner. 1989. *Project Management: A Systems Approach to Planning, Scheduling and Controlling, Third Edition*. New York: Van Nostrand Reinhold, pp. 260–261.
14. H.J. Thamhain, and G.R. Gemmill. 1974. Influence Styles of Project Managers: Some Project Performance Correlates. *Academy of Management Journal* (June).
15. Joan Knutson and Ira Bitz. 1991. *Project Management: How to Plan and Manage Successful Projects*. New York: AMACOM, pp. 17–35.
16. D.L. Wilemon and Jane Wilemon. 1984. *Project Management, Team Building and Leadership Workshop*. Philadelphia, PA: Presented at the 1984 International Project Management Institute Symposium.
17. G.H. Varney. 1977. *Organization Development for Managers*. Reading, MA: Addison Wesley Publishing Company, pp. 151–152.
18. This section is based upon ideas from Linn C. Stuckenbruck and David Marshall, 1985, *Team Building for Project Managers*, Drexel Hill, PA: Project Management Institute, pp. 16–24, 39–45; and Vijay K. Verma, 1996, Achieving Project Excellence in Culturally Diverse Teams, *Proceedings of the 1996 Project Management Institute Seminars & Symposium*, Project Management Institute, Upper Darby, PA: pp. 869–874.

274

19. Vijay K. Verma. 1995. *Human Resource Skills for the Project Manager.* Upper Darby, PA: Project Management Institute, pp. 33–35. Also Thomas L. Quick, 1992, *Successful Team Building.* New York: AMACOM, pp. 67–71.

20. Hans J. Thamhain and David L. Wilemon. 1975. Conflict Management in Project Life Cycles. *Sloan Management Review 12*: pp. 31–50. As quoted in Harold Kerzner, *Project Management: A Systems Approach to Planning, Scheduling and Controlling,* pp. 253–264; Thamhain and Wilemon, Conflict Management in Project-Oriented Work Environments, *Proceedings of the 1974 Project Management Institute Seminar/Symposium,* pp. 88; and Harold Kerzner, *Project Management: A Systems Approach to Planning, Scheduling and Controlling,* pp. 415–424.

21. Eschman and Lee. 1977. Conflict in Civilian and Air Force Program/Project Organization. *A Comparative Study* (September): LSSR 3–77B, A047230, p. 168.

22. B. Posner. 1986. What's All the Fighting About? Conflict in Project Management. IEEE Transactions on Engineering Management, EM–33 (4) (November): pp. 207–211.

23. Vijay K. Verma. 1995. *Human Resource Skills for the Project Manager.* Upper Darby, PA: Project Management Institute, pp. 117–127.

24. Robert R. Blake and Jane S. Mouton. 1964. *The Managerial Grid.* Houston, TX: Gulf Publishing. Also in application by Hans J. Thamhain and David L. Wilemon, 1975, Conflict Management in Project Life Cycle, *Sloan Management Review 16* (spring): pp. 31–50.

25. Vijay K. Verma and R.M. Wideman. 1994. Project Manager to Project Leader? and the Rocky Road Between. *Proceedings of the 25th Annual Seminar/Symposium.* Upper Darby, PA: Project Management Institute, pp. 627–633.

26. J.D. Batten. 1989. *Tough-Minded Leadership,* AMACOM; W. Benis, 1989, *On Becoming a Leader,* Addison Wesley. Also S.R. Covey, 1991, *Principle-Centered Leadership,* Summit Books; Robert L. Dilenschneider, 1991, A Briefing for Leaders, *Harper Business;* J.W. McLean and W. Weitzel, 1991, *Leadership, Magic, Myth or Method?* AMACOM; and Kimball Fisher, 1993, *Leading Self-Directed Work Teams: A Guide to Developing New Team Leadership,* New York: McGraw-Hill.

27. Batten. *Tough Minded Leadership,* p. 35.

28. McLean and Weitzel. *Leadership, Magic, Myth or Method?* P. 90.

29. Jeffrey K. Pinto. 1994. *Successful Information System Implementation: The Human Side.* Upper Darby, PA: Project Management Institute, p. 159.

30. Robert Townsend. 1984. *Further Up the Organization.* New York: Alford A. Knopf, p. 123.

31. Dennis P. Slevin. 1983. Leadership and the Project Manager. *Project Management Handbook,* edited by Cleland and King, New York: Van Nostrand Reinhold Co., p. 574.

32. Thomas V. Bonoma and Dennis P. Slevin. 1978. *Executive Survival Manual.* Belmont, CA: Wadsworth Publishing Company.

33. William G. Dyer. 1978. *Team Building: Issues and Alternatives.* Reading, MA: Addison-Wesley Publishing Company, p. xi.

Chapter 4

1. David L. Wilemon and Hans J. Thamhain. 1979. Team Building in Project Management. *Proceedings of the 11th Annual Seminar/Symposium.* Drexel Hill, PA: Project Management Institute, pp. 373–380, later published in 1983, *Project Management Journal* (June): pp. 73–81.

2. Joan Knutson and Ira Bitz. 1991. *Project Management: How to Plan and Manage Successful Projects.* New York: AMACOM, pp. 3, 17–35.

3. This section is based upon Linn C. Stuckenbruck and David Marshall, 1985, *Team Building for Project Managers,* Drexel Hill, PA: Project Management Institute, pp. 31–39.

4. Robert B. Maddux. 1986. *Team Building: An Exercise in Leadership.* Los Altos, CA: Cris Publications, Inc., p. 47.

5. Thomas L. Quick. 1992. Successful Team Building. New York: AMACOM, *American Management Association,* pp. 55–66.

6. Vijay K. Verma. 1995. *Human Resource Skills for Project Managers.* Upper Darby, PA: Project Management Institute, pp. 32–38, 40–49.

7. Robert L. Montgomery. 1981. *Listening Made Easy.* New York: AMACOM, pp. 13–15.

8. K. Davis. 1978. *Human Relations at Work, Fifth Edition*. New York: McGraw Hill Book Company.

9. J. Kostner and C. Strbiak. 1993. Inspiring People and Performance. San Diego, CA: Workshop presented at the Annual Seminar/Symposium, pp. 61–87.

10. 1995. Interpersonal Communication Skills Workbook. CO: Career Track Inc., pp. 4–22.

11. Peter F. Drucker. 1974. *Management Tasks, Responsibilities, Practices*. New York: Harper & Row, pp. 465–471.

12. Paul C. Dinsmore. 1990. *Human Factors in Project Management, Revised Edition*. New York: AMACOM, pp. 200–211.

13. Stephen P. Robbins and Robin Stuart Kotze. 1986. *Management Concepts and Practices. Canadian Edition*, Toronto, Canada: Prentice Hall Canada Inc., pp. 93–138.

14. D.C. Kinlaw. 1991. *Developing Superior Work Teams: Building Quality and the Competitive Edge*. Lexington, MA: Lexington Books. Also R.A. Cook and J.A. Kernagan, Estimating the Difference between Group versus Individual Performance on Problem-Solving Tasks, *Group and Organization Studies* 12: pp. 319–342.

15. Don Hellreigel, John W. Slocum, Jr., and Richard W. Woodman. *Organizational Behavior, Sixth Edition*. St. Paul, MN: West Publishing Company, pp. 332–342.

16. Charles Wilson and Marcus Alexis. 1962. Basic Frameworks for Decision. *Academy of Management Journal* 5: pp. 151–164.

17. Ernest Dale. 1973. *Management: Theory and Practice*. New York: McGraw-Hill, pp. 548–549. This section of Dale's test is based on Erich Fromm, *Man for Himself*, New York: Holt, Rinehard & Winston, pp. 62–117.

18. W.C. Morris and M. Sashkin. 1976. *Organization Behavior in Action: Skill Building Experiences*. St. Paul, MN: West Publishing Company, p. 3.

19. Rick Roskin and R. Stuart Kotze. 1983. *Success Guide to Managerial Achievement*. Reston, VA: Reston Publishing Co.

20. William Ouchi. 1981. *Theory Z*. Reading, MA: Addison Wesley Publishing Co, pp. 4–43.

21. Robert B. Duncan. 1972. Characteristics of Organizational Environments and Perceived Environmental Uncertainty. *Administrative Science Quarterly* 17: pp. 313–327.

22. R.B. Gallupe, L.M. Bastianutti, and W.H. Cooper. 1991. Unblocking Brainstorms. *Journal of Applied Psychology* 76: pp. 137–142.

23. L.M. Jessup, T. Connolly, and J. Gelegher. 1990. The Effects of Anonymity on GDSS Group Process with an Idea-Generating Task. *MIS Quarterly*, pp. 313–321.

24. Frederick Brooks. 1982. *The Mythical Man-Month: Essays on Software Engineering*. Reading, MA: Addison Wesley Publishing Company.

25. F.L. Harrison. 1985. *Advanced Project Management, Second Edition*. New York: John Wiley and Sons.

26. W. Richard Plunkett. 1986. *Supervision: The Direction of People at Work, Fourth Edition*. Dubuque, IA: Wm. C. Brown Publishers, pp. 220–224.

27. R.E. Lefton, V.R. Buzzotta, and Mannie Sherberg. 1978. *Dimensional Management Strategies*. St. Louis: Psychological Associates, pp. 6–11.

28. Robert R. Blake and Jane S. Mouton. 1978. *The New Managerial Grid*. Houston, TX: Gulf Publishing, p. 11.

Chapter 5

1. This section is based upon J. Kostner and Christy Strbiak, 1993, Openness: The Gateway to Top Performance, *PM Network* (November): pp. 25–29; and Kostner and Strbiak, 1993, Inspiring People and Performance, workshop materials presented at the Annual Seminar/Symposium of the Project Management Institute, pp. 61–87.

2. Fernando Bartholomew. 1989. Nobody Trusts the Boss Completely: Now What? *Harvard Business Review* 67: pp. 135–142.

3. Craig A. Russell. 1989. Openness and Trust. *Executive Excellence* 6: p. 12. Also Alan Farnham, 1989, Trust Gap, *Fortune*, pp. 56–78.

4. J. Kostner and C. Strbiak. 1993. *Inspiring People and Performance*, San Diego, California: PMI'93 Workshop, 94–95.

5. Kurt Lewin. 1967. Frontiers in Group Dynamics. *Human Relations 1*. Also 1951, New York: Field Theory in Social Science, Harper.

6. H.S. Dugan, H.J. Thamhain, and D.L. Wilemon. 1977. Managing Change in Project Management. *Proceedings of the 9th Annual Seminar/Symposium*, Project Management Institute, pp. 178–188.

7. R. Levering. 1989. *A Great Place to Work*. New York: McGraw-Hill, p. 15. See also M.R. Weisbord, 1990, *Productive Workplaces*, San Francisco, CA: Jossey-Bass.

8. Joseph A. Patrick and George E. Manning. 1991. How to Manage Morale. Costa Mesa, CA: *Personnel Journal,* later reprinted in *Inside Guide*, Toronto, ON: Inside *Guide Magazine Limited*, pp. 41–46.

9. D.T. Hall. 1976. Careers in Organizations. *Pacific Palisades*. CA: Goodyear Publishing.

10. R.M. Steers and L.W. Porter. 1983. *Motivation and Work Behavior, Third Edition*. New York: McGraw-Hill Publishers.

11. J.M. Kouzes and B.Z. Posner. 1987. *The Leadership Challenge: How to Get Extraordinary Things Done in Organizations*. San Francisco, CA: Jossey-Bass Publishers. Also A. Zaleznik, 1989, *The Managerial Mystique: Restoring Leadership in Business*, New York: Harper & Row, Publishers, Inc.; G.A. Yukl, 1989, *Leadership in Organizations*, Englewood Cliffs, NJ: Prentice-Hall.

12. P. Drucker. 1974. *Management Tasks and Responsibilities*. New York: Harper & Row, Publishers, Inc. Also W.E. Deming, 1982, *Quality Productivity and Competitive Position*, Boston, MA: MIT Press.

13. J.M. Ivanivich, A.D. Szilagyi, and M. Wallace Jr. 1977. *Organizational Behavior and Performance*. Santa Monica, CA: Goodyear Publishing Company Inc., p. 162. Also R.N. Ford, 1973, Job Enrichment Lessons from AT&T, *Harvard Business Review* (January/February): pp. 97–106.

14. L.W. Porter and E.E. Lawler. 1968. *Managerial Attitudes and Performance*. Homewood, IL: Dow Jones Irwin. Also T. Matsui and M. Terai, 1975, A Cross-cultural Study of the Validity of the Expectancy Theory of Work Motivation, *Journal of Applied Psychology* 60: pp. 263–265.

15. G.S. Odiorne. 1987. *The Human Side of Management: Management by Integration and Self-control*. San Diego, CA: University Associates. Also C.M. Kelly, 1968, *The Destructive Achiever: Power and Ethics in the American Corporation*, Reading, MA: Addison-Wesley.

16. B.F. Skinner. 1969. *Contingencies of Reinforcement: A Theoretical Analysis*, Englewood Cliffs, CA: Prentice-Hall. Also Fred Luthans and Robert Kreitner, 1975, *Organizational Behavior Modification*, Glenview, III; Scott, Foresman.

17. Charles L. Buck, Jr. 1981. Managing the Most Valuable Resource: People, A Decade of Project Management selected readings from the *Project Management Quarterly*, 1970 through 1980, published by the Project Management Institute, Drexel Hill, PA, pp. 92–95.

18. Robert B. Maddux. *Team Building; An Exercise in Leadership*. Los Altos, CA: Crisp Publications, Inc., pp. 58–59.

19. Don Hellriegel, John W. Slocum, Jr., and Richard W. Woodman. 1992. *Organizational Behavior, Sixth Edition*. St. Paul, MN: West Publishing Company, pp. 266–271. Also Linn C. Stuckenbruck and David Marshall, 1985, *Team Building for Project Managers*, Drexel Hill, PA: Project Management Institute, pp. 39–40.

20. Vijay K. Verma and R. Max Wideman. 1994. Project Manager to Project Leaders, and the Rocky Road Between ...., *Proceedings 25th Annual Seminar/Symposium*, Vancouver, Canada, (October): pp. 627–633.

21. John Adair. 1986. *Effective Team Building*. Gower Publishing Company Ltd., Ch. 10, pp. 117–125.

22. Ken Blanchard. *One Minute Manager*.

23. Linn C. Stuckenbruck and David Marshall. 1985. *Team Building for Project Managers*. Upper Darby: PA: Project Management Institute, p. 42–43.

24. William G. Dyer. 1978. *Team Building; Issues and Alternatives*. Reading, MA: Addison Wesley Publishing Company, p. xi.

References

25. Dennis P. Slevin. 1983. Leadership and the Project Manager, *Project Management Handbook.* Eds. D. Cleland and W. King. New York: Van Nostrand Reinhold Company, p. 574.

26. Thomas V. Bonama and Dennis P. Slevin. 1978. *Executive Survival Manual.* Belmont, CA: Wadsworth Publishing Company.

27. Pamela Poseyy and Janice Klein. 1990. Traditional vs. New Work System Supervision: Is there a difference? *Revitalizing Manufacturing: Text and Cases,* Janice Klein, Ed. Homewood, IL: Irwin Publishing Co.

28. Fisher. *Leading Self-Directed Work Teams.* New York: McGraw-Hill, Inc. pp. 97, 105–119, 255–258.

29. Sheila Murray Bethel. 1990. New York: Bentley Books.

Chapter 6

1. Richard S. Wellins, William C. Byham, and Jeanne M. Wilson. 1991. *Empowered Teams.* San Francisco, CA: Jossey-Bass Inc., pp. XVII-XV, 5–13.

2. Project Management Institute. 1994. *A Guide to the Project Management Body of Knowledge (Exposure Draft).* Upper Darby, PA: Project Management Institute, p. 4.

3. Kimball Fisher. 1993. *Leading Self Directed Work Teams.* New York: McGraw-Hill, Inc., pp. 4–23.

4. Jack Sherwood. 1983. Presented this idea (as a Consultant) at Tektronix.

5. Richard Wellins *et al.* 1990. Self Directed Teams: A Study of Current Practice. *Industry Week.* The Association of Quality and Participation (AQP) and Development Dimensions International Study.

6. Robert F. Hicks and Diane Bone. 1990. *Self Managing Teams.* Menlo Park, CA: Crisp Publications, Inc., p. 4.

7. Richard S. Wellins, William C. Byham, and Jeanne M. Wilson. 1991. *Empowered Teams.* San Francisco, CA: Jossey-Bass Inc., pp. 3–5.

8. R.E. Walton. 1985. From Control to Commitment in the Workplace. *Harvard Business Review.* (March–April): pp. 77–84.

9. Louis Harris. 1988. What Workers Want: The Gap in Management's Perception. 1988. *Behavioral Sciences Newsletter.* (June 27): p. 1.

10. A.P. Carnevale, L.J. Gainer, and A.S. Meltzer. 1988. *Workplace Basics: The Skills Employers Want.* American Society for Training and Development and U.S. Department of Labour Report, 0–225-795–QL.2, Washington, D.C.: Government Printing Office, p. 1.

11. 1993. *Implementing Self Directed Work Teams Work Book.* Boulder, CO: Career Track Inc., pp. 2–4.

12. Eric Trist. 1950. *The Relation of Social and Technical Systems in Coal Mining.* A paper presented to the British Psychological Society, Industrial Section.

13. John Cotter. 1983. Designing Organizations that Work: An Open Sociotechnical Systems Perspective. John J. Cotter and Associates, Inc.

14. Richard S. Wellins, William C. Byham, and Jeanne M. Wilson. 1991. *Empowered Teams.* San Francisco, CA: Jossey-Bass Inc., pp. 21–23.

15. Cynthia D. Scott and Dennis T. Jaffe. 1991. *Empowerment.* Menlo Park, CA: Crisp Publications, Inc., pp. i–ii, 4–16, 29–37.

16. Diane Tracy. 1990. *The Power Pyramid.* New York: William Morrow, P. 163.

17. Erica Jones. 1994. Workbook on Outwitting Organizational Politics and Bureaucracy to Get Results. *Workshop presented at PMI'94 Annual Symposium.* Upper Darby, PA: Project Management Institute, pp. 25–38.

18. This section is based upon ideas and check lists in Robert F. Hicks and Diane Bone. 1990. *Self Managing Teams.* Menlo Park, CA: Crisp Publications, Inc., pp. 7–18.

19. James L. Huskett. 1990. *Service Breakthroughs.* New York: The Free Press, pp. 227–228.

20. Fisher. *Leading Self Directed Work Teams,* pp. 164–172.

21. Robert F. Hicks and Diane Bone. 1990. *Self Managing Teams.* Menlo Park, CA: Crisp Publications, Inc., pp. 66–83.

22. Fisher. *Leading Self-Directed Work Teams*. New York: McGraw-Hill, Inc., pp. 97, 105–119, 255–258.
23. Wellins. *Empowered Teams*, pp. 30–41.
24. H.R. Jessup. 1990. New Roles in Team Leadership. *Training and Development Journal* (November): pp. 79–83.
25. Wellins. *Empowered Teams*, pp. 127–138.
26. Wellins. *Empowered Teams*, pp. 138–142, 223–236.
27. This section is based upon Kimball Fisher. 1993. *Leading Self Directed Work Teams*. New York: McGraw-Hill, Inc., pp. 120–133.
28. Ralph Stayer. 1990. How I Learned to Let My Workers Lead. *Harvard Business Review* (November-December)
29. Fisher. *Leading Self Directed Work Teams*, pp. 131–133.
30. Fisher. *Leading Self Directed Work Teams*, pp. 44–53.
31. Fisher. *Leading Self Directed Work Teams*, pp. 255–258.
32. A. Toffler. 1990. *Powershift: Knowledge, Wealth and Violence at the Edge of the Twenty-First Century*. New York: Bantam Books.
33. B. Dumaine. 1990. Who Needs a Boss? *Fortune* (May 7): pp. 52–55, 58–60.
34. R. Howard. 1990. Values Make the Company. *Harvard Business Review* (September–October): pp. 132-145.
35. S.C. Gwynne. 1990. The Right Stuff. *Time* (October 29): pp. 74–84.
36. America's Choice: High Skills or Low Wages. 1990. Report published for the National Center of Education and the Economy, cited in Richard S. Wellins, William C. Byham, and Jeanne M. Wilson. 1991. *Empowered Teams*. San Francisco, CA: Jossey-Bass Inc., p. 230.
37. J. Hoerr. 1990. Sharpening Minds for a Competitive Edge. Business Week (December 17): pp. 72–78.
38. Fisher. Leading *Self Directed Work Teams*, pp. 217–221.

Appendix

Self-Assessment Exercise A

Questionnaire for Evaluating Your Behaviors as a Team Member

1 = Never   2 = Seldom   3 = Often   4 = Always

Task-oriented behaviors: In a team, I...

1. Initiate ideas or actions	1	2	3	4
2. Facilitate the introduction of facts and information	1	2	3	4
3. Clarify issues	1	2	3	4
4. Evaluate task structures and constraints	1	2	3	4
5. Summarize and pull together various ideas	1	2	3	4
6. Keep the group working on the task	1	2	3	4
7. Ask to see if the group is near a decision (determine consensus)	1	2	3	4
8. Request further information	1	2	3	4

Relations-oriented behaviors: In a team, I...

9. Support and encourage others	1	2	3	4
10. Reduce tensions	1	2	3	4
11. Harmonize (keep the peace)	1	2	3	4
12. Compromise (find common ground)	1	2	3	4
13. Encourage participation	1	2	3	4

Self-oriented behaviors: In a team, I...

14. Resolve conflicts promptly	1	2	3	4
15. Express hostility	1	2	3	4
16. Seek recognition	1	2	3	4
17. Avoid participation	1	2	3	4
18. Dominate the group	1	2	3	4
19. Nitpick and hold back the information	1	2	3	4
20. Reject views of others	1	2	3	4

Total Score: _____

Scoring Key:
Too much or too little of certain behaviors can adversely affect the efficiency and effectiveness of a team. A score of 24–32 on task-oriented behaviors, 15–20 on relations-oriented behaviors, and 7–14 on self-oriented behaviors would suggest an effectively functioning team.

Source: Don Hellreigel, John W. Slocum, Jr., and Richard W. Woodman, Organizational Behavior, Sixth Edition, St. Paul, MN; West Publishing Company, p. 323. By permission of publisher.

Self-Assessment Exercise B

The Cultural Awareness Quiz

1. Which country do people not expect to be paid for overtime?
   a. United States
   b. Korea
   c. Canada
   d. Saudi Arabia

2. Chewing gum is illegal in which of the following cities?
   a. Bangkok
   b. Manilla
   c. Singapore
   d. Budapest
   e. Venice
   f. Lisbon

3. How many countries are in the Middle East?
   a. 23 countries
   b. 16 countries
   c. 14 countries
   d. 17 countries

4. In what country would you have trouble conducting business, if you were a recovering alcoholic?
   a. Brazil
   b. France
   c. South Africa
   d. Vietnam
   e. Canada

5. What is the only official bilingual province in Canada?
   a. British Columbia
   b. Saskatchewan
   c. Quebec
   d. New Brunswick
   e. Yukon

Appendix

6. The flicking out of a thumb on your front teeth is not considered an insult in which culture?

   a. Deaf
   b. Slavic
   c. Italian
   d. Prussian
   e. Mongolian

7. What time of the year is Yom Kippur?

   a. August/Sept.
   b. Nov./Dec.
   c. Dec./Jan.
   d. Sept./Oct.

8. In what country are cows sacred?

   a. Turkey
   b. Malaysia
   c. Nigeria
   d. India
   e. Tanzania

9. It is illegal to consume alcohol in:

   a. Bolivia
   b. Sweden
   c. Iran
   d. Kuwait
   e. Libya

10. During a social visit in Korea your host asks you to dinner. At the dinner you propose a toast to a senior partner in the firm. Do you ...

    a. Toast holding the glass in two hands.
    b. Toast holding the glass in right hand, supporting the arm with the left.
    c. Toast with the left hand.

11. What number is considered lucky and prosperous in Chinese culture?

    a. 8
    b. 4
    c. 5
    d. 3
    e. None of the above

12. When meeting your Korean business partner, Lo Tom Wong, for the first time, you would address him as:

    a. Mr. Tom
    b. Mr. Lo
    c. Mr. Wong
    d. Partner
    e. Any of the above

13. What are the languages spoken in the Middle East?

    a. Arabic
    b. Persian
    c. Turkish
    d. Hebrew
    e. Greek
    f. All of the above

14. Where would a Taiwanese businessman prefer to go to talk about a contract?

    a. Buddhist temple
    b. Beer hall
    c. Businessman's residence
    d. At a party
    e. None of the above

15. In which country is it considered more appropriate (but not law) for women to wear skirts (medium/long) instead of shorts?

    a. Mexico
    b. El Salvador
    c. Columbia
    d. None of the above
    e. All of the above

16. In which of the following countries would tipping be considered rude?

    a. Canada
    b. United States
    c. Japan
    d. Spain
    e. Mozambique
    f. Burma
    g. None of the above

17. What is the most popular spoken language in Hong Kong?
    a. Mandarin
    b. Cantonese
    c. English
    d. None of the above

18. An unofficial "payment" to a customs official would be customary in:
    a. Canada
    b. Germany
    c. Denmark
    d. Mexico
    e. None of the above

19. In which country would Ramadan (a month of fasting) be celebrated by the majority of people?
    a. Saudi Arabia
    b. India
    c. Singapore
    d. Korea
    e. All of the above

20. In Japan it is important to:

    a. Present your business card only after you have developed a relationship with your host
    b. Present your card with both hands
    c. Put your company name on the card, but never position or title
    d. All of the above

21. Which would be inappropriate when you are *first meeting* a Taiwanese businessman?
    a. Presenting your business card
    b. Asking if he wants a cigarette
    c. Shaking hands
    d. Asking if he's had a meal
    e. All of the above are fine

22. As a Canadian business involved in a business venture with a company in Hong Kong, which of the following languages would be appropriate for presenting documents?
    a. English
    b. Chinese
    c. Both English and Chinese
    d. Doesn't matter which language

284

23. "Nodding the head" is a sign of comprehension only in which of the following countries?

    a. United States
    b. France
    c. Chile
    d. Japan
    e. South Africa

24. In which country is it appropriate to bring your own alcohol to restaurants?

    a. Canada
    b. Australia
    c. France
    d. Saudi Arabia
    e. None of the above

25. If you take your hat off and place it on the bar in an Australian outback pub, you are saying you're:

    a. Available
    b. Thirsty
    c. Looking for directions
    d. Looking for a fight
    e. Following house rules

26. What is the most popular spoken language in Hong Kong?

    a. Mandarin
    b. Cantonese
    c. English
    d. None of the above

Answer Key

1. b	6. d	11. b	16. b	21. e
2. c	7. d	12. f	17. b	22. a
3. d	8. d	13. b	18. d	23. d
4. d	9. b	14. e	19. a	24. b
5. a	10. a	15. c	20. b	25. d

Scoring Key: A score of 19–25: you are culturally literate; 14–18: you have some cultural awareness, but could improve; 13 or less: better pack your suitcase and start learning!

Self Assessment Exercise C

Team Readiness Survey

Question: When does it make sense to start work teams in your
organization?

Answer: When the conditions are right.

To help you determine how conducive your organization is to the implementation of teams, you might want to give some thought to key situational issues. Seventeen questions to assess team readiness are given below. Readiness assessment does not have to be an exhaustive analysis. These questions relate to the organization's culture, practices, work environment and goals. Answers should be based on how you think the situations *are*, rather than how they *should* be.

Using the scale below each item, give yourself a "5" for yes (if you strongly agree with the item), a "1" for no (if you strongly disagree with the item), or a "2," "3," or "4," depending on how close you are to either end of the scale. When you are finished, total your scores for an indication of your organization's readiness to accept work teams.

1. Management believes that front-line employees can and should make the majority of decisions that affect how they do their work.

    1   2   3   4   5
   STRONGLY DISAGREE   STRONGLY AGREE

2. Employees can suggest and implement improvements to their work without going through several levels of approval.

    1   2   3   4   5
   STRONGLY DISAGREE   STRONGLY AGREE

3. The union is likely to agree to renegotiate traditional work rules and job classifications to permit greater flexibility and autonomy.

    1   2   3   4   5
   STRONGLY DISAGREE   STRONGLY AGREE

4. The nature of the work in your organization lends itself to a team-based approach rather than to individual effort.

    1   2   3   4   5
   STRONGLY DISAGREE   STRONGLY AGREE

5. Your technology is flexible enough to permit restructuring or reorganization based on the needs of your teams. The physical design of your workplace lends itself to working in teams.

    1   2   3   4   5
   STRONGLY DISAGREE   STRONGLY AGREE

286

6. It is possible to organize work so that teams of employees can take responsibility for entire jobs.

1   2   3   4   5
STRONGLY DISAGREE   STRONGLY AGREE

7. There is enough complexity in jobs to allow for initiative and decision-making.

1   2   3   4   5
STRONGLY DISAGREE   STRONGLY AGREE

8. Your employees would be interested or willing to organize into teams.

1   2   3   4   5
STRONGLY DISAGREE   STRONGLY AGREE

9. Your overall organizational culture, vision, and values support teamwork and empowerment.

1   2   3   4   5
STRONGLY DISAGREE   STRONGLY AGREE

10. Your organization has a history of following through on initiatives such as empowerment.

1   2   3   4   5
STRONGLY DISAGREE   STRONGLY AGREE

11. Management in your organization is willing to adjust responsibility downward and radically change its own roles and behavior.

1   2   3   4   5
STRONGLY DISAGREE   STRONGLY AGREE

12. Your company is secure enough to guarantee a period of relative stability during which the teams can develop.

1   2   3   4   5
STRONGLY DISAGREE   STRONGLY AGREE

13. You have adequate support functions, such as human resources, engineering, and maintenance, that can help teams by providing information, coaching, and training.

1   2   3   4   5
STRONGLY DISAGREE   STRONGLY AGREE

14. Management understands that developing teams is a lengthy, time-consuming, and labor-intensive process. It is willing and able to make the investment.

1   2   3   4   5
STRONGLY DISAGREE   STRONGLY AGREE

15. Your organization has systems that provide timely information to front-line employees.

1	2	3	4	5
STRONGLY DISAGREE			STRONGLY AGREE	

16. Your employees have the skills needed to take greater control of their jobs.

1	2	3	4	5
STRONGLY DISAGREE			STRONGLY AGREE	

17. You are willing to invest in training your front-line employees.

1	2	3	4	5
STRONGLY DISAGREE			STRONGLY AGREE	

Your Total Score: _____

Scoring Key:

Score	Actions
Above 65	You are on solid ground. Teams stand a good chance of taking root if properly implemented.
40–64	There are some weaknesses in your culture's policies, processes and procedures. Work on these weak areas before proceeding.
Below 40	Teams will have difficulty taking hold. Reexamine your culture and explore a more gradual course toward empowerment.

Source: Richard S. Wellins, William C. Byham, Jeanne Wilson. 1991. Empowered Teams. San Francisco, CA: Jossey-Bass, Inc. pp 95-99. By permission of publisher.

Self-Assessment Exercise D

Team Effectiveness Inventory

Instructions: Think of a group or team in which you are currently or have been a member. Please respond on the basis of your degree of agreement or disagreement with each statement. Use the following scale: strongly disagree (SD), disagree (D), undecided/neutral (U), agree (A), strongly agree (SA).

Statements	SD	D	U	A	SA
Task Performance					
1. We plan ahead for problems that might arise	1	2	3	4	5
2. We are an effective problem-solving team	1	2	3	4	5
3. We achieve high performance goals	1	2	3	4	5
Influence					
4. Team members are willing to listen to and understand each other	1	2	3	4	5
5. Members are active in influencing the future of the team	1	2	3	4	5
6. Members are willing to disagree and make suggestions to each other	1	2	3	4	5
Satisfaction					
7. I enjoy working with my team members	1	2	3	4	5
8. I am able to make good use of my skills and abilities on this team	1	2	3	4	5
9. Considering everything, it is a pleasure to be a member of this team	1	2	3	4	5
Member Relations					
10. I trust the members of my team	1	2	3	4	5
11. There is no free riding by members	1	2	3	4	5
12. We are a cooperative and cohesive group	1	2	3	4	5
Creativity					
13. Divergent ideas are encouraged	1	2	3	4	5
14. Our norms encourage change and the exploration of new ideas	1	2	3	4	5
15. The creative talents of members are drawn on to improve the quality and quantity of the team's outputs	1	2	3	4	5

Interpretation: Add the point values for each scale:

Task Performance = _____

Influence   = _____

Satisfaction   = _____

Member Relations = _____

Creativity   = _____

Total = _____

Scoring Key: Point values of 12 to 15 suggest the team is effective on that dimension, whereas point values of 3 to 8 suggest ineffectiveness. Point values of 9 to 11 suggest uncertainty and ambiguity on that dimension. Total point values for items 1 through 15 of 60 to 75 suggest a highly effective team, whereas a total score of 15 through 30 suggests a team that is probably ineffective.

Developed from I.T. Kaplan. 1989. Measuring Work Group Effectiveness: A Comparison of Three Instruments. *Management Communication Quarterly*, 2 pp. 424-448; F. Friedlander. 1966. Performance and Interactional Dimensions of Organizational Work Groups. *Journal of Applied Psychology*, 50, pp. 257-265; Wilson Learning Corporation. 1988. *Team Interaction Profile is Valid and Reliable*. Eden Prairie, Minn: Wilson Learning Corporation; Honeywell Inc. 1985. *Job Reaction Questionnaire User's Guide*. Minneapolis: Honeywell, Inc.

Self-Assessment Exercise E

Is Your Team a High Performance Team?

Rate your current team on each of the five following points. Circle the number rating you give your team for each statement.

1	2	3	4	5	6
worst I've seen	needs much improve-ment	needs some improve-ment	about average	good/ better than average	best I've seen

1. Acceptance, openness, respect and trust are words I'd use to describe relationships within our team.

    1   2   3   4   5   6

2. There is high motivation for productivity and excellence in all team members.

    1   2   3   4   5   6

3. Conflicts and disagreements are dealt with by seeking the best possible solution rather than blame-placing.

    1   2   3   4   5   6

4. Team members see the "big picture" and put the overall company needs and priorities over their own agendas.

    1   2   3   4   5   6

5. If a team member has problems or gets into difficulty, others fully and willingly step in to help.

    1   2   3   4   5   6

Score:
- 25-30   You're a good coach and a team leader. Use this day for reinforcement and recognition of what you're doing right.
- 21-24   You have a better than average team.
- 15-20   You're right. Your team can do better.
- 5-15   You need to work on team building. Refer to this book and other literature. Then why your team is experiencing difficulties should hopefully become clear very soon.

Source: H. Rhea Gray. 1991. *Models of Excellence.* By permission of publisher.

Self-Assessment Exercise F

Readiness Assessment

Answer the following questions and discuss them with other team members to determine how ready you are to form a Self-Motivated Project Team (SMPT).

1. Are you willing to succeed or fail as a team?
2. Does your project have a sponsor or a leader who is supportive of SMPTs?
3. To what extent do you function without management now?
4. Do you possess the required technical, administrative, and interpersonal skills you need?
5. Are you willing to recognize peer pressure as a means of control within the team?
6. Have you clearly discussed your expectations, and are they realistic?
7. Do you each have personal and/or professional benefits to gain from working in an SMPT?
8. Are you willing to pay attention to HOW you do things as well as WHAT you do?
9. Is there a climate of trust within the team?
10. Are you willing to engage in developing creative solutions?

Exercise:

a. What is the important information you discovered in your readiness assessment?
b. How would you use this information?
c. Identify areas that you need to discuss further to gain more information. How would you proceed with this and solve existing problems?

Index

Aesthetics 90

Assembling the project team 13, 126–127
composition 68, 75, 88
checklist for selecting team members 128–129

Backlash against teams 264

Baseline changes 43, 45–46, 49

Boundary management 255, 258–259

Change
diagnosing need for 19–20, 22, 24
dynamics of 16–18, 20, 204
managing changes
in a project 42
types of 21
pressure for 18, 28, 30
principles of 19, 52
procedures for managing 44, 49

Change agent, project manager as 20–21

Characteristics of effective teams 37–38, 68

Cohesiveness, in teams 84–88
consequences of 86–87

Communication (SEE ALSO LISTENING)
teamwork and 35
communication blockers 113, 168–169
channels and links 41, 113, 136, 160, 162, 164
creating openness 13, 194, 216

Committee, difference from team 66–67

Conflict resolution 119, 139–141, 143, 186, 203, 237–238, 255

Conformity 82–83

Confronting poor performance 198, 201–203

Cross cultural settings 104

Cultural orientation model 97–98

Cultural variables 94, 97–98

Culture
elements of 89, 92
low/high-context 95
definition of 89

Culture shock 92

Decision-making
rational decision–making model 176
rational decision–making process 175, 181
decision situations 174

Decision styles 13, 152–153, 179
factors affecting 180

Developmental sequence of teams 40, 68–69, 80

Diversity 19, 33, 34, 35, 37, 59—103, 205, 261

Empowerment
continuum 227, 257, 265
variables of 234, 265
principles of 236, 266

Facilitative skills 251–252, 266

Figures 23,27,32,35,38,39,40,46,47,48,54, 69, 71, 77, 85, 87, 90, 90, 98, 106, 108, 117, 118, 119, 124, 127, 131, 132, 133, 149, 156, 161, 164, 166, 172, 181, 184, 188, 189, 197, 207, 210, 212, 215, 219, 223, 227, 231, 233, 240, 250

Force field analysis 28, 204

Gender role identification 93

Globalization 18–19, 55, 105–106,

Groups, and project teams 13, 60–62

Guidelines for
team decision making 180
team management 251
team building 5, 133
overcoming resistance to change 29

Human resource management 34–35, 37, 298

"I" statements 198, 200

Individualism 60, 98

Integrated project team 13, 64, 66

International projects 58–59, 101, 105–106, 212

Kick–off meeting 135, 150, 245, 250

Language 25, 34, 90, 92, 96, 102–104, 107, 162, 165, 284–286

Listening
effective listening 36, 164–165, 167

Leadership
styles 37, 146, 218–220
project leadership 36, 54, 68, 143–147, 150, 185, 206, 215
qualities of leaders 175, 221

Learning objectives 13

Management support 41, 137, 148, 150, 155, 189, 244, 246, 251

Managerial grid 187–189

Matrix structure 24–25, 135, 141

Money, and team motivation 45, 91, 94, 103, 138, 206, 213, 217

Morale
managing 206, 216

Negotiations 28, 89, 91, 95, 103, 123, 162
of SMPT leaders 256, 260

Organization development 22

Organizational climate 13, 23, 116–117, 176, 220, 236, 240, 242, 266

Overtime, effect of 185

Performance
drivers and barriers to 12, 34, 120
measuring team performance 119

Personal qualities, and leadership 175, 181

Power and authority 13, 152–153, 155, 189, 248

Power distance 92, 98–99

Praise 28, 78, 82, 133, 138, 196, 198, 211–212, 217–218

Problem–solving abilities 157, 189

Problem–solving styles 77–78

Process activities 118, 149

Process management 244, 254–255

Product obsolescence 19, 55

Project life cycle 34, 36, 43, 67, 105–107, 136–137, 140, 146, 150, 154, 172, 182, 184, 204, 215, 257

Project meetings 113, 138, 160, 170–171

Quality of life 93–94, 99

Religion 89, 91–92, 103

Resistance to change 16–17, 20, 25–33, 52, 54–56,

Responsibility matrix 13, 130, 132–133, 149, 298

Rewards and recognition 41, 118, 121, 138, 150, 183, 196, 206, 210–211, 214

Roles and responsibilities of leaders 220

Roles of team members 68, 75, 77–78, 80, 88

Sandwich approach 200

Scope changes 43–45

Selective perception 26, 55

Self Assessment Exercises 280–291

Self–directed teams 65, 263

Self–motivated project teams 13, 220, 225, 227, 229–231, 233, 235, 237, 239, 241, 243, 245, 247, 249, 251, 253, 255, 257, 259, 261, 263, 265, 267
problems during transitions 260
readiness for SMPT 243–244
main characteristics of SMWT 227

Self–reference criterion 91

Setting project goals 13, 122

Sharing power 236–237

Skills inventory matrix 130, 132

SMART goals 122, 197, 216

SMPT culture 5, 235–236, 239–241, 265–266
components of SMPT culture 236, 239–240

Sources of power 236–238, 266

Space 94, 96–97, 138, 165–166, 213

Stages of maturity 249

Stages of team development 13, 41, 55, 70–72, 84, 88

Stewardship 146

Synergy 22, 33–34, 36–37, 53, 55, 58–60, 68–69, 72, 86, 92, 97, 100, 122, 126, 133–134, 148, 159, 194, 205, 220, 234, 255, 261, 263

Tables 25, 41,62, 73, 76, 99, 125, 129, 142, 144, 145, 165, 203, 205, 218, 241, 263

Task activities 118, 149, 221

Team building
five stages of team development 40
definition 39, 114
model 105, 117–118, 149
process 34, 39–40, 114, 116–117, 122–123, 134–135, 148
outcomes of 13, 115
types of interacting teams 64–65

Team climate 30, 123, 126, 159, 259

Team conflicts 139–140, 150

Team decision making 13, 152–153, 171–174, 177–178, 180, 208
advantages and disadvantages of 173, 179

Team management styles 186, 218

Motivation, in teams 159, 203–206, 208

Team norms 74, 80–84, 86, 88

294 ———————————————————————

Teamwork
    and cultural ambiance 37
    and leadership 34, 36–37, 144

Thinking styles 77–78, 94, 97–98, 138, 157, 159, 167, 169, 221

Tight matrix 74, 85, 87, 169

Time horizon 93, 141

Tradeoff analysis 43, 50–51

Traditional management model 230

Trust, developing 34, 201–203

Uncertainty avoidance 93, 98–99

Value of time 93–94

Visioning 216

War room 170

Work force changes 19

The Human Aspects of Project Management Series

Book 1: Organizing Projects for Success

There is no exercise better for the heart than reaching out and lifting people up.

— Anonymous

This book presents an overview of project human resource management, a model for effective management of project human resources, tips for managing external and internal project stakeholders, and organizational design strategies.

Readers will learn to develop an appropriate project organizational strategy, one that effectively interfaces project stakeholders and organizes human resources in a way that inspires high performance among all participants.

Book 2: Human Resource Skills for Project Managers

I will pay more for the ability to deal with people than any other ability under the sun.

— John D. Rockefeller

People are the backbone of projects and the most important resources in a project. To survive and grow in the 21st century, project managers must learn and use appropriate human skills to motivate and inspire all those involved in the project. This book focuses on major human skills: communication; motivation; negotiation; conflict resolution; managing conflict and stress; leadership; and power, influence and politics in a project environment.

Readers are presented an overview of major human relations topics along with practical guidelines that can be used to develop and implement the human skills appropriate to project management.

Book 3: Managing the Project Team

Working together, ordinary people can perform extraordinary feats. They can lift things that come into their hands a little higher, a little further on toward the heights of excellence.

Today project managers operate in a global environment and work on joint projects characterized by cultural diversity. Teamwork is the key to project success. This book focuses on developing and sustaining the project team throughout the project life cycle and promotes working together interdependently in a climate of mutual trust and a win/win atmosphere.

This book will help readers to understand the stages of team development; build strong project teams by eliminating barriers to high performance; select and organize the project team for success by gaining commitment through participative decision-making; and develop a matching skill and responsibility matrix. After reading this book, project leaders should be able to create an environment to facilitate open and effective communication; develop trust and motivation within the project team; and develop appropriate team leadership styles and strategies to suit the project.